LIFE SCIENCE LIBRARY

FOOD AND NUTRITION

LIFE SCIENCE LIBRARY

CONSULTING EDITORS
René Dubos
Henry Margenau
C. P. Snow

FOOD AND NUTRITION

by William H. Sebrell Jr., James J. Haggerty
and the Editors of TIME-LIFE BOOKS

TIME-LIFE BOOKS   NEW YORK

ABOUT THIS BOOK

EVERY HUMAN BEING needs food to survive. By putting food to use man builds his body's cells and keeps them in good repair and functioning properly. This book explains how man finds the food he needs in every part of the globe. It gives clear, detailed accounts of the processes of nutrition, by which the body breaks food down to essential nutrients, and it discusses the diseases caused by a lack or oversupply of nutrients. It examines the fads and fancies that have influenced man's choice of foods throughout history, and draws sober conclusions about the state of the world's food supplies in an era of rapid population growth.

Each chapter in the book is complemented by a picture essay. Chapter 4, for example, tells how the body digests and assimilates food; Essay 4 shows the functioning of the digestive tract in a series of unusual color pictures.

THE AUTHORS

WILLIAM H. SEBRELL JR. is internationally recognized as a leader in nutritional science, public health and medical research. He is Robert R. Williams Professor Emeritus of Public Health Nutrition at Columbia University, and has been director of the National Institutes of Health, Assistant Surgeon General of the United States, nutrition consultant to the World Health Organization and UNICEF and member of the Executive Committee of the Food and Nutrition Board. Among his posts today are: Director of Columbia's Institute of Human Nutrition and Chairman of the Committee on Recommended Dietary Allowances of the International Union of Nutrition Sciences. Among Dr. Sebrell's contributions to science are his identification of the ailments caused by riboflavin deficiency and his studies on the relation of nutrition to liver disease and blood disorders.

JAMES J. HAGGERTY is a freelance writer. He is the author of the LIFE Science Library volume *Flight*, which won the Aviation Space Writers' award for 1966, and has received other prizes for his aviation and space writing.

THE CONSULTING EDITORS

RENÉ DUBOS, a member and professor emeritus of The Rockefeller University, is a distinguished microbiologist and experimental pathologist who was awarded the Arches of Science Award in 1966 and the Pulitzer Prize in 1969 for his book *So Human an Animal: How We Are Shaped by Surroundings and Events*. He also authored *Mirage of Health* and *Man Adapting* and co-authored *Health and Disease* in this series.

HENRY MARGENAU is Eugene Higgins Professor Emeritus of Physics and Natural Philosophy at Yale, and an authority in spectroscopy and nuclear physics. He wrote *Open Vistas*, *The Nature of Physical Reality*, and is coauthor of *The Scientist* in this series.

C. P. SNOW has won an international audience for his novels, including *The New Men*, *The Affair* and *Corridors of Power*, which explore the effects of science on today's society.

ON THE COVER

Since prehistoric times, bread has been Western man's staff of life. Yet even this traditional staple has been improved by the science of nutrition, for the flour with which today's bread is made is enriched with vitamins and other nutrients essential to health. The design on the back cover symbolizes the eating utensils used by many of the world's peoples.

© 1967 Time Inc. All rights reserved.
Published simultaneously in Canada. Reprinted 1971.
Library of Congress catalogue card number 67-23026.
School and library distribution by Silver Burdett Company, Morristown, New Jersey.

CONTENTS

TIME-LIFE BOOKS

EDITOR
Jerry Korn
EXECUTIVE EDITOR
A. B. C. Whipple
PLANNING DIRECTOR
Oliver E. Allen
TEXT DIRECTOR   ART DIRECTOR
Martin Mann   Sheldon Cotler
CHIEF OF RESEARCH
Beatrice T. Dobie
DIRECTOR OF PHOTOGRAPHY
Melvin L. Scott
Associate Planning Director: Byron Dobell
Assistant Text Directors:
Ogden Tanner, Diana Hirsh
Assistant Art Director: Arnold C. Holeywell
Assistant Chief of Research: Martha T. Goolrick

PUBLISHER
Joan D. Manley
General Manager: John D. McSweeney
Business Manager: John Steven Maxwell
Sales Director: Carl G. Jaeger
Promotion Director: Paul R. Stewart
Public Relations Director: Nicholas Benton

LIFE SCIENCE LIBRARY

SERIES EDITOR: Martin Mann
Editorial Staff for *Food and Nutrition:*
Associate Editor: Robert G. Mason
Text Editors: William K. Goolrick,
William Frankel
Picture Editor. Edward Brash
Designer: Charles Mikolaycak
Assistant Designer: Raymond Ripper
Staff Writers: George Constable, John von Hartz
Chief Researcher: Marjorie Pickens
Researchers: Sarah Bennett, Irene Yurdin,
Suzanne Braun, Elizabeth A. Freilich,
Melvin J. Ingber, Alice Kantor,
Cynthia J. MacKay, James MaHood,
Brooke Newman

EDITORIAL PRODUCTION
Production Editor: Douglas B. Graham
Quality Director: Robert L. Young
Assistant: James J. Cox
Copy Staff: Rosalind Stubenberg,
Madge Raymond, Florence Keith
Picture Department: Dolores A. Littles,
Merry Mass
Art Assistant: Gloria Cernosia

This book, from its conception to its final editing, was under the professional direction of William H. Sebrell Jr. The text chapters were written by James J. Haggerty, the picture essays by the editorial staff. The following individuals and departments of Time Inc. were helpful in producing the book: LIFE staff photographers Alfred Eisenstaedt, Ralph Crane, J. R. Eyerman, Robert W. Kelley, Arthur Rickerby; Editorial Production, Norman Airey, Margaret T. Fischer; Library, Peter Draz; Picture Collection, Doris O'Neil; Photographic Laboratory, George Karas; TIME-LIFE News Service, Murray J. Gart. Revisions staff: Paula Arno (editor), Alice Kantor (assistant editor).

INTRODUCTION

An interesting and unique book, *Food and Nutrition* is concise, clear in its suggestions for practical guidance, and is written with sufficient historical perspective to answer three important questions: "How did we get here?"; "Where are we now?"; and "What do we see ahead?" It traces the improvement in understanding of nutritional needs from prehistoric times, when primitive man chose his foods with little regard to their nutritional value. His primary guide was his own pleasure, influenced by the experience of others in the common struggle for survival. The lessons he learned in this way were costly, for he had no way of identifying the delicate connections between nutrition and human wellbeing. And yet, some ancient people did recognize that certain foods could protect against specific diseases: the Greeks learned to avoid goiter by eating seafood, and the American Indians knew how to cure scurvy with fresh plant extracts.

Why such diets were useful could not be explained, however, until the 20th Century. The science of nutrition is still very young, and many problems remain to be solved. But it is important that everyone should have a working knowledge of the field, both for his own personal guidance and for an understanding of public policy. Many critical problems at home and abroad revolve around food and nutrition. In our own country agricultural subsidies and the development of food resources are matters of vital concern. Here and in other technologically advanced nations, excessive consumption of calorie-rich foods constitutes a major hazard to health. In technologically handicapped nations, on the other hand, food deficiencies—particularly of food containing high-quality protein—seriously impair the health of millions of children and adults.

In this book Dr. Sebrell and Mr. Haggerty have provided a useful guide to the food problems—scientific, political and humanitarian—facing the world today, as well as delightful accounts of some of the pioneers who have revealed the intricate ways in which food influences human life.

—C. G. KING

Former President, International Union of Nutritional Sciences
Professor Emeritus of Chemistry, Columbia University

1

From Soup
to Nuts

United Nations donations of milk to youngsters of Chad, in northern Africa, are part of an international effort to provide sufficient protein-rich food and a properly balanced diet for the millions of hungry children throughout the world.

AT NEW YORK'S Waldorf-Astoria Hotel some time ago, a group of gourmets called the Confrérie des Chevaliers du Tastevin sat down to a meal fit for a king—a meal, indeed, far better than some kings have ever been lucky enough to taste. On the same day, a group of Masai herdsmen, 8,100 miles away in the tropical grasslands of eastern Africa, sat down to a feast that most gourmets would find unpalatable or even nauseating. A greater food contrast—in materials, preparation and flavor—is hard to imagine. Yet nutritionally there would be little to choose between the meals.

The gourmets' dinner was varied and rich. The first of its eight courses was an *amuse-bouche*, or "palate-teasing," offering of Gardner Bay oysters, Beluga caviar, snails from France and cheese-flavored puff pastry. Then came a spicy consommé, a fish course and a meat entrée: leg of lamb, accompanied by braised lettuce and *pommes Champs-Élysées*—mashed potatoes with truffles and mushrooms. The Chevaliers went on to their fowl: Brittany chicken with truffles, accompanied by a salad and a selection of cheeses. Finally, for the *apothéose*, or "glory," of dessert, the gourmets had a soufflé of strawberries served with the little pastries known as *petits fours*.

No such culinary masterpieces grace the daily diet of the Masai. Their vegetable food consists of corn mush, wild berries and green plants, honey and a few plantains. The Masai kill and eat a few goats and sheep from their herds, but they rarely slaughter their cattle, for a Masai tribesman reckons his wealth and status by the number of bulls and cows in his herd. Yet these cattle do provide food; they are, in fact, the Masai's major source of food. Every herdsman milks his cows and regularly draws blood from their jugular veins; he drinks a mixture of this milk and the fresh blood several times a week.

The contrasts in composition—and the similarities in nutritional value—between the gourmet and Masai dinners could easily be matched in comparisons of many other meals around the world. People eat almost anything that grows on this planet, and their enormously diverse diets— whether based on beef and potatoes, rice and fish, seal meat and blubber, or tortillas and beans—are all capable of meeting the basic human need for food.

Recognition of this need is instinctive; a baby cries from hunger without being taught. But instinct cannot supply understanding of the reasons behind the need or of effective ways to satisfy it. This knowledge was hard won. To meet the need for food, men have sought for millions of years to increase their food supplies, inventing hunting tools, developing agriculture and devising storage methods. Their ancient successes in this endeavor, improved upon and added to over the millennia, have provided the foundation for the settled way of life that is the basis of our civilization. Only recently, however, has man been able to comprehend why he requires food. Not until the great expansion of science in the late 18th Century did men begin to discover how food is consumed in the body or show the results of this consumption. And it is barely a hundred years since scientists realized that the need for food is actually composed of two interlocking requirements. No matter how great the quantity, food will not keep a man alive unless it is of the right quality —that is, unless it contains certain specific chemical ingredients. And neither will high-quality food sustain a man unless it simultaneously meets his requirements for quantity.

Energy for the human engine

Food is the fuel that makes the human machine work. Like an engine, when the human body is functioning, it is expending energy; energy is required to breathe, to walk, to stand, to move a finger, even to think. Man obtains this energy from the foods he eats: he burns food, much as an automobile burns gasoline or a steam engine burns coal. The energy that foods can provide determines the quantity of food that is required by the body. In making this calculation, the total potential energy is measured in a heat unit called a food calorie. The calorie rating given to food—63 calories for a slice of white bread, for example—simply indicates the amount of heat energy theoretically contained in that food. A total of about 2,900 calories of food are needed every day by an average American man.

The food in that single dinner of the Chevaliers du Tastevin provided each diner with more than 2,500 calories, and the gourmets undoubtedly more than satisfied their remaining need for calories with the other meals they ate that day. How many calories the Masai get is not known; they keep no regular schedule of meals but eat whenever they are hungry. Nevertheless it is obvious from the energetic life of these hardy people that their diet is adequate in quantity. A typical Masai herdsman may walk as far as 60 miles a day; a young tribesman may kill a lion with a crude iron spear. Such expenditures of energy simply could not be maintained on insufficient food.

While the quantity of food is measured by its energy content, the quality of food is determined by its chemical ingredients. Specific compounds and elements are needed to nourish the uncountable number of individual cells—blood cells, nerve cells, muscle cells—that make up the human body. Each kind of cell has a job to do, and each cell must "eat" to do its job.

The whole man eats food; the cells take from that food the specific substances they require. The cells of the thyroid gland, for example, must have the element iodine, which they use to control the body's processing of nutrients. At least 45 chemical compounds and elements are believed to be needed by human cells. Each of these 45 substances, called essential nutrients, must be present in adequate diets, either directly, when the nutrient itself is in the food, or indirectly, as a raw material in food that can readily be converted to bodily use.

All 45 of these nutrients are of absolutely vital importance: the absence of any of them leads to illness and eventually to death. No single food offers all 45 nutrients and one of the main tasks of the nutritionist,

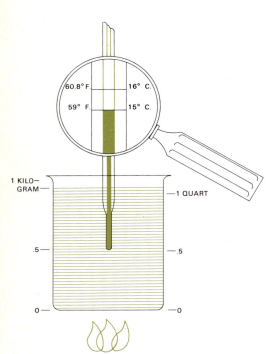

THE CALORIE RATING OF FOOD measures its energy content in terms of heat, as shown by the arrangement of flame, water and magnified thermometer above. The heat that is needed to raise the temperature of one kilogram of water (about one quart) from 15° C. to 16° C. is equal to one food calorie. Thus an apple, rated at 87 calories, releases enough heat energy when consumed in the body to warm 87 kilograms of water 1° C.

a scientist specializing in the nourishment of plants, animals and humans, is to identify balanced diets of different food that, in combination, make available adequate amounts of the essential 45.

Such balanced diets can be supplied by fare as diverse as that of the Masai and the Chevaliers du Tastevin. The gourmets' cheese and sherbet correspond, in nutrient content, to the Masai's milk; the lamb, fish and chicken to goat meat and animal blood, the strawberries and lettuce to plantains and wild plants, the bread and pastry to corn mush. Foods even more varied furnish the essential nutrients for people in other parts of the world. The source of the vital ingredients in milk and milk products eaten by the Masai and the Chevaliers, for example, need not be the cow: in Arab countries, it might be the camel; in parts of Africa, the buffalo; in Mongolia, the mare; in Tibet, the yak; in Lapland, the reindeer; in Peru, the llama. Throughout most of the Orient rice is a staple that supplies the nutrients obtained elsewhere from bread and cereals, while in Italy spaghetti and noodles serve the same function.

Until modern times, the *balance* of nutrients was given little scientific thought. For hundreds of centuries men knew only of their need for enough food. To satisfy the nutritional requirement of quantity, they gathered as much food as they could, wherever they could find it; they collected wild fruits and vegetables, caught fish, killed animals. Then, some 10,000 to 12,000 years ago, inhabitants of Middle Eastern lands learned to plant seeds and domesticate animals; for the first time, mankind had a dependable source of nourishment, an alternative to the never-ending nomadic quest for food. Still later, men learned to process food in ways that slowed the rate at which it spoiled so that the products of the hunt and the harvest could be stored for subsequent use. And finally, modern science and technology were applied to the problem of getting enough food. Fertilizers to enrich the soil, new types of plants and animals bred for greater yield, farm machinery to cultivate land on a large scale—developments like these have so enormously increased food production that in the more advanced parts of the world, at least, no one need go hungry.

Purges and prescriptions

During these millennia of increases in the total supply of food, concern for its quality was not entirely ignored. The ancient Egyptians, according to Herodotus, the Greek historian of the Fifth Century B.C., thoroughly purged their bodies every month because they believed that all disease originated in food. A more positive view was expressed at about the same time by the Greek physician Hippocrates, who considered a proper combination of foods the key to good health and regularly prescribed certain diets as part of his therapy. But it was only toward the end of the 18th Century that such vague generalizations gave way to a scientific approach.

Advances in the science of chemistry gave birth to scientific nutrition, for nutrition is concerned with the chemical constituents of food and

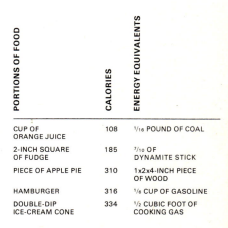

PORTIONS OF FOOD	CALORIES	ENERGY EQUIVALENTS
CUP OF ORANGE JUICE	108	1/16 POUND OF COAL
2-INCH SQUARE OF FUDGE	185	7/10 OF DYNAMITE STICK
PIECE OF APPLE PIE	310	1x2x4-INCH PIECE OF WOOD
HAMBURGER	316	1/8 CUP OF GASOLINE
DOUBLE-DIP ICE-CREAM CONE	334	1/2 CUBIC FOOT OF COOKING GAS

THE ENERGY IN FOOD, listed in the table above, is so great that some foods generate as many calories of heat *(middle column)* as do quantities of materials used as fuels or even explosives *(right-hand column)*. The energy contained in foods is far less noticeable than that of certain other substances—dynamite, for example—because it is released slowly at many points in the body, rather than instantly as in the case of explosives.

the complex chemical processes by which food is put to use. The first great discoveries were made by the Frenchman Antoine Lavoisier, who has been called the father of modern chemistry. Lavoisier is remembered for giving the element oxygen its name and for his demonstration that fire consists of the combination of oxygen with a fuel material. Less well known is his use of his discovery to explain how air and the processes of burning are related to the consumption of food.

Before Lavoisier's time, most scientists believed that men and animals breathed air simply to ventilate or cool their bodies. Lavoisier proved that, in effect, the opposite was true: breathing helps keep the body warm. He established this fact in a series of experiments conducted in collaboration with Pierre Simon de Laplace, the great French mathematician-astronomer. The two scientists analyzed the air inhaled and exhaled by guinea pigs, and compared their analyses with the amounts of heat given off by the animals' bodies. Lavoisier and Laplace already knew that air is essentially a mixture of oxygen and nitrogen. They found, however, that in the process of respiration a dramatic change took place: most of the oxygen in the inhaled air disappeared, to be replaced in the exhaled breath by carbon dioxide gas. What was more, the amount of oxygen replaced during an animal's respiration was almost exactly the amount required to sustain a fire yielding as much heat as did the animal's body. (Lavoisier and Laplace proved this by burning charcoal in a chamber and measuring its "respiration" of oxygen.)

Now the two men made a great deductive inference from their findings. They argued that the lost oxygen was combining with some substance or substances inside the guinea pig's body. In effect, substances within the body were burning. In the process some of the oxygen was consumed and the heat released by the burning sustained the body temperature of the animal. As Lavoisier put it, in a paper published in 1783: "Respiration is . . . a combustion, admittedly very slow, but otherwise exactly similar to that of charcoal."

"Life is a chemical function"

Now, Lavoisier began to work with a human subject. In a series of experiments that lasted 10 years, he studied human respiration under a variety of conditions—at different temperatures, at mealtimes and when fasting, at rest and at work. The results showed clearly that as a human body expended effort or encountered a need for heat, it used up more oxygen to burn more food. Lavoisier reported that his subject used 10 per cent more oxygen when cold than when warm. Oxygen intake went up 50 per cent after a meal (the process of digestion is work). And the subject who was both digesting food and performing mechanical work needed two or three times as much oxygen as a man who was resting.

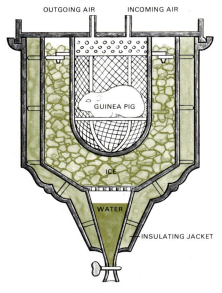

A KEY NUTRITIONAL EXPERIMENT was performed in 1783 by Antoine Lavoisier and Pierre de Laplace of France. They surrounded a guinea pig with ice and gauged the animal's heat output by the amount of melted water. Then they measured the animal's carbon dioxide production. When an experiment with burning charcoal produced the same proportions of heat and carbon dioxide, they concluded that the body "burns" food much as a fire does.

OUTGOING AIR   INCOMING AIR

GUINEA PIG

ICE

WATER

INSULATING JACKET

Later investigators found that the figures Lavoisier gave for oxygen intake were inaccurate, but the principles he uncovered were both true and important. Lavoisier had shown that oxygen must be considered an essential nutrient even though it is not ordinarily thought of as a food. And he had laid a foundation of research on which other scientists were to build. "Life is a chemical function," Lavoisier wrote, and later students of nutrition have depended largely upon chemical analysis to learn more about the body's need for food.

Hunting the fuels in food

Soon after Lavoisier's death, scientists discovered that the body is very sensitive to the chemical composition of its fuel. They began to take food apart in their laboratories to find out which nutrients are essential to human life and in what foods these nutrients may be found. They quickly identified four different groups of nutrients—carbohydrates, fats, proteins and minerals—each corresponding to a distinct class of chemical compounds.

The fats and carbohydrates furnish most of the calories the body needs. They are the primary sources of fuel for the body's heat and energy. The carbohydrates—the sugars and starches in vegetables and fruits—are chemical compounds composed of the elements carbon, hydrogen and oxygen. The carbohydrate compounds are easily broken down in reactions that eventually give off carbon dioxide and water and release energy for use in the body. Even more energy is released by the consumption of fats—butter, oils and similar foodstuffs—which are made up almost entirely of energy-producing carbon and hydrogen.

Some energy is also provided by the third group of nutrients, the proteins, but their main function is quite different. They are responsible for the growth and repair of the body itself, since skin, bones, muscles and all other parts of the body are built of protein compounds. Proteins are among the largest of all chemical molecules, very long structures built up by the linking together of many smaller chemical units. These units, composed mainly of carbon, oxygen, nitrogen and hydrogen, are called amino acids, and these acids are essential to human nutrition. The proteins from meat, fish and vegetables are separated into their constituent amino acids by digestion, and then the amino acids, or subgroups within them, are reassembled in new combinations to form the distinctive human proteins that make up a man's body.

While proper nutrition requires proteins, fats and carbohydrates in large quantities, small amounts of a fourth group of nutrients are also necessary. This group consists of the minerals, such as the calcium that makes bones and teeth hard, and the iron that, combined into a complex blood substance, carries oxygen throughout the body.

LAVOISIER'S EXPERIMENTS showed that man—as well as the guinea pig shown opposite —"burned" his food and that the amount burned varied with physical exertion. He fitted his co-worker Armand Séguin with a face mask attached to flasks measuring air consumption and found that Séguin converted more air into carbon dioxide when working than when at rest. Madame Lavoisier (right) recorded the results and also painted this picture showing her husband's experiment.

A fifth group of essential nutrients, the vitamins, also occurs in food—in amounts so small that they could not be detected until the 20th Century. As early as 1880, however, there were hints of their existence. In that year, a young Estonian biochemist named Nikolai Lunin reported a puzzling series of experiments. Lunin had fed mice pure food concentrates containing all the then-known nutrients. Within a few weeks, the mice sickened and died. At the same time, he fed a second group of mice on milk alone—and these mice thrived. Cautiously Lunin suggested that since mice "cannot subsist on [the known nutrients,] it follows that other substances indispensable for nutrition must be present in milk."

The elusive vitamins

Nikolai Lunin's theory of "other substances" was ignored for decades. But soon after the turn of the 20th Century, several investigators, working independently, found evidence of Lunin's "other substances." In 1906 the British biochemist F. G. Hopkins (who was to receive a Nobel Prize in 1929) suggested that the diseases of scurvy and rickets were caused by the lack of unknown nutrients that he later called "accessory food factors." Six years later the mysterious "substances" and "factors" were even given a name. A Polish chemist, Casimir Funk, had isolated a chemical compound called an amine, which he used to cure beriberi disease in experiments with pigeons. Funk went on to suggest that a whole family of amine compounds played a role in nutrition so vital that the lack of any of them could lead to fatal illness. And he proposed that the whole family be called vitamines, from *vita*, the Latin word for "life," plus *amine*. Later research showed that not all such substances were amines, and to prevent confusion the final "e" was dropped to create the modern word vitamin.

With the discovery of vitamins—complex chemical compounds that play key roles in regulating bodily processes—the groups of essential nutrients had been identified. By the 1960s, scientists had refined these groups into the present—and perhaps still incomplete—catalogue of 45 known essential nutrients and had come a long way toward an understanding of their functions.

The list of essential nutrients includes oxygen and water, which are not usually thought of as foods. But as Lavoisier proved almost 200 years ago, oxygen is essential to nutrition because it is the prerequisite to the combustion of food in the body. Water is equally essential, for water solutions carry nutrients through the body.

The other 43 essential nutrients are still conveniently classified into five main groups: carbohydrates, fats, proteins, minerals and vitamins. The carbohydrate sugars and starches are the source, either directly or through chemical conversion inside the body, of a single essential nutrient, a type of sugar called glucose. Fats provide two essential nutrients: calorie-yielding substances called triglycerides and a compound called linoleic acid, which was identified as an essential nutrient in 1932, but for which no precise function has yet been discovered.

From proteins, the body gets the element nitrogen and the amino acid compounds it needs for building and repairing tissues. Eight amino acids must be provided directly in protein food (children need a ninth, called histidine). These are considered essential nutrients because they cannot be manufactured by the body; other amino acids are also necessary to good health, but these acids are not counted as essential nutrients, because they can be manufactured within the body from other food ingredients.

In the list of 45 essential nutrients, 17 are minerals. Calcium, chlorine, iron, magnesium, phosphorus, potassium, sodium and sulfur are required in amounts that range from 1/30 to 1/30,000 of an ounce per day. Far smaller allotments—as little as a few millionths of an ounce per day—fulfill the body's need for the nine so-called trace elements: chromium, cobalt, copper, fluorine, iodine, manganese, molybdenum, selenium and zinc.

Even the minute requirements of trace elements seem large compared with the amounts of some vitamins believed necessary. Less than .0001 ounce of vitamin A, which helps activate the light-sensitive cells in the eyes, is enough for one day; the allotment of vitamin B_{12}, which helps form the red blood cells, is 141 *billionths* of an ounce per day. Today 13 vitamins—A, C, D, E, K and the eight members of the "vitamin B complex"—are believed essential to human health; all play a vital part in body chemistry, and the lack of any will lead to disease.

Tragedies of poverty—and of wealth

These 45 essential nutrients make up the diet that keeps human beings active and healthy. All 45 are abundant in foodstuffs that can be found from Iowa to India. Yet there is no part of the world in which everyone gets the right amounts of the right kinds of food.

In the United States some people follow fad diets that unnecessarily deprive them of high-quality food. Many other Americans are too well fed. Their overeating—particularly of some types of foodstuffs—harms their health, for excess nutrition is now blamed for the rising incidence of serious heart ailments.

In parts of India, babies go blind because their diets lack vitamin A— a tragedy that could be prevented if their mothers recognized the problem, for vegetables, which could supply vitamin A, are easily obtainable in the area.

In all the underdeveloped countries, an uncountable number of children waste away and die because ignorance and poverty combine to deprive them of the foods their growing bodies need. And in some nations, farms are so unproductive that the ancient terror of famine continues to haunt their populations.

In the 20th Century, as at the beginning of human history, man's oldest problem remains. It will be removed only when the worldwide application of the knowledge and skill of modern science brings to all people the food quantity and food quality that they need.

CARBOHYDRATE

PROTEIN

THE MAJOR NUTRIENT GROUPS— carbohydrates, proteins and fats—are each composed of carbon (C), hydrogen (H), and oxygen (O), although proteins also contain a fourth element, nitrogen (N). The nutrients act differently because their elements are assembled in distinctly different patterns, shown here by simplified diagrams. In simple carbohydrates, the elements are linked in a short chain *(top)*. Proteins *(middle)* and fats *(below)* are much larger; only small portions of their typical patterns are shown. Proteins are twisted combinations of oxygen, carbon, hydrogen and nitrogen atoms, while fats are three-pronged assemblages of hydrogen, oxygen and carbon groups.

FAT

One Man's Meat . . .

Only because man is so omnivorous has he been able to dom-inate this planet. Capable of living on nearly anything that grows, he has settled the entire globe and developed a bal-anced diet with the materials at hand. An anecdote from World War II underscores this fact. A botanist serving in the Japanese army found himself and his unit cut off by Allied troops in a remote area of the Philippines. The unit would have starved but for the botanist's understanding of human nutrition: although a man must have a balanced diet in order to survive, all 45 essential nutrients can be found in some form in most parts of the world. The botanist-officer searched his wild and seemingly barren refuge and discovered 25 dif-ferent varieties of edible plants, on which he kept himself and 60 soldiers alive for 16 months.

In similar fashion, men in different parts of the world have developed diets of striking diversity. The islands of Polyne-sia, for example, rely on seafood, breadfruit, taro and coco-nuts. The French favor chicken, artichokes and snails, while Americans like sweet corn, tomatoes and juicy steaks. Yet much as these diets differ, they all have one thing in com-mon: men have thrived on and enjoyed every one of them.

THE MANY WAYS OF DINING
Eating utensils (opposite) may be chopsticks, fingers or silverware, and mealtimes may come at any hour of the day, but people the world over share the same nutritional require-ments. How this need can be met by varied diets—in Polynesia, Guatemala, the U.S., France, Kenya, northern India and Japan (pins on map)—is shown on the following pages.

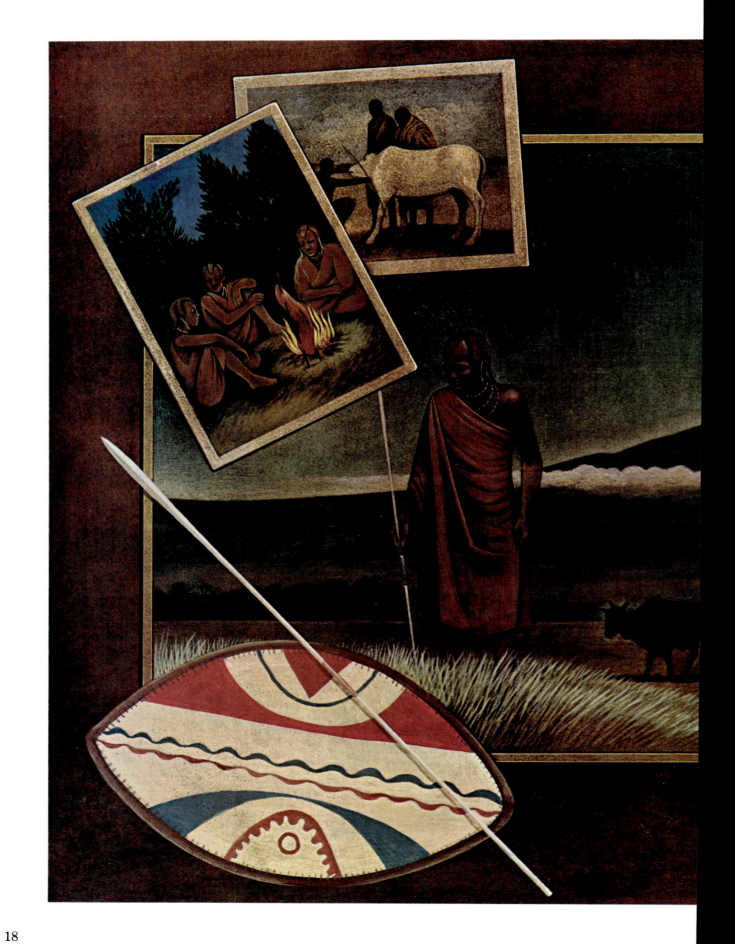

18

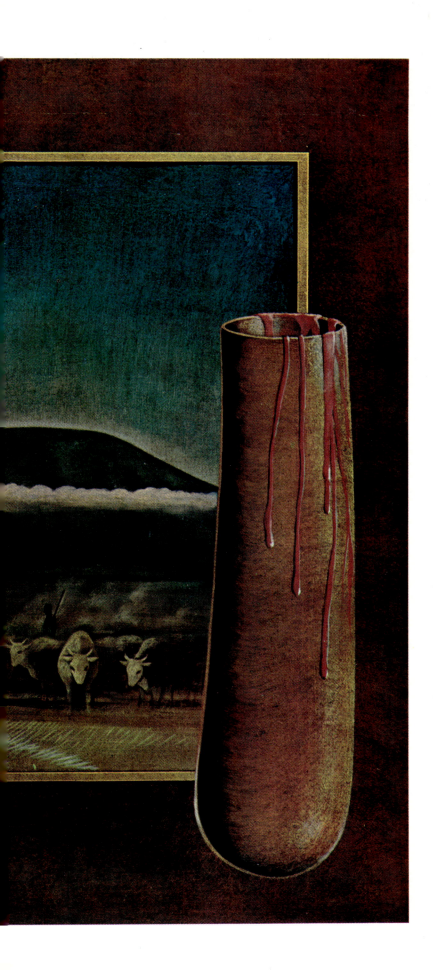

Africa: Thriving on Blood and Milk

The powerful young men of the cattle-herding Masai tribes in the East African grasslands are famous for their bravery and endurance. These warriors, known as the *Moran*, get their great strength from a balanced diet *(chart below)*, which is one of the strangest in the world. The Moran eat meat and a little fruit, drink as much as four and a half quarts of milk a day but also consume blood taken from their living cattle.

Their diet agrees with the Moran. Although they rely on foods often blamed for circulatory ailments, they rarely fall prey to heart disease. They walk as much as 60 miles a day, and when tested they were able to jog along much longer than young Americans who took a similar test.

SOURCES OF NUTRIENTS IN MASAI DIET

CARBOHYDRATES	MILK
FATS	MEAT, MILK
PROTEIN	MILK, MEAT, BLOOD
VITAMINS	MILK, MEAT, WILD FRUITS
MINERALS	MILK, BLOOD, MEAT

A WARRIOR'S NUTRITIOUS MEAL
When the Moran, shield-bearing warriors of the East African Masai, eat roast sheep *(opposite, extreme left)*, they gain about a quarter of the protein they need. The rest comes mainly from milk, but during certain seasons, the Moran drink cattle blood. The blood, drawn from a live animal by shooting an arrow into its jugular vein *(opposite, top left)*, is caught in a gourd *(left)*.

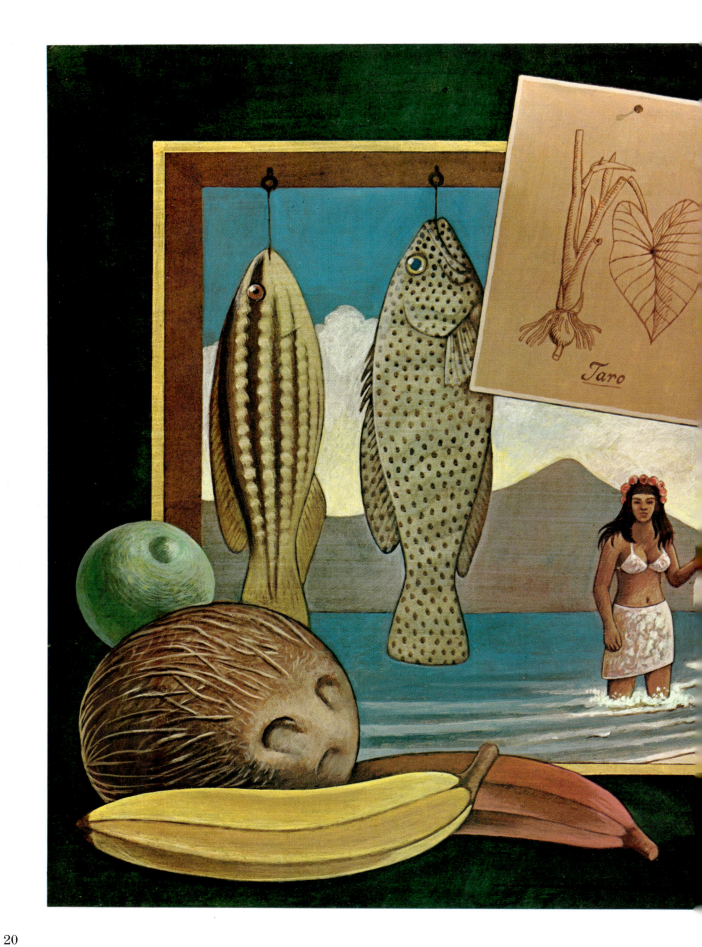

Taro

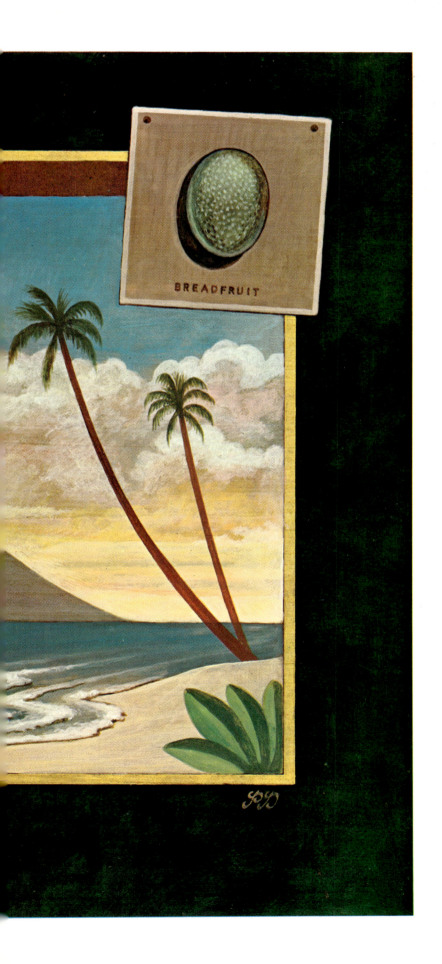

BREADFRUIT

Polynesia: Exotic Vegetables

In the lush South Pacific islands of Polynesia the seas teem with fish, which the Polynesians eat cooked or raw. Waiting to be picked from trees is breadfruit, which when cooked tastes like newly baked bread.

But the mainstay of the Polynesian diet is a plant called taro, and it requires effort to grow and process. A highly versatile potatolike vegetable, taro must be cultivated in the ground, then either baked or boiled, after which it may be eaten whole or pounded into a paste. The leaves are also eaten as a green vegetable. The Polynesians start the day with a light breakfast of taro and fruit, eat a coconut or bananas for lunch and then an hour before sundown enjoy a feast of breadfruit, taro, fish and fruit.

SOURCES OF NUTRIENTS IN POLYNESIAN DIET

CARBOHYDRATES	TARO, BREADFRUIT, BANANAS
FATS	FISH, COCONUTS
PROTEIN	FISH, COCONUTS
VITAMINS	FISH, TARO LEAVES, LIMES, BREADFRUIT, TARO
MINERALS	TARO LEAVES, FISH BONES

FOOD FOR AN ISLANDER'S DINNER
A young Polynesian woman, wearing a modernized version of traditional dress, emerges from the sea with a string of fish that are usually eaten whole and raw when small. Polynesians cook such fish as the spotted grouper, but the staples of their diet are taro and breadfruit. To supplement these foods, they eat limes, coconuts and red and yellow bananas *(lower left)*.

21

India: Vegetarians and a Holy Fruit

Many people in India refrain from eating meat for religious reasons. They get their nutrition from rice or from *chapati*, a flat bread made from wheat flour. This they supplement with *dahl*, made of chick-peas, and with fruits, vegetables and dairy products such as curds, butter, milk and a clarified butter called *ghee*. Those Indians who eat meat—Moslems and some Hindus—prefer lamb.

The mango tree is sacred because Buddha found repose in mango orchards. Nutritionists also honor the melonlike fruit for its vitamin A.

In the past, these foods have usually provided a nutritious diet for the Indian people. Today, however, overpopulation and droughts are straining food supplies, causing famine.

SOURCES OF NUTRIENTS IN NORTH INDIAN DIET

CARBOHYDRATES	CHAPATI, MANGOES, POTATOES, DAHL, PEARS, ORANGES
FATS	GHEE, LAMB
PROTEIN	LAMB, DAHL, CHAPATI, CURDS
VITAMINS	LAMB, CHAPATI, DAHL, CABBAGES, CURDS, CARROTS, ORANGES, POTATOES, MANGOES, GHEE
MINERALS	DAHL, CURDS, CHAPATI

FLAT BREAD AND CHICK-PEAS
A north Indian woman kneads wheat-flour dough to make *chapati,* a flat bread that supplies carbohydrates, proteins, vitamins and iron, as does a puree of chick-peas called *dahl (in pan near chick-peas).* Additional protein comes from curds *(in large bowl),* and, for some, from lamb. Vitamins abound in the exotic mango *(far left), ghee (in jar near woman),* vegetables and fruit.

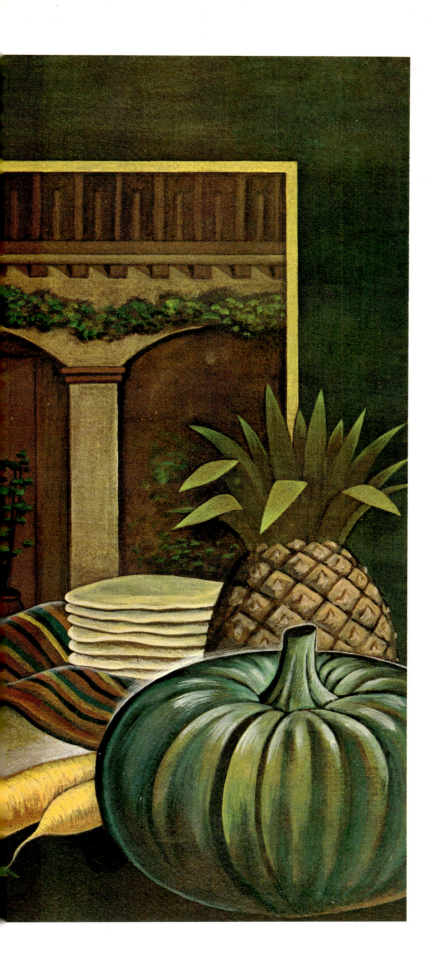

Guatemala: A Corn-based Diet

In most parts of the world, a balanced diet centers around a grain food: rice in Asia, wheat in Europe and North America. Latin Americans, 7,000 years ago, developed their own grain, corn, which was so vital it was considered sacred. To this day its planting and harvesting are often accompanied by religious observances. In Guatemala, seeds are blessed at masses and incense burned in cornfields. Today corn is used in porridge and tortillas, thin, flat bread served at every meal.

Despite its undoubted value, corn is not a wholly satisfactory grain. It contains less of certain essential protein ingredients than rice and wheat. To help make up these deficiencies the Latin Americans consume cheese and large quantities of black beans.

SOURCES OF NUTRIENTS IN GUATEMALAN DIET

CARBOHYDRATES	TORTILLAS, BLACK BEANS, PINEAPPLE, PAPAYA, GUICOY
FATS	CHEESE, CHICKEN
PROTEIN	CHICKEN, BLACK BEANS, CHEESE, TORTILLAS
VITAMINS	BLACK BEANS, TORTILLAS, CHICKEN, CHARD, PAPAYA, CARROTS, CHEESE, PINEAPPLE
MINERALS	BLACK BEANS, CHARD, TORTILLAS, CHEESE

A LAND OF TORTILLAS AND BEANS

The Guatemalan diet is largely vegetarian; meat or chicken is a costly rarity. Tortillas *(stacked behind pineapple)* and black beans *(in large bowl)*, supplemented by a squash called *guicoy*, supply carbohydrates, protein, vitamins and minerals. Cheese also furnishes protein. Carrots and chard contain vitamin A, while papaya *(far left)* and pineapple provide vitamin C.

25

Paul Davis

Japan: Enjoying Fruits of the Sea

Japan is an island nation, and much of its food comes from the ocean—fish, shrimp, squid and oysters, as well as mineral-rich seaweed. Yet the staple of the diet is rice, steamed or boiled, which most Japanese eat with every meal. So important is rice that many Japanese villages have shrines devoted to the Shinto goddess Ugano-Mitama, who is associated with rice growing.

While rice remains the main item in the Japanese diet, the eating habits of the Japanese have changed significantly since the end of World War II. Milk, first introduced by American relief programs, has become a popular beverage, and the Japanese eat other dairy products as well as enriched bread and canned preserves.

SOURCES OF NUTRIENTS IN JAPANESE DIET

CARBOHYDRATES	RICE, MANDARIN ORANGES
FATS	RAW AND COOKED FISH, SOYBEAN SOUP
PROTEIN	RAW AND COOKED FISH, SHRIMP, SOYBEAN SOUP
VITAMINS	SEAWEED, RAW AND COOKED FISH, RICE, SHRIMP, MANDARIN ORANGES, STRAWBERRIES
MINERALS	SHRIMP, RAW AND COOKED FISH, SEAWEED, GREEN ONIONS, SOYBEAN SOUP

FOODS FROM NEIGHBORING WATERS
Ever present in Japanese meals is rice *(seen in sheaves)*, a source of carbohydrates, niacin and some protein. Soybean soup *(in bowl, the beans nearby)* and seafood, such as tuna and shrimp, also supply protein. Seaweed, being poled up by men in the background furnishes both vitamins and minerals. Tea *(being picked)* is the national beverage but milk is also consumed.

France: Snails and Artichokes

The haute cuisine of elegant restaurants in Paris is not the daily fare of most Frenchmen. But their meals, too, set an enviable standard for flavor and nutrition. A farmer in Burgundy enjoys fine dishes. The main course may be *coq au vin* (chicken cooked in wine) with artichokes and a spinachlike vegetable called *blette*.

The most unusual dish, to many Americans, would be snails, a favorite of the French. They eat 600 million a year, enough to stretch around the world one and a half times. To supply this tremendous demand, French growers raise snails like livestock, nourishing them on special feed and penning them in small "parks" whose loose, moist soil is favored by snails for their winter nests.

SOURCES OF NUTRIENTS IN FRENCH DIET

CARBOHYDRATES	BREAD, POTATOES, ARTICHOKES, TURNIPS, WINE
FATS	CHEESE, CHICKEN
PROTEIN	CHICKEN, CHEESE, SNAILS, BREAD
VITAMINS	BLETTE, SNAILS, BREAD, TOMATOES, CHEESE, POTATOES, ARTICHOKES
MINERALS	ARTICHOKES, SNAILS, BREAD, BLETTE, CHEESE

THE MATERIALS OF FRENCH MEALS

The main course of chicken provides a provincial French meal with a rich supply of protein, fats, vitamins and minerals. Potatoes and turnips give carbohydrates, while snails and bread have vitamins, minerals and protein. Other vitamins and minerals are found in artichokes *(behind bread), blette (in bowl)* and tomatoes. The wine in the chicken sauce contains carbohydrates.

United States: Meals on the Hoof

When an Illinois farmer and his family sit down to Sunday dinner they can dine on foods from their own fields: roast beef from a well-fattened Hereford steer; and, to go with it, potatoes, tomatoes and sweet corn.

This meal differs from one that would have been eaten on the same farm 50 years ago. Americans today eat more meat than their grandfathers, and they insist that it be tenderer and tastier than in days gone by. To fill that order, farmers now bring beef to a high point of perfection by keeping the animals relatively immobile in small enclosed fields where they are fattened on corn, hay and soybean meal. These pampered steers enjoy a richer diet than people in some sections of the world.

SOURCES OF NUTRIENTS IN U.S. DIET

CARBOHYDRATES	BREAD, CORN, POTATOES, APPLES, CUCUMBERS
FATS	BEEF, BUTTER, MILK
PROTEIN	BEEF, BREAD, MILK, CORN
VITAMINS	BREAD, STRINGBEANS, POTATOES, CORN, BEEF, MILK, TOMATOES, BUTTER, CUCUMBERS
MINERALS	BREAD, MILK, BEEF, CORN

THE BOUNTY OF AMERICA

An American meal is incomplete without meat, usually protein-rich beef. Potatoes give carbohydrates; both corn on the cob *(growing in background)* and bread provide protein and carbohydrates. Butter has quantities of vitamin A, and tomatoes are rich in vitamin C. Milk is almost a meal in itself, while string beans, apples and cucumber salad add some vitamins.

2
Filling
the Larder

Eskimos of northwestern Canada, following ancient fishing methods in a land too cold for
farming, spear char trapped behind stone dams
during the upstream migration. The fish will be
stored, and eaten cooked or raw in the winter.

In the scale by which human history and prehistory are measured, man mastered the technique of food production relatively recently. Agriculture began only within the last 12,000 years—a period that comprises less than 1 per cent of the time since man first appeared on earth. Even after the invention of agriculture, thousands of years went by without significant changes in domesticated animals and plants or in methods of raising them. Not until the 19th Century—only yesterday in mankind's history—did the Industrial Revolution on the farm drastically increase the output of food. In our own century, chemical and biological sciences have further revolutionized agriculture with fertilizers, insecticides, and new breeds of plants and animals. Today, man has the capacity to raise enormous quantities of food on every acre of arable and grazing land on the planet.

By contrast, early man took his food where he could find it. He was a random collector of plant foods, a vagabond hunter, a scavenger. In Africa, for example, manlike creatures who lived some two million years ago gathered fruits, roots and berries during the wet season; in the dry season, they ate small game and the remains of kills left by larger carnivores. By about 10,000 B.C., men hunted with bows and arrows, and caught fish with hooks, traps and nets. They apparently dried their fish for future use and had learned to store wild fruits and berries. Gradually, man built up herds of domesticated animals—first sheep, then goats, then cattle—to provide a captive source of food on the hoof.

Far more important to prehistoric man than any of these developments, however, was his new understanding of the way vegetable food comes into existence. At some point—archeologists date it variously between 40,000 and 10,000 B.C.—nomadic hunter-gatherers presumably began to recognize patterns of vegetable growth and to schedule their wandering to coincide with the seasonal flourishing of plants. Then came another discovery—the fact that seeds knocked to earth later sprouted into new plants.

About the Eighth or Seventh Millennium B.C., man began to sow seeds in methodical fashion. By planting crops and domesticating animals, he had changed himself from a food gatherer to a food producer. Some archeologists call this development the "Agricultural Revolution"; others the "Great Transition." All agree that it was one of the most gigantic single leaps forward in man's long history. For the first time, man could settle in one place. One part of the population could provide food for the entire group, leaving a nonfarmer contingent free to pursue other occupations. Law, religion, science and every facet of technology from the primitive mud hut to the modern moon shot have their origins in the stable societies that grew out of the Agricultural Revolution.

Archeologists have worked long and hard to pinpoint the exact date and place of the Agricultural Revolution. There is no written record of it, for writing itself came in the train of the revolution. Food production began independently in a number of places at different times, but the oldest sites so far discovered are in the part of southwest Asia that

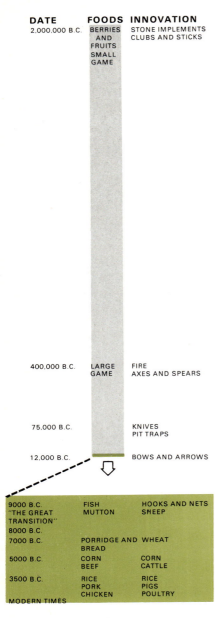

DATE	FOODS	INNOVATION
2,000,000 B.C.	BERRIES AND FRUITS SMALL GAME	STONE IMPLEMENTS CLUBS AND STICKS
400,000 B.C.	LARGE GAME	FIRE AXES AND SPEARS
75,000 B.C.		KNIVES PIT TRAPS
12,000 B.C.		BOWS AND ARROWS

9000 B.C. "THE GREAT TRANSITION"	FISH MUTTON	HOOKS AND NETS SHEEP
8000 B.C.		
7000 B.C.	PORRIDGE AND BREAD	WHEAT
5000 B.C.	CORN BEEF	CORN CATTLE
3500 B.C.	RICE PORK CHICKEN	RICE PIGS POULTRY
MODERN TIMES		

DISCOVERING NATURE'S BOUNTY was a slow process over nearly two million years of human existence *(upper chart)*. Only with the mastery of fire, around 400,000 B.C., did man make his first important advance from the gathering of berries and hunting of small game toward the beginnings of civilized life. Later, the invention of spears, knives, bows and arrows brought large game within his reach. About 9000 B.C., man took his most crucial single step when he learned to domesticate animals and raise crops *(lower chart)*. This "Great Transition" made him a farmer and rapidly increased his food stores.

includes modern Israel, Jordan, Lebanon, Syria, Iran, Iraq and Turkey.

One such site is northern Iraq's Shanidar Valley, 75 miles from the Tigris River. There in 1951, archeologist Ralph Solecki, now at Columbia University, began excavating two long-vanished communities of prehistoric men: Shanidar Cave, in the foothills of the Zagros Mountains, and the valley community of Zawi Chemi Shanidar, two and a half miles away. Both were modest settlements. The cave, only 130 feet long, 25 feet high, and 135 feet across at its widest point, rarely sheltered more than 30 or 40 residents at any one time; Zawi Chemi was little more than the open-air encampment of a seminomadic people. But both provide evidence of that crucial point in the Agricultural Revolution when man first domesticated animals and was about to cultivate crops.

The slaughtered sheep of Shanidar

The story has been reconstructed from the layers of ancient refuse unearthed at Shanidar. Careful counts of discarded animal bones show that for centuries the people of the valley hunted wild goats and, more rarely, wild sheep. Suddenly, soon after 9000 B.C., a dramatic change took place. The bones of sheep began to outnumber those of goats by 16 to one; among the sheep remains, the proportion of yearling lambs shot up from 25 to 60 per cent. These statistics carry an unmistakable message: sheep had been domesticated (apparently the first modern food animal to be so utilized), and the yearlings were being systematically slaughtered for food.

The people of Shanidar do not seem to have grown their own crops —no traces of cultivated grains have been found there—but they were almost ready to do so. They gathered and used wild plants more skillfully than had any earlier men. Deep pits at the sites were apparently the first crude granaries; fragmentary remains of woven twigs, the oldest yet discovered, suggest that baskets were used for collecting food; pieces of a primitive sickle and stone mortars—perhaps the first ever made by man—show that plants were reaped and acorns and cereals ground into flour. Most significantly, the discovery of such luxury items as beads, pendants and inscribed slates hints that some of the Shanidarians could afford to take time off from food gathering and turn to the fashioning of nonessentials.

In the language of archeology, Shanidar represents the first "culture horizon" in the great food-producing revolution—a distinct level of achievement leading to further progress. From this level man went on to plant and grow vegetable foods, starting with wild grasses that may have been brought under cultivation as early as 7500 B.C. The most important of these grasses was wheat, and the first certain evidence of wheat farming was found at the Jarmo excavation, not far to the south of Shanidar and Zawi Chemi. Jarmo dates back to about 6750 B.C. and, like its neighboring settlements, it was a small community; it never consisted of more than about 25 mud-walled houses, rebuilt again and again over 300 years of habitation. In the remains of these houses, however, are the broken fragments of implements used by the world's first farmers. There are sickle blades of flint for harvesting grain, mortars for cracking it, ovens for parching it, stone and pottery bowls for holding the porridge into which it was made. And more important, there is archeological evidence that this grain was deliberately cultivated, not gathered from wild plants.

Embedded in the floors of Jarmo's ovens are the remains of wheat that shows a sharp change from the wild wheat of the region. Its stems are tougher and its husks more fragile. The product of unpredictable natural mutations, this changed wheat was better suited than wild varieties to cultivation, for the fragile husks were easier to thresh and the tough stems prevented loss of the kernels during harvesting. The discovery at Jarmo of wheat with characteristics particularly useful to farmers suggests that the grain was not harvested wild but was cultivated. Starting with two members of the wild-wheat family called emmer and einkorn, farmers like those of Jarmo laid the foundation for nearly 9,000 years of cultivation and improvement.

In time, man added other crops to his larder: rye, fruits, nuts and oil-yielding plants. From his domesticated animals he learned to take not only meat but also milk and cheese. To his earliest farming implement, the sickle, he added the hoe and the plow; and to lessen the labor of preparing his ground for seeding, he harnessed draft animals like the ox. Larger communities found ways of diverting the waters of rivers and springs into canals for irrigation.

None of these developments came swiftly or easily, but all of them contributed to a single result: the improvement of man's nutritional supply, either quantitatively or qualitatively. At the same time, the range and variety of food products was constantly increased as man brought more and more species of animals and plants under cultivation. By modern times, the diversity of individual food items had become enormous.

Man-made evolution

Consider three components of the main course in a traditional American dinner: a juicy, marbled beefsteak, an ear of large-kernel corn, firm white bread. None of these foods ever existed in nature in the forms we know. Each is the product of centuries of evolution—man-made evolution, dependent largely upon the deliberate combination and recombination of different strains of plants and animals. And the ways in which man consciously alters his foods can be summarized in the histories of these three basic foodstuffs: wheat, beef and corn. In each case, the history begins with a single wild ancestor brought under man's control at a specific time and place. Over the years, man improves and diversifies the parent stock, and increases the area of cultivation or domestication. Eventually, farmers produce foods that bear little resemblance to the original ancestor.

The history of wheat follows this pattern in every respect. From the valley of the Tigris, the cultivation of wheat spread as civilization itself spread—first to other parts of Asia Minor; then southward to Egypt; then, by the Fifth Millennium B.C., to Europe. Each move meant a change of climate, of soil, of habitat; and every change led to new varieties. In comparatively recent times, men began to cross different strains of wheat, deliberately creating new types that possess the most desirable characteristics of their parents. Today, many thousands of strains of wheat are grown.

Adaptable to an amazing variety of soils and climates, wheat is the most widely grown of all food plants, raised almost everywhere that men have settled, from steppes and tundras to tropical rain forests. It ranks high among plant foods as a source of proteins; it also contains a high proportion of carbohydrates, some fat and minerals, and several vitamins of the B complex. And it is raised in such great quantities— 270 million tons each year—that it provides the people of the world with one fifth of their total calorie supply.

Cultivating wheat was relatively easy; by comparison, the domestication of beef cattle must have been a fearsome task. The common ancestor of all modern breeds of cattle was a fierce animal, far bigger and stronger than any man, and difficult to capture and to raise. Some experts argue that, with so many other animals abundantly available, cattle were probably not originally domesticated for food. The first cattle to be tamed may have been sacrificial animals sacred to the goddess of the moon (the bull's curved horns, of course, bear an obvious resemblance to the crescent moon). Later, these experts suggest, cattle may have been harnessed to wagons or to sleighs used in religious processions, and later slaughtered for food.

Archeological evidence does little to clear up the question of cattle's earliest use. What is certain is that by the Fifth Millennium B.C., beef cattle were domesticated in parts of western Asia. The wild ancestor of these domesticated cattle was the aurochs, or *Bos primigenius*. A huge, blackish, longhorned beast, sometimes almost seven feet tall at the shoulders, the aurochs ranged over vast regions of Asia, Europe and Africa, but no domestic animal of its type lives on the earth today. The last surviving aurochs died in captivity in Poland in 1627, though some reasonably successful attempts have been made in recent times to "reconstruct" the breed. All existing domestic cattle derive from *Bos primigenius*, but differ from it in varying degrees.

Humpbacks, piebalds, high foreheads

From the beginning, the derived breeds were smaller than their original ancestor, possibly because early herdsmen could not get enough forage to keep larger animals alive. By 2500 B.C., several distinct breeds had become well established in various parts of the world. In India and Mesopotamia, for example, there were (and still are) herds of cattle with a distinctive humped back—a feature that may have developed as early as 2,000 years before. Egyptian cattle included one breed that was horn-less and another that was piebald, or parti-colored. In Europe, cattle tended to be small in stature, with high foreheads and short, incurved horns.

Exactly when the breeding of cattle began to be controlled by man is unknown, but planned breeding was well underway by the time of the Roman Empire. By the 19th Century, superb standardized breeds of beef stock and milk cows had been developed. In Europe alone, there were beef breeds such as the Aberdeen Angus, Shorthorn and Hereford, dairy breeds such as the Guernsey, Jersey and Holstein, and dual-purpose breeds such as the Red Poll, Brown Swiss and Ayrshire.

Coddling a steer

Beef cattle are not only carefully bred but also carefully grown; their rich, tender, juicy meat is as much a product of special handling and feeding techniques as of heredity. When cattle were allowed to live in open pasturage, eating only grass and getting plenty of exercise, they produced tough, stringy beef. Today, male beef cattle (cows' meat is generally considered inferior, and is used mainly for lower grades of beef) receive special treatment. To begin with, they are turned into steers by castration soon after birth, because steers are much more manageable than bulls and steer meat is more tender. The steers are taken from the range during their first year of life, penned up to prevent them from exercising, and fed specially grown corn and alfalfa enriched with mixtures of proteins, minerals and vitamins. The meat of such coddled animals "marbleizes"; that is, strings of fat develop between the muscle fibers to create the tender beef called "prime." To bring prime beef to market at the peak of perfection, cattlemen slaughter most steers when the animals are no more than 18 months of age.

Both in quantity and quality, man's centuries of improving his cattle have yielded a rich nutritional harvest. Modern beef and dairy cattle produce far greater quantities of meat and milk than their forebears. Beef is one of the richest natural sources of proteins, and also provides fats for energy, many of the B vitamins and several essential minerals, particularly iron and phosphorus. Milk is even more nutritious. It contains well-balanced proportions of proteins, carbohydrates and fats, provides most of the vitamins (it is a major source of vitamins A and B_2) and is especially rich in essential minerals. Cow's milk is an excellent food; for children, to whom it is fed for its easy digestibility, it can be very nearly a complete food.

Corn, the third component of the steak-dinner course, has certain resemblances to wheat and beef. Like them, it is grown on every inhabited continent and plays a significant part in the world's diet. Like them, too, it derives from a single wild ancestor and was developed through millennia of improvement and diversification. In its modern forms, cultivated corn, like wheat and beef, is largely a product of man's ingenuity and effort.

MODERN CATTLE'S ANCESTOR, the aurochs, shown here in a drawing adapted from an old painting, was domesticated in Asia at least 6,000 years ago but roamed the forests of Europe until comparatively recent times. The last of the species—an old cow—was found dead by keepers in 1627 in the Jaktorowka Forest, a royal game preserve in western Poland that was the refuge of the world's last herd.

But corn—unlike wheat, beef and many other present-day foods that were first domesticated in southwest Asia—originated in the New World. There a completely independent food-producing revolution took place. In parts of Middle America (including most of Mexico and sections of what are now Guatemala, Honduras, Nicaragua and Costa Rica), corn evolved from a wild plant gathered by wandering bands to a domesticated crop cultivated in farming villages. Excavations of the last two decades, particularly in the valleys of southern Mexico, have traced this evolution in great detail. We know, for example, that the cultivation of corn began about the Fifth Millennium B.C., at least 2,000 years after the first cultivation of wheat in the Old World, and that the improvement of the plant under cultivation was a slow and difficult affair.

One reason for the difficulty may have been the plant with which early corn farmers had to work. The wild ancestor of cultivated corn was quite different from the plant that produces the big golden ears that grace today's tables. The first corncobs were less than an inch long. They bore about 50 tiny kernels, or less than a thimbleful of nourishment (a modern cob bears about 500 to 1,000 relatively huge kernels). The kernels of the early plant were only loosely attached to the cob, and the husk opened at maturity to leave the kernels unprotected (unlike its present-day counterpart, which completely encloses the cob). Yet the very characteristics that made the plant unrewarding to cultivate apparently aided its evolutionary development. The naked seeds of mature corn, lying open to the weather, could easily be jarred loose and scattered by the wind to new locales.

"A . . . grain they call mahiz"

Once human beings took over, the plant changed radically. Cultivated corn, unlike other grains, will not grow wild. Its seeds are too heavy and too tightly held by the husk to be scattered by the wind, and they must be sowed by man every year if the plant is to survive. By the 15th Century, when Christopher Columbus sailed to America, the cultivation of corn had spread over most of the New World. In Cuba, Columbus saw and described "a sort of grain they call mahiz, which was well tasted baked or dried and made into a flour," and on his return to Spain he presented a handful of the kernels to Queen Isabella. The queen, who had expected him to bring back spices and gold, was not especially interested; but European farmers began to cultivate mahiz, or maize. Eventually, the plant made its way to North Africa, and then to the rest of the world.

In the New World, corn became the primary crop of North America. During the 19th Century, American farmers developed new strains that were enormously improved in appearance and in taste. But there was little improvement in yields—in 1916 the farmers were still producing little more than 25 bushels of corn per acre, about the same as half a century before. One reason was the farmers' interest in breeding ears for show purposes rather than for yield. Most of the new strains were un-

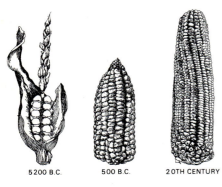

5200 B.C.   500 B.C.   20TH CENTURY

THE EVOLUTION OF CORN to the modern fruitful version required 7,000 years of radical change, as indicated by these three samples. The inch-long ear of wild maize *(left)*—a Central American plant now extinct—dates from around 5200 B.C.; it has only eight rows of kernels with five to six kernels on each row. By 500 B.C., Mexicans were growing four-inch-long ears called Nal-Tel *(center)* that had some 11 rows of small kernels per cob. Today, one of the most widely cultivated corn plants in Mexico is Chalqueño *(right),* eight inches long, with 17 rows of narrow kernels.

stable, losing any ability to produce greater yields after the first growing season. Not until the early years of the 20th Century was the cycle of improvement and degeneration broken; and it took a new breed of men —plant geneticists—and a completely new kind of corn to do it.

The development of hybrid corn, one of the greatest advances in the history of food production, was based upon the laws of inheritance first propounded in 1865 by the Austrian monk Gregor Mendel. In modern form, these laws state that plant and animal genes, transmitted from parents to offspring, carry specific characteristics. The genes of corn, for example, determine such characteristics as appearance, disease resistance, growing season—and yield. Normally, corn plants are not uniform because genes from a variety of strains take part in the process of fertilization. But geneticists realized that uniformly good characteristics could be selected and perpetuated if the corn could literally mate with itself.

The idea was not as farfetched as it sounds. Corn plants contain both male and female reproductive cells on a single stalk—the male cells in the tassel at the top of the stalk, the female in the silks, or fine hairs, sprouting from the ears. To mate corn with itself, a way had to be found to pollinate the silks directly from the plant's own tassel. The job, carried out largely by George Harrison Shull of the Carnegie Institute and Edward Murray East of the Connecticut Agricultural Experiment Station, was not an easy one. Both tassels and silks had to be enclosed in paper and glassine bags to prevent indiscriminate fertilization by other plants. Pollination itself had to be done by hand, one plant at a time. Developing a pure strain of corn—a strain that showed practically no variation in characteristics among individual plants—called for five to eight "self-fertilized" generations. And then, once these pure strains had been developed they generally showed a marked decrease in vigor and productivity. After generation upon generation of inbreeding, the plants were small and weak.

Boosting yield by a "double cross"

Then the geneticists made an extraordinary discovery. When a pure inbred plant was mated with another from a different inbred strain, their offspring, called hybrids, were bigger and stronger than either of the parent lines. A "single cross" of two pure lines created a hybrid corn superior to any then in existence; a "double cross" of two such hybrids was still better. And since the characteristics of each line had been carefully predetermined, the geneticists could "custom build" their hybrid corn, selecting genes for protein content, disease resistance, adaptability to specific soils or climates and—above all—yield. From the first, the productivity of the new hybrid plants, particularly in fertilized soil, was electrifying. In nearly every case, experimental plants yielded at least double the going rate of 25 bushels per acre. Today 98 per cent of all corn acreage in the United States is planted in hybrids, and the average acre can produce about 70 bushels—nearly three times the prehybrid yield.

In the United States, 90 per cent of the corn crop is fed to livestock;

EMMER, 6750 B.C.

DURUM, 100 B.C.

KANSAS HARD RED WINTER,
20TH CENTURY

THE EVOLUTION OF WHEAT during 9,000 years has resulted in better grain plants, but has not radically altered the plants' appearance —contrary to the case with corn *(opposite)*. Emmer *(top)*, a wheat that grew wild in eastern Iraq 8,700 years ago, is a brittle strain that breaks apart in the wind and loses its edible seeds. Durum macaroni wheat *(middle)* that has thrived in Italy since 100 B.C. and modern bread wheats, like Kansas hard red winter wheat *(bottom)*, have the tough heads and stems that keep their seeds until they are harvested and threshed.

it contributes to human nutrition indirectly, in the form of meat. But in some countries of Africa corn is the food crop that directly supplies more than half the total calorie consumption, and in Latin America corn has always been a basic foodstuff. For all the people who eat it, corn provides energy in the form of carbohydrates and fats; it also contains proteins (though of a lower quality than those of beans, beef or wheat).

Dramatic events, like the development of hybrid corn, that suddenly multiply the supply of an existing food are rare. Throughout history, the world has generally increased its food supply by putting more land under cultivation and putting more farmers to work. Until very recent times farmers worked the land by hand, using the simplest of tools. In the days of Napoleon, French farmers still broke the soil with wooden plows that differed little from the ones used in the 11th Century.

Agriculture's Industrial Revolution

Little more could be done to increase the supply of food until the techniques that had brought about the Industrial Revolution were applied to agriculture. But the time was ripe for the application of mechanical technology to the farmer's ancient tasks.

The great breakthrough came in the 1830s, when a young Virginia farmer named Cyrus McCormick invented a harvesting machine and solved a problem that had hampered wheat growers since the days of Jarmo. Unless wheat is reaped within a few days after it ripens, its tiny grains fall from the stalk to the ground and are lost to man. No American farmer had ever dared to plant more wheat than he and his hired hands could harvest with scythes in those few days' time. So, although more than 80 per cent of the American people farmed the land in the 1830s, millions of acres lay fallow for want of men to work them. The McCormick reaper changed that situation.

McCormick was not the first to patent a mechanical reaper; he was in fact, the 47th. But the earlier tries failed because they did not properly combine the essential functions of holding, cutting and gathering the plants. McCormick's own father, Robert, had tried to build a successful reaper for 15 years, becoming a neighborhood joke in the process. But young Cyrus learned from his father's mistakes. In 1831, at the age of 22, he came up with a horse-drawn contraption that was clumsy and broke down regularly, but worked. In its first public demonstration, at the village of Steele's Tavern, Virginia, the reaper cut six acres of oats in a single afternoon, doing the work of five men.

The farmers of Virginia were slow to accept the newfangled device. By 1844 McCormick had sold fewer than 90 reapers. But in 1847, he made a business decision that was to change the history of the nation: he moved from Virginia to the then-small lakeside village of Chicago, Illinois.

DEVELOPMENT OF THE PLOW, which went hand in hand with the growth of agriculture, began in Neolithic times with a stick *(below)*, pulled backward along the ground. The first great improvement came in the Bronze Age, when the plow was hooked to oxen *(below, right)* by a wooden yoke, and the plowman followed, guiding it with a handle. Later, around the Tenth Century B.C. a metal tip was added to the front of the plow to strengthen it.

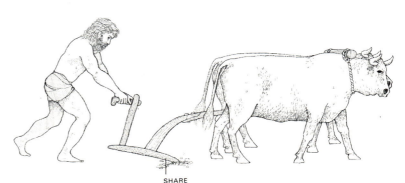

SHARE

Here he could sell reapers in the setting for which they were ideally suited—the vast, rich prairies west of the Appalachians. Within two years McCormick's company was manufacturing more than a thousand reapers annually; by 1862, he and his competitors were turning out no fewer than 20,000 improved models a year, each machine capable of doing the work of eight farmhands.

Machines for the mammoth farms

Though it played a decisive role, McCormick's reaper was only one of the devices that mechanized American farming. After the Civil War the western plains saw the first "combines"—composite machines that reaped, bound and threshed great quantities of grain. Early combines were monstrosities, big as houses and demanding the help of five or six men and 20 or more mules or horses. But they ushered in the era of the mammoth farm. Today, a combine operated by one man and powered by a gasoline engine can harvest 65 acres a day.

Hard on the heels of the mechanizers came the scientists. During the late 19th Century, chemists developed artificial fertilizers that enormously increased agricultural production by providing essential plant nutrients—particularly nitrogen, phosphorus and potassium—needed for growth. Plants get these nutrients from the soil, but cultivation, grazing or erosion can deplete soil nutrients and leave the land "dead," incapable of supporting a crop. The nutrient-rich fertilizers produced by the agricultural chemists rejuvenate exhausted land and increase the yield of good land. And research into fertilizers has led to other chemical means of increasing food production, such as synthetic pest killers that now save billions of dollars worth of crops every year.

Some countries, such as the United States, got the full benefit of all these developments; in a single century, the United States transformed itself into the greatest exporter of food the world has ever known. Canada, Australia and Argentina, which experienced similar but somewhat later developments, are now the only other exporters of grain in significant amounts. But elsewhere, particularly in parts of Africa and the Middle East, agriculture never went through an Industrial Revolution and food supplies are never quite adequate. There are even parts of the world where the Agricultural Revolution never took place: some Australian aborigines, for example, have no domesticated plants or animals, but live by hunting and by gathering berries and roots.

Today, world agriculture has the quality of a historical museum, with exhibits ranging from Paleolithic food gathering to the mechanized large-scale farm. But museum exhibits belong in museums. Mankind needs modern agriculture, which has provided the means for producing abundance the world over.

THE MODERN PLOW first appeared in the early 18th Century *(left, below)*. It incorporated three older elements—a blade called the coulter (100 B.C.), an iron share (900 B.C.) and an earth-turning moldboard (1000 A.D.), the last greatly improved in design. With these features it could dig a deeper furrow and turn back the soil at the same time. Today's tractor-drawn plows *(below)* are arranged in a series that plows several furrows at a time.

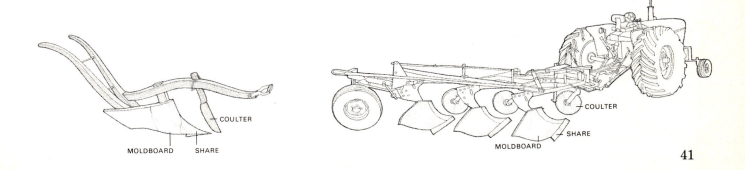

COULTER

MOLDBOARD   SHARE

COULTER

SHARE

MOLDBOARD

The American Cornucopia

The United States is far and away the greatest food producer the world has ever known: each year its farmers send to market more than half a ton of food for every citizen. A certain measure of this abundance was inevitable, considering America's birthright of almost a billion acres of land suitable for agriculture. The explanation of the nation's food-growing capacity, however, is to be found not only in land and climate but also in enlightened management.

From pioneering days to modern times, the prevailing pattern of American agriculture has been the family farm, rather than the huge corporate or collective farm. Long before the land was filled, farsighted officials realized that only if the individual farmer had a strong personal incentive could he be enlisted to develop the nation's natural fertility. Legislation like the Homestead Act, which offered land at almost no cost, drew farming families westward. At the same time, agricultural colleges, demonstration farms and advisory programs were set up to educate farmers in the efficient use of new machines and techniques. They met the challenge. In 1870 one farmer could produce enough food for only five people *(graph opposite)*. Today, the average U.S. farmer feeds 39 people.

THE GREAT LEAP IN EFFICIENCY
In the past hundred years, American farmers have left behind their horse-drawn plows and hand-pushed cultivators *(right)*, and have entered an age of machinery, fertilizers, pesticides, hybrid plants, irrigation and business management techniques. And the efficiency of farmers—in terms of the mouths that each can feed—has increased nearly eightfold.

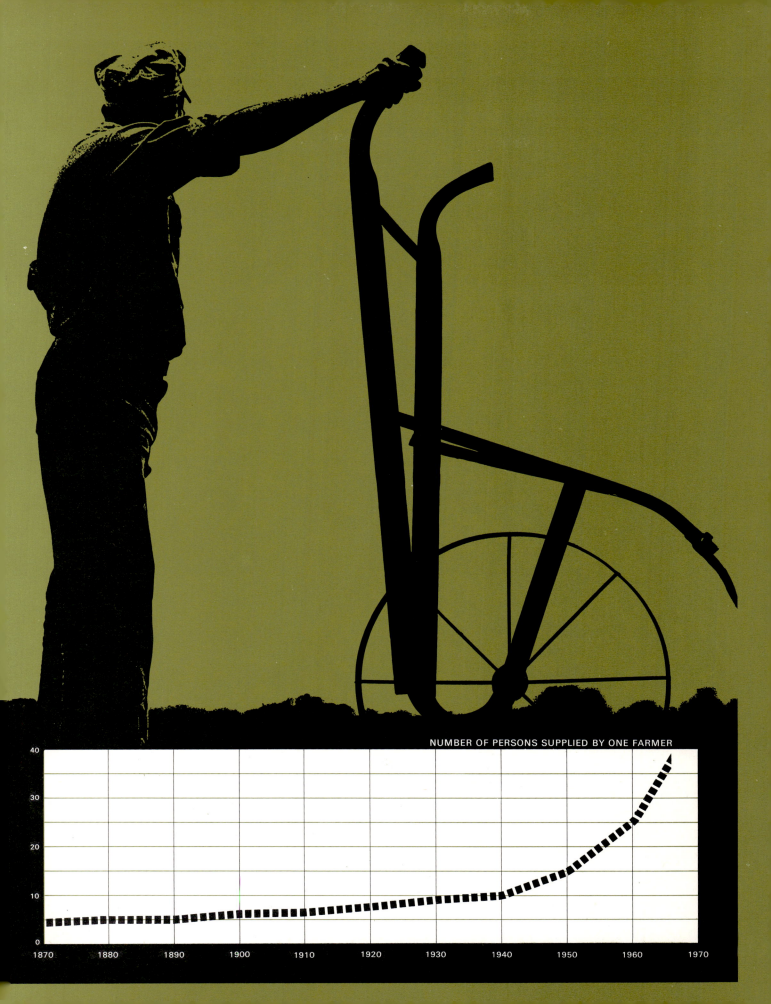

NUMBER OF PERSONS SUPPLIED BY ONE FARMER

40

30

20

10

0

1870   1880   1890   1900   1910   1920   1930   1940   1950   1960   1970

America's Surging Food Production

While the output of American farms has doubled and redoubled, the nature of their output has changed sharply. As the graphs here show, new foodstuffs have become important and older ones have lost their former prominence—readjustments influenced by changes in demand and in the plants themselves.

Yield per acre of corn, for example, increased at a fairly steady pace up until the early 1940s. Then, following the introduction of hybrid seed and chemical fertilizers, yields doubled within two decades.

Soybeans saw an even swifter rise. The soybean plant, native to Asia, was introduced to American farmers for commercial growing around 1900. By 1930 it was coming into its own. Today, soybeans provide 60 per cent of the high-protein feed for livestock; vast quantities of oil pressed from the beans go into margarine, shortening, salad oils and other products.

The consumption of potatoes, on the other hand, has not kept pace with the rise in population. Americans, with more money to spend, have shown an increasing preference for high-protein foods, such as meat, over carbohydrates.

The benevolent flood that fills up warehouses (background) will continue to rise. Food output is expected to jump 50 per cent by the 1980s to meet the needs of an expanding and ever more affluent population.

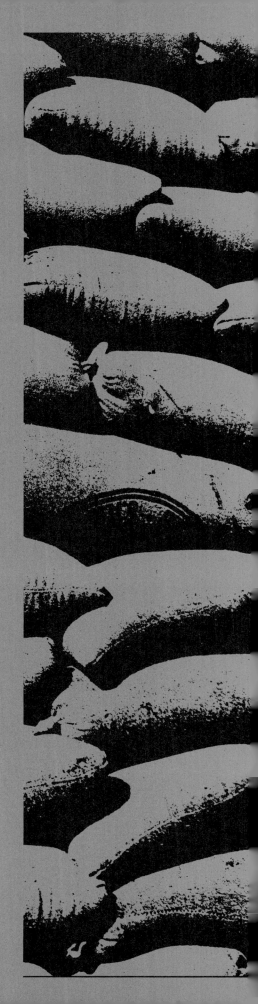

CORN
(MILLIONS OF TONS)

1866	1900	1930	1966
20.5	74.5	58.2	114.9

SORGHUM GRAIN
(MILLIONS OF TONS)

1930	1966
1.1	20.2

WHEAT
(MILLIONS OF TONS)

1866	1900	1930	1966
5.1	18	26.6	39.3

RICE
(THOUSANDS OF TONS)

1930	1966
1	4.3

SOYBEANS
(MILLIONS OF TONS)

1930	1966
0.4	27.9

HAY
(MILLIONS OF TONS)

1866	1900	1930	1966
21.3	49.8	74.5	120.9

POTATOES
(MILLIONS OF TONS)

1866	1900	1930	1966
3.3	7.8	10.3	15

PEANUTS
(MILLIONS OF TONS)

1900	1930	1966
0.3	0.3	1.2

CATTLE
(MILLIONS ON FARMS)

1866	1900	1930	1966
28.6	59.7	61	106.6

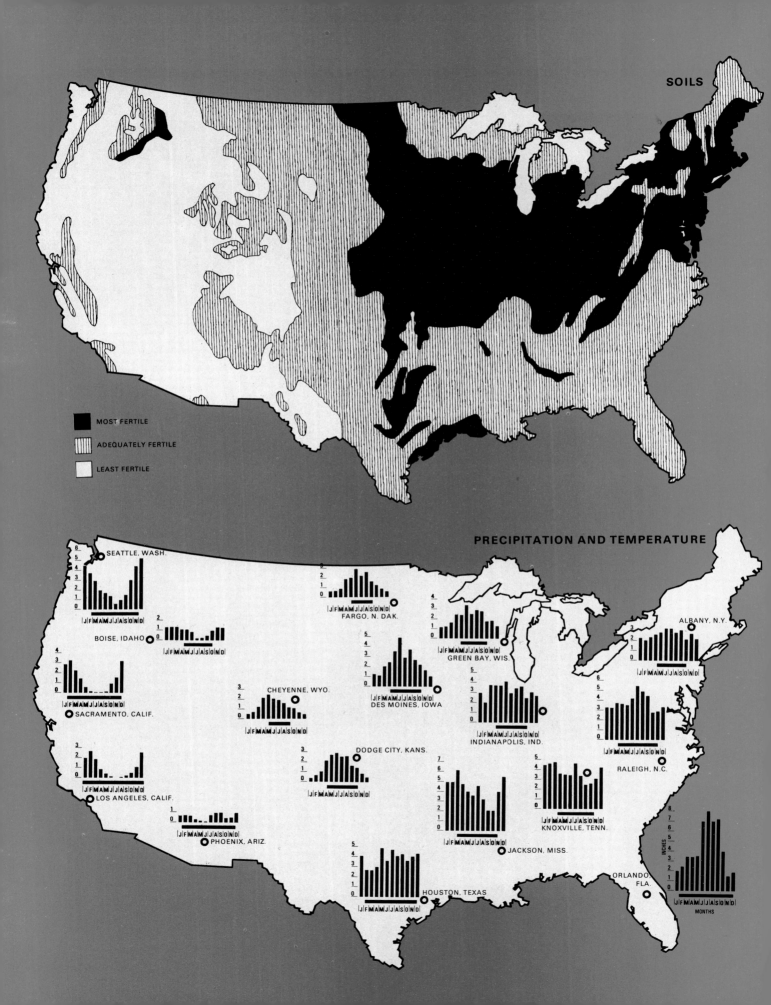

SOILS

MOST FERTILE

ADEQUATELY FERTILE

LEAST FERTILE

PRECIPITATION AND TEMPERATURE

The Ingredients of Agricultural Might

America is blessed with remarkable agricultural resources. The three maps on these pages reveal how soil and climate have interacted to permit the development of an agriculture unexcelled in its diversity.

The map at left shows the distribution of soil riches. The climate map *(below, left)* indicates the average monthly rainfall *(12 vertical bars)* and the average length of the frost-free growing season *(horizontal bar)* at 17 regional centers. These two factors —soil and climate—determine which crops can be grown in each section of the nation, as shown on the map below. Green Bay, Wisconsin, for example, is a dairy center *(map below)* because its soil is fertile *(map at left)* and it enjoys two to three and a half inches of rainfall during each frost-free month between May and October *(map at left, below)*.

In the Northeast, Great Lakes and North Pacific Coast regions, a cool climate, plentiful year-round moisture and good—if hilly—soil have fostered dairy farming. The fruit and truck crops of the South and the West Coast require, most of all, high moisture, often necessitating irrigation. Though infertile and dry, enormous tracts of the West and Southwest support enough forage to serve as rangeland. Cotton, whose seed yields flour and oil, is king in the moist, fairly fertile South. On the Great Plains, wheat flourishes despite uncertain rainfall, a short frost-free season and only adequate soil. And at the heart of the continent is the Corn Belt, whose rich soil, good rainfall and vast unwooded expanse make it perhaps the most highly favored single agricultural area in the world.

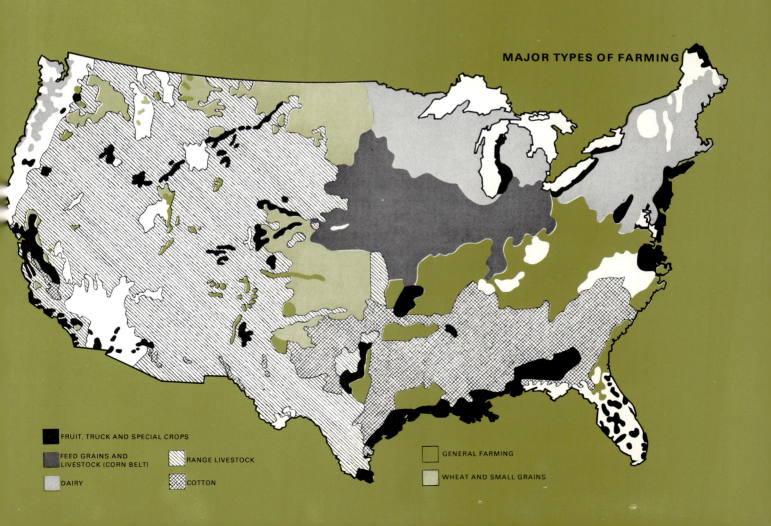

MAJOR TYPES OF FARMING

■ FRUIT, TRUCK AND SPECIAL CROPS

■ FEED GRAINS AND LIVESTOCK (CORN BELT)

▨ RANGE LIVESTOCK

□ GENERAL FARMING

□ DAIRY

▨ COTTON

□ WHEAT AND SMALL GRAINS

The Factors That Spur Efficiency

In the early years of the United States, 90 per cent of all workingmen were farmers. Today, fewer than 10 per cent are engaged in farming—versus 40 per cent in the U.S.S.R. and 80 per cent in China. This efficiency came slowly, as the graph directly to the right shows. Farm population did not begin its precipitous decline until the 1930s, when machinery like the wheat-harvesting combines *(below)* sharply reduced the need for muscle power. And land devoted to farming increased steadily until about 1950.

The six graphs at center indicate how both men and land were made more efficient: between the World Wars, tractors supplanted horses; after World War II came machinery like corn harvesters—which can reap and bag three acres of corn in one hour—as well as chemical fertilizers and pesticides.

A coordinated effort by many public and private agencies, notably the federal Department of Agriculture, made these advances available to farmers throughout the nation. The Department, which began with nine employees and a $64,000 budget in 1862, by 1966 employed approximately 119,000 people and spent almost eight billion dollars annually in its program of aid to U.S. agriculture.

The result of the past century's interacting changes in farming labor, agricultural techniques and governmental effort is shown at far right in sharp rises in production per acre.

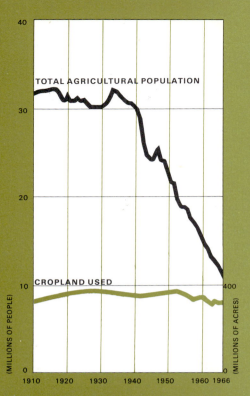

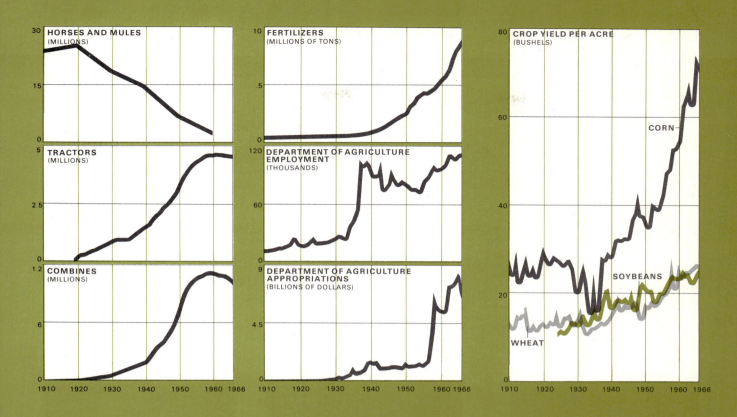

| HORSES AND MULES (MILLIONS) | FERTILIZERS (MILLIONS OF TONS) | CROP YIELD PER ACRE (BUSHELS) |

30
15
0

10
5
0

80
60
40
20
0

CORN
SOYBEANS
WHEAT

TRACTORS (MILLIONS)
5
2.5
0

DEPARTMENT OF AGRICULTURE EMPLOYMENT (THOUSANDS)
120
60
0

COMBINES (MILLIONS)
1.2
.6
0

DEPARTMENT OF AGRICULTURE APPROPRIATIONS (BILLIONS OF DOLLARS)
9
4.5
0

1910 1920 1930 1940 1950 1960 1966   1910 1920 1930 1940 1950 1960 1966   1910 1920 1930 1940 1950 1960 1966

Knowledge to Fire a Revolution

At the time of the American Revolution, farmers were tilling their land in a fashion that would have looked remarkably familiar to the husbandmen of ancient Rome. However, U.S. agriculture was soon to undergo its own revolution. President George Washington saw it coming and recommended to Congress the establishment of a Board of Agriculture to "assist a spirit of discovery and improvement." His advice was not heeded, but the spirit of science spread through the farmers' ranks nonetheless. Agricultural societies, founded as early as 1785, concerned themselves with improved methods; at first aristocratic in makeup, these soon became broadbased in membership, and their programs of continuous study helped set the pattern for American agriculture. Farm journals

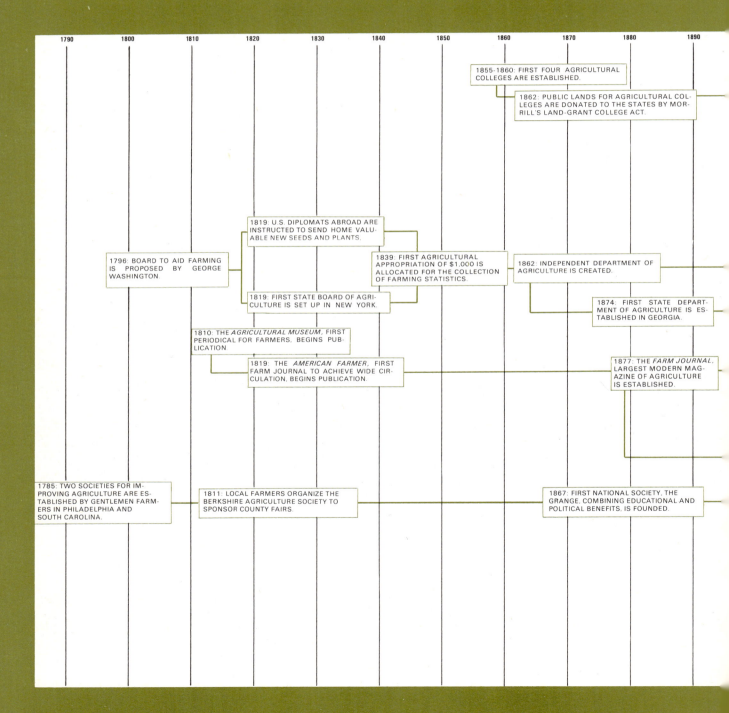

1855-1860: FIRST FOUR AGRICULTURAL COLLEGES ARE ESTABLISHED.

1862: PUBLIC LANDS FOR AGRICULTURAL COLLEGES ARE DONATED TO THE STATES BY MORRILL'S LAND-GRANT COLLEGE ACT.

1819: U.S. DIPLOMATS ABROAD ARE INSTRUCTED TO SEND HOME VALUABLE NEW SEEDS AND PLANTS.

1796: BOARD TO AID FARMING IS PROPOSED BY GEORGE WASHINGTON.

1839: FIRST AGRICULTURAL APPROPRIATION OF $1,000 IS ALLOCATED FOR THE COLLECTION OF FARMING STATISTICS.

1862: INDEPENDENT DEPARTMENT OF AGRICULTURE IS CREATED.

1819: FIRST STATE BOARD OF AGRICULTURE IS SET UP IN NEW YORK.

1874: FIRST STATE DEPARTMENT OF AGRICULTURE IS ESTABLISHED IN GEORGIA.

1810: THE *AGRICULTURAL MUSEUM*, FIRST PERIODICAL FOR FARMERS, BEGINS PUBLICATION.

1819: THE *AMERICAN FARMER*, FIRST FARM JOURNAL TO ACHIEVE WIDE CIRCULATION, BEGINS PUBLICATION.

1877: THE *FARM JOURNAL*, LARGEST MODERN MAGAZINE OF AGRICULTURE IS ESTABLISHED.

1785: TWO SOCIETIES FOR IMPROVING AGRICULTURE ARE ESTABLISHED BY GENTLEMEN FARMERS IN PHILADELPHIA AND SOUTH CAROLINA.

1811: LOCAL FARMERS ORGANIZE THE BERKSHIRE AGRICULTURE SOCIETY TO SPONSOR COUNTY FAIRS.

1867: FIRST NATIONAL SOCIETY, THE GRANGE, COMBINING EDUCATIONAL AND POLITICAL BENEFITS, IS FOUNDED.

appeared; fairs were held regularly at which prizes were given for outstanding produce, thus stimulating a healthy competition; and U.S. diplomats were encouraged to bring home useful plants they came across during their foreign tours.

Under President Lincoln, the U.S. Department of Agriculture was established. It was Lincoln, too, who in 1862 signed the Morrill Act, which granted land to every state for colleges of agriculture and mechanics. From these colleges sprang experiment stations—devoted to research in scientific farming. Many other programs followed: the extension service that sends county agents out into the field to give farmers expert advice; the industry-financed demonstration farms; and 4-H Clubs that encourage youngsters to raise improved livestock or grow better crops. Listed below are significant events in this continuing educational process.

Today, with about 40,000 agricultural college graduates every year, with radio and television programs, newspapers, industrial bulletins and with farmers' organizations spreading knowledge, American agriculture is firmly wedded to the science that promises ever-increasing abundance.

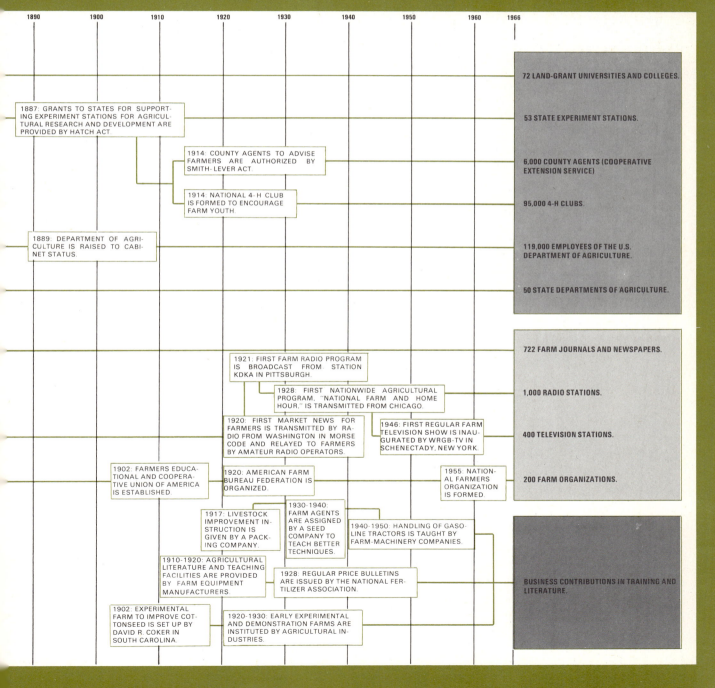

The Triumph of the Family Farm

The awesome productivity of American agriculture is largely the doing of a small elite group of farmers. Some rent their land, some own it; some "farmers" are huge corporations. Together they work only 15 per cent of all American farms, but they account for 65 per cent of gross farm revenue; each grosses at least $20,000 a year.

The most surprising thing about these flourishing farms is that so many are relatively small. There are a few enormous operations whose revenues run into the millions, but the typical success story in U.S. agriculture involves a one-family farm like the one whose financial statement appears on the opposite page. The family farm has not been left behind by modern technology. Although the individual farmer works hard, he lives well—and he puts something in the bank at the end of the year.

65% OF ALL FARM REVENUES

15% OF ALL FARMS

THE BUSINESS OF A TYPICAL SUCCESSFUL ONE-FAMILY FARM IN THE CORN BELT

THE FARM AND ITS PRODUCTS

Total land	295 acres
Crops harvested	
Corn	10,107 bushels
Wheat	1,260 bushels
Soybeans	1,072 bushels
Oats	355 bushels
Hay	57 tons
Animals	
Chickens	50
Cattle	2
Tractors	3

THE VALUE OF THE FARM

Land and buildings	$158,710
Machinery and equipment	16,700
Crops	430
Livestock	370

THE FARMER'S ANNUAL CASH RECEIPTS

Crops	$20,326
Poultry and eggs	203
Cattle	0
Other (including government payments)	2,524
Value of homegrown food consumed plus rent saved through occupancy of farmhouse	1,514
Gross farm income	$24,567

THE FARMER'S ANNUAL CASH EXPENDITURES

Machinery, buildings and fences	$5,692
Taxes	1,840
Fertilizer and lime	1,296
Miscellaneous crop expenses	1,119
Labor hired	347
Feed purchased	160
Livestock purchased	26
Other	572
Total operating expenses	$11,052
THE FARMER'S INCOME	$13,515

Breadbasket for the World

In 1966, even after feeding all U.S. citizens, the overflowing American cornucopia was able to send about six billion dollars' worth of food overseas; agricultural imports, largely such things as coffee and sugar, totaled about four billion dollars. U.S. farm exports go all over the world, as the listing at right shows, in amounts and varieties suited to many needs: the Democratic Republic of the Congo needed such basic foods as wheat and rice, while Norway was supplied only feed grains, fruits and vegetables.

Almost 20 per cent of U.S.-grown animal feed is shipped abroad. Two thirds of American wheat production finds an international market, and the purchasers include such grain-growing centers as France and even, in some years, the U.S.S.R.

Yet this great outflow of foodstuffs scarcely strains America's agricultural capacity. And if further technical advances are applied, output may be raised even further. In the United States there are more than 50 million acres of fertile land that currently lie untilled; millions of additional acres of wasteland may in the future be reclaimed for agriculture by irrigation or drainage. America's role as breadbasket for the world will probably expand: food exports are expected to rise another billion dollars by 1970. But the product that the U.S. most wants to export is its agricultural expertise, which will help developing nations achieve their own abundance.

FEED GRAINS

TOTAL EXPORTED $1,350,989
(THOUSANDS OF DOLLARS)

BELGIUM AND LUXEMBOURG	$ 89,718
CANADA	102,073
DENMARK	7,563
EGYPT	284
FRANCE	4,892
GREECE	19,084
INDIA	52,801
IRELAND	9,446
ISRAEL	25,129
ITALY	154,027
JAPAN	233,590
KENYA	10,385
MEXICO	9,183
NETHERLANDS	179,242
NORWAY	9,662
POLAND	1,601
SOUTH KOREA	571
SOUTH VIETNAM	1,905
SPAIN	106,223
SWITZERLAND	6,105
TUNISIA	1,225
UNITED KINGDOM	116,813
VENEZUELA	3,557
WEST GERMANY	110,138
OTHER COUNTRIES	95,772

WHEAT GRAIN AND FLOUR

TOTAL EXPORTED $1,403,094
(THOUSANDS OF DOLLARS)

ALGERIA	$ 16,303
BELGIUM AND LUXEMBOURG	10,044
BOLIVIA	5,945
BRAZIL	49,451
CANADA	18,397
CEYLON	2,204
CHILE	1,972
COLOMBIA	11,883
CONGO, (DEMOCRATIC REPUBLIC OF)	6,600
COSTA RICA	1,009
EGYPT	82,845
FRANCE	17,574
GREECE	1,221
GUYANA	1,987
INDIA	430,185
IRAN	15,272
ISRAEL	13,494
ITALY	11,716
JAMAICA	1,618
JAPAN	114,081
JORDAN	7,346
LEBANON	3,018
MEXICO	81
MOROCCO	10,992
NETHERLANDS	43,202
PAKISTAN	56,680
PHILIPPINES	26,501
PORTUGAL	6,877
SAUDI ARABIA	5,906
SOUTH KOREA	37,270
SOUTH VIETNAM	6,493
SUDAN	1,989
TAIWAN	16,803
TRINIDAD, TOBAGO	1,274
TUNISIA	3,634
TURKEY	23,105
UNITED KINGDOM	41,359
VENEZUELA	23,100
WEST GERMANY	22,886
YUGOSLAVIA	86,733
OTHER COUNTRIES	164,044

FRUITS AND VEGETABLES

TOTAL   EXPORTED $496,385
(THOUSANDS OF DOLLARS)

AUSTRALIA	$ 2,230
AUSTRIA	1,963
BELGIUM AND LUXEMBOURG	14,583
BRAZIL	518
CANADA	194,705
DENMARK	7,376
DOMINICAN REPUBLIC	3,629
FINLAND	7,290
FRANCE	16,228
HONG KONG	10,001
IRELAND	2,404
ISRAEL	521
ITALY	4,712
JAMAICA	1,544
JAPAN	17,538
MALAYSIA	3,277
MEXICO	7,478
NETHERLANDS	24,416
NEW ZEALAND	2,091
NORWAY	7,774
PANAMA	3,930
PERU	1,195
PHILIPPINES	4,679
SAUDI ARABIA	1,118
SOUTH AFRICA	685
SPAIN	3,003
SWEDEN	19,130
SWITZERLAND	7,906
UNITED KINGDOM	43,923
VENEZUELA	14,505
WEST GERMANY	39,296
OTHER COUNTRIES	26,737

MEAT

TOTAL   EXPORTED $366,204
(THOUSANDS OF DOLLARS)

BELGIUM AND LUXEMBOURG	$ 1,571
BRAZIL	1
CANADA	27,728
CHILE	2,219
COLOMBIA	1,747
DENMARK	225
EGYPT	8,445
FRANCE	19,647
GREECE	1,992
HONG KONG	3,157
INDIA	3,681
IRAN	2,159
ISRAEL	6,513
ITALY	13,428
JAMAICA	1,541
JAPAN	47,879
MALAYSIA	1,059
MEXICO	5,832
NETHERLANDS	33,746
PAKISTAN	2,830
PANAMA	947
PERU	4,397
PHILIPPINES	2,089
POLAND	5,643
SOUTH AFRICA	2,493
SOUTH KOREA	3,533
SOUTH VIETNAM	64
SPAIN	9,141
SWEDEN	1,657
SWITZERLAND	5,517
TAIWAN	3,206
TRINIDAD, TOBAGO	1,276
TURKEY	3,633
U.S.S.R.	11,294
UNITED KINGDOM	38,974
VENEZUELA	3,251
WEST GERMANY	34,355
YUGOSLAVIA	1,350
OTHER COUNTRIES	47,984

RICE

TOTAL   EXPORTED $221,506
(THOUSANDS OF DOLLARS)

BELGIUM AND LUXEMBOURG	$ 1,332
CANADA	8,189
COLOMBIA	80
CONGO, (DEMOCRATIC REPUBLIC OF)	6,110
DOMINICAN REPUBLIC	1,224
FRANCE	2,336
GHANA	5,575
GUINEA	3,495
HAITI	1
INDIA	1,240
ISRAEL	2,902
ITALY	2
IVORY COAST	3,564
JAMAICA	3,869
JAPAN	38,606
KUWAIT	2,793
LIBERIA	6,248
MEXICO	133
NETHERLANDS	3,618
PANAMA	67
PERU	2,102
PHILIPPINES	4,847
SAUDI ARABIA	7,909
SOUTH AFRICA	12,590
SOUTH VIETNAM	45,326
UNITED KINGDOM	6,305
VENEZUELA	1,062
WEST GERMANY	7,623
OTHER COUNTRIES	42,358

3

Fire, Spice and Ice—the Preservers

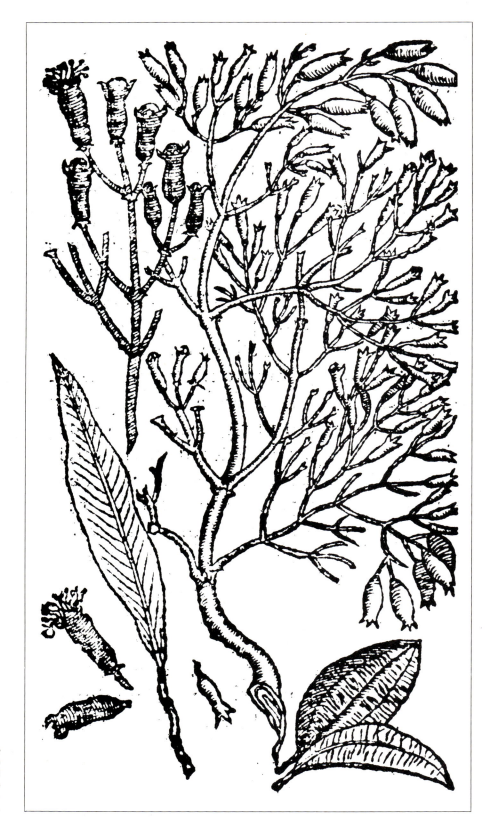

Cloves were among the spices used to preserve food before refrigeration. Shown in this 16th Century drawing, these dried buds of an evergreen were mixed into foodstuffs, there to release eugenol, a preservative that delayed spoilage for months.

IN 1497, FIVE YEARS after Christopher Columbus discovered the New World, four tiny ships sailed southward from the port of Lisbon, Portugal. Like Columbus, their captain Vasco da Gama was searching for a new route to the spice lands of Asia. But while Columbus failed to achieve that goal, da Gama succeeded. In a two-year, 24,000-mile round trip, he took his ships around the continent of Africa to India and back to Lisbon. Only two of the four ships survived to reach their home port. But those two ships brought back a cargo of spices and other products worth 60 times the cost of the voyage.

The spices of the East were valuable in da Gama's time, as they had been for centuries, because they could be used to stretch Europe's always inadequate supply of food. During the Middle Ages, a pound of ginger was worth a sheep; a pound of mace, three sheep or half a cow. Pepper, the most valuable spice of all, was counted out in individual peppercorns, and a sack of pepper was said to be worth a man's life. Da Gama's successful voyage intensified an international power struggle over spices. For three centuries afterward the nations of Western Europe—Portugal, Spain, France, Holland and Great Britain—fought bloody wars for spice-producing colonies and the control of the spice trade.

The people of those times used spices as we do today, to enhance or vary the flavors of their food, but they were ready to fight over them for a different reason. Spices were flavor-disguisers, masking the taste of tainted food that was still nutritious but would, if unspiced, have to be thrown away. And some spices were also preservatives that helped men to keep meat for a year or more without refrigeration. Cloves, for example, contain a chemical called eugenol that inhibits the growth of bacteria (it is still used to help preserve some modern foods, such as Virginia ham). When spices were unavailable, people often went hungry because they could not store enough food to carry them over the winter. In medieval England, before the use of spices became widespread, farmers who could not accumulate enough fodder to keep all their cattle alive through the winter months slaughtered all but their breed stock in the fall, but the meat soon began to deteriorate and by mid-winter no edible-flesh foods could be had. For such men, new methods of processing food for greater storability helped stave off starvation.

Spicing foods to preserve them is only one of many processing methods; others include cooking, drying, canning, and chilling or freezing. All of these methods of processing food have certain objectives in common, and all of them are important today. Processing for palatability increases the pleasure of eating food and hence aids digestion. And processing for nutritive quality contributes to good health by making essential nutrients more available.

Of all processing methods, cooking—the oldest and the most common —exemplifies these objectives best. By simply applying heat to foods, and thus changing their chemical composition, man improves his diet in a number of ways. Cooking transforms raw food into subtle, appetite-teasing delights and elevates the brute function of eating to a high place among civilized diversions. As a counteragent to the factors that cause food spoilage, it acts as a method of preservation. By breaking down some of the complex substances in raw food, it makes food easier to digest—and converts almost-inedible plants into nutritious foods, extending man's food resources. Even the most obvious effects of cooking, such as the softening of most foods under heat, help some people who would otherwise suffer from malnutrition because they cannot chew easily. For infants and the elderly, with few or no teeth and underdeveloped or failing digestive systems, food must be soft and easily digestible.

Cooking began at least 400,000 years ago, invented by modern man's ancestors. The evidence comes from an ancient cave near Peking, China —remnants of charred bones attesting that the long-extinct Peking men who lived there had already made one of the greatest technical innovations of all time. By accident or design, these primitive hunters had learned to tend a fire, and, most important of all, to use it to roast their meat. They were able not only to soften meat and improve its flavor, but to slow its decay; with the help of cooking, a hunter could get meals for several days from today's kill. Though roasting meat before an open fire is a crude method of cooking, it met man's needs for hundreds of thousands of years. Then, with the invention of agriculture about 12,000 years ago, new methods and new implements appeared. The Stone Age cook used clay pottery and ovens; his successors had metal pots and pans. By the beginning of recorded history, cooking had been adapted to a variety of foods and included all of today's basic techniques.

While cooking methods have hardly changed in thousands of years, the understanding of exactly what cooking does to food is very new. We now know that the chemical effects of cooking vary from food to food— boiling a potato causes one kind of reaction, boiling meat another. The cooking reactions differ among the categories of essential nutrients— carbohydrates, fats, proteins, minerals and vitamins—and even among members of the same category. Carbohydrates are a case in point.

Breaking big sugars into little ones

One type of carbohydrate, simple sugar, is easily digested just as it is; that is why many fruits and such compounded foods as candy and ice cream, which are high in sugar content, require little or no cooking. Yet the carbohydrates also include starches, which are forms of sugar— but sugar that occurs in complex compounds made up of chemically linked simple sugars. These complex sugars, called polysaccharides, are in insoluble granules in raw food and cannot normally be absorbed by the human body; at best, they are digested with great difficulty. These granules must be broken down before the digestive tract can handle them. Cooking is a simple but effective way of breaking them down.

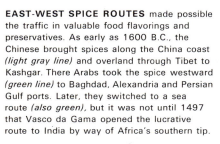

EAST-WEST SPICE ROUTES made possible the traffic in valuable food flavorings and preservatives. As early as 1600 B.C., the Chinese brought spices along the China coast *(light gray line)* and overland through Tibet to Kashgar. There Arabs took the spice westward *(green line)* to Baghdad, Alexandria and Persian Gulf ports. Later, they switched to a sea route *(also green)*, but it was not until 1497 that Vasco da Gama opened the lucrative route to India by way of Africa's southern tip.

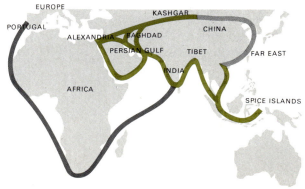

Anyone who has ever eaten a raw potato has a vivid memory of a case of indigestion—or, more correctly, of incomplete digestion. The cause of the trouble is the potato's starch, a substance consisting of white, tasteless, microscopic particles that make up nearly a fifth of the potato's weight. Cooking the potato makes these granules swell and, eventually, burst open, making the starch more easily digestible. In digestion, the constituents of the granules, complex sugars called amylose and amylopectin, are hydrolized into glucose, an easily absorbed sugar.

Fats, the second important nutrient group, are generally fairly easy to digest and little affected by normal cooking. Overcooking can reduce their nutritive value, and prolonged overcooking can actually render them inedible by driving off their oxygen and hydrogen atoms, reducing them to a carbon residue. But by far the most important result of cooking with fats is not the effect on the fats but on the other foods cooking in them, for the fats add essential nutrients. The Chinese practice of cooking vegetables in soybean or peanut oil, for example, adds vitamin E and linoleic acid to the finished dish. In the same way, frying an egg in butter or margarine adds a whole cluster of nutrients, including vitamins A, D and E and the triglycerides. All cooking with fat also adds a high proportion of calories to food.

Preparing the proteins

For most high-protein foods, particularly meat and such vegetables as peas and beans, cooking is usually essential. To begin with, it enhances the taste of these foods. More important, it prepares them for digestion. In their raw state, many protein foods are too tough for the human digestive system to handle; the body's digestive juices cannot get through to start work. The heat of cooking softens the meat so that it can be chewed to make the protein available for digestion. The same job can sometimes be done without cooking; in hamburger, beefsteak is broken by chopping and the meat can be eaten raw as "steak tartare." And some flesh—that of fish and shellfish particularly—is naturally so soft that it is often eaten raw; raw fish is a staple in Japan and raw oysters and clams are delicacies all over the world.

While cooking makes protein, fat and carbohydrate foods far more useful to mankind, it does not do the same for the remaining two nutrient groups, the minerals and the vitamins. They would serve man better, in fact, if cooking had never been invented. They do not need to be cooked, for they are used by the body in almost the same forms they take in raw food, and cooking may deplete or destroy them. Cooking with bicarbonate of soda, which is often added to vegetables to improve their color, creates an alkaline solution that accelerates losses of vitamin C. Worst of all is the use of large amounts of water in cooking;

the water dissolves, or leaches, essential minerals and vitamins and they are left behind in the pot.

The dangers of leaching were pointed out as recently as the 1920s, when public-health officials were puzzled by the strange pattern of malnutrition in the South. Impoverished sharecroppers there ate poorly—grits, corn mush and molasses, greens, with a bit of fatback. The diet for white and Negro sharecroppers was much the same. But, oddly enough, the whites suffered more severely from deficiency diseases; the Negroes, also ill-fed, were relatively unaffected. The mystery was not solved until the scientists learned that both whites and Negroes boiled their staple foods for long periods to improve the palatability of the somewhat tasteless provender. But then the whites threw away the cooking water; using the so-called potlikker was socially unacceptable. With the discarded liquid went the nutrients that had been leached away by long boiling. The Negroes, uninfluenced by the social stigma attached to potlikker, drank it and used it to soak corn bread, recapturing the essential vitamins and minerals. The lesson this incident taught has not been lost on modern housewives, who conserve vitamins and minerals in two ways: they save potlikker (dignified by the name of "stock") for soups and gravies, and they reduce leaching by cooking food in the least possible water.

Besides enhancing or preserving nutritional quality, proper cooking increases the available quantity of food by effectively controlling two of the major causes of spoilage: microorganisms and enzymes.

Slowing the speed of spoilage

Enzymes are complex organic compounds that speed up the chemical reactions of decay. They are part of all living cells, including the cells of plant and animal foods, but they are normally locked within the tissues of the foods. Even the most gentle handling, however, can release them. When an apple is peeled, for example, the pressure of the knife breaks cell walls and exposes the enzymes within to the air. In the presence of oxygen, the enzymes go to work almost immediately. By the time the apple is completely peeled, the part first touched has turned brown; in a few moments, the entire apple will turn brown and begin to soften. A similar sequence begins whenever food is handled before cooking; the freed enzymes, if unchecked, will cause the food to change color, lose flavor and, eventually, become inedible. Cooking prevents this deterioration because its heat destroys most of the enzymes.

Bacteria, molds and yeasts, the microorganisms that are found in plants, animals, water and air, also contain enzymes—enzymes vital to their owners but dangerous to human beings. When these enzymes are turned loose on human food they may create obnoxious, even poisonous, substances and decompose the food to unusable forms. A foul smell and rotten appearance clearly announce this decay—and the layman knows, as well as any nutritionist does, that he eats such food at his peril. But the heat of cooking kills most microorganisms, and checks the progress of putrefaction. Though new organisms will eventually attack cooked food, the gain in preservation is considerable. Raw meat spoils in a few hours, but roasted it stays fresh at least a day and in some parts of the world it is considered edible after even longer storage.

To preserve foods for still longer periods, other methods of processing must be used. The oldest of them after cooking itself is dehydration, the removal of water from a solid or liquid food. Dehydrated foods resist spoilage because both enzymes and microorganisms require moisture. But while preserving food, dehydration also affects its taste—usually adversely, though prunes and raisins, which are dehydrated plums and grapes, have agreeable flavors—and it almost always causes some loss of nutritional quality. A few vitamins, particularly, tend to be destroyed or depleted by the light of sun-drying.

A meal from mare's milk

These disadvantages are far outweighed by dehydration's usefulness and simplicity. Sun-drying was invented at about the same time as agriculture. In Mesolithic Denmark and China, men sun-dried fish, meat and fruit to save them for another day. As long ago as the 13th Century, men were using dried food that could be reconstituted in somewhat the same way modern milk powder is. The nomadic warriors of Genghis Khan, who spent long hours on horseback, sun-dried mare's milk to a light-weight powder, and put some of the powder in a water-filled saddle bottle at the beginning of each day's journey. Stirred throughout the day by the jogging of the horse, the mixture became a thin porridge by nightfall.

Today, sun-drying for preservation is especially important to under-developed nations. In modern Turkey, for example, many villagers eat a complex sun-dried mixture called *tarhana*, based on powdered yogurt made of cow or buffalo milk. To the yogurt are added wheat flour and bits of carrots, beans or peppers. The resultant chalky powder can be stored almost indefinitely. It is reconstituted by boiling it in water to produce a stew containing most of the original nutrients—except for vitamin C, which is destroyed by the light of the sun.

In industrialized nations, some of this loss of nutritional quality and flavor is prevented by newer drying techniques. Foods are frozen, then placed for varying periods of time in a chamber from which the air has been exhausted. With air pressure reduced to the vanishing point, the water in the food evaporates quickly, preserving much of the flavor and nutrients of even such delicate fruits as strawberries.

Only in comparatively recent times have new preservative methods been devised to rival cooking and dehydration. The canning of food was developed little more than 150 years ago, by a man who set out to solve a specific problem in the spirit of modern science and technology. In the 1790s, during the wars that followed the French Revolution, the armies of France fought on battlefronts all over Europe. Thousands of soldiers in those armies were disabled, not in combat, but by slow starvation and by deficiency diseases induced by a diet of smoked fish, salt meat and hardtack. In desperation, the French government offered 12,000 francs (nearly a quarter of a million dollars today) for a practical way to preserve enough food to supply a large, constantly moving army.

An inventor named Nicolas Appert took up the challenge. A man of all food trades, Appert had been variously a chef, confectioner, wine maker, brewer and distiller and had dabbled in food preservation. Now, spurred by the prize offer, he embarked upon a series of tests that occupied him for more than a decade. Appert knew nothing of enzymes or bacteria, nor did anyone else in his day. He did know one fact—that heat neutralizes whatever it is that causes food to spoil—and he set out to make this neutralization permanent. After 14 years of trial and error, he arrived at a process that did the job. The food—vegetables, fruit, fish or meat—was sealed in stoppered bottles and the filled bottles were immersed in boiling water; the heat sterilized bottles and contents alike. The food then remained edible until the bottles were opened. The technique was effective enough to win Appert his prize in 1809; he started a canning factory and went on to found a family canning dynasty that continued the business into the 20th Century.

Appert's bottles were expensive, heavy and fragile; their indispensable airtight seals were uncertain. But improvements were not long in coming. By 1810 other inventors had produced more reliable canisters made of tin, and in 1847, the invention of a mass-produced stamped-out can made large-scale inexpensive canning possible. By the time of the American Civil War, canning was a major method of food preservation, widely used to feed the armies of both the Union and the Confederacy.

Recent improvements have made canning still cheaper and more popular; the United States alone now uses 26 billion cans and jars of food a year. The process is extraordinarily effective. A four-pound can of roast veal, put up in 1824, was not opened until 1938; it was then fed to 12 rats for 10 days without ill effect.

Frozen mammoth steaks, 50,000 years old

Cold alone is a wonderfully effective means of preservation: in Siberia, 50,000-year-old steaks cut from frozen mammoths have been eaten in the 20th Century by men and dogs. Chilling was used as a preservative even by the ancients. The Romans brought snow, insulated with straw or chaff, from the mountains to preserve perishable foods. Later, men stored foods in wells, cellars and springhouses, and cut natural ice in wintertime to keep in insulated rooms for summer use. By 1890 mechanical refrigeration had been developed, and 50 years later the refrigerator had become a standard piece of kitchen equipment in the American home. In a modern home refrigerator, which maintains a temperature between 38° F. and 42° F., a housewife can safely keep such food as dairy

THE FIRST ICEBOX, an insulated wooden cabinet holding chunks of ice, was developed in the early 1800s (the box above dates from about 1880). Large blocks of ice were chopped from frozen rivers and lakes in winter *(right)*, stored in warehouses and delivered to household consumers in summer by wagon. In the 1860s mechanical refrigeration was developed to manufacture ice for iceboxes. The next breakthrough in food preservation had to wait until the 1920s, when mechanical refrigerators were developed for kitchen use.

products and meats for a week, and many housewives store food longer.

Chilling in a refrigerator simply slows down the activity of the enzymes and microorganisms that cause decay. Freezing stops most of this activity altogether, preserving nearly all the food's nutrients and flavor. Even its texture is usually protected; temperatures as low as −320° F. produce almost instantaneous freezing and prevent the formation of the large ice crystals that change the food's physical structure.

Freezing provides one of the best means of food preservation yet found. One potential rival in recent years has been the irradiation of food by radioactive materials, a process which for a time held out the hope of preserving foods so that they could be stored indefinitely without the need for refrigerators or freezer cabinets. However, irradiation was found to destroy flavors and nutrients, and, despite some years of experimentation, the method has yet to find extensive practical use.

Adding chemicals to block disease

One food-processing method that has become increasingly important in recent years is an old idea adapted to a new purpose. This is the use in foods of chemical "additives." Some of these compounds are preservatives, such as the sodium propionate included in bread to retard its spoilage, but many additives serve a quite different purpose: they supply ingredients that people need for good health but might not otherwise get from their diets. Thanks to additives, deficiency diseases that once were common in the United States have now almost disappeared.

As early as the 1920s, "iodized salt"—salt containing an iodine compound—appeared on American tables as a preventive against goiter, a thyroid ailment afflicting many people who lived in sections of the Midwest and Northwest. A decade later, dairymen began to add vitamin D to milk to guard children against the bone-deforming disease called rickets. Vitamin A, essential for normal vision, occurs naturally in butter; for families who prefer margarine, which does not contain it, the vitamin is artificially added. "Enriched" bread and flour contain a whole assortment of nutrient additives (thiamine, niacin, riboflavin and iron) to prevent an equally large number of diseases (beriberi, riboflavin deficiency and iron-deficiency anemia). In the southern United States, enriched bread helped wipe out pellagra in a single generation.

With additives to guarantee the quality of food, cooking to make it more edible, and freezing, canning and drying to preserve it, man has acquired a formidable arsenal of food-processing methods. The old problem of saving today's meat for next week is long solved; today's housewife expects to serve July-fresh strawberries in December. For with modern processing, the produce of every season and every country can always be as close as the nearest supermarket.

Food from the Factory

A century ago most American families ate food that they had grown at home. They picked fruit from the backyard trees, cooked vegetables from the garden and often even slaughtered their own meat. The produce of nearby fields and barnyards usually came straight into the kitchen, its only stop a brief stay in the pantry or root cellar.

Today most food comes from fields thousands of miles distant, and it reaches the family table only after detouring through a factory for processing. Complex machines wash and grade, wrap or peel, prepare and preserve the fresh products of the farm, transforming them into handy, packaged foodstuffs that not only save the housewife time and effort but also make available the widest possible variety of foods in every locality and every season. Even the simplest foods now undergo some kind of treatment in a factory. Apples are washed and bagged in plastic before they are placed on the produce shelf. And entire dinners wait in the freezer, needing only to be heated before they can be eaten. Every day American families consume the contents of 70 million cans and jars, and 32 million pounds of freezer packages; as a result, the food industry has become the largest in the country.

CHOPS ON THE HOOF
Crowding up the chute to a waiting freight car, lambs leave a railhead in the Far West for the extended journey that will take them through packing plant, refrigerated warehouse and meat-cutting room, and convert them into chops and roasts for hungry Americans. Today, not just lamb but all meat is processed before it is sold to the housewife at the market.

DELIVERED FOR PROCESSING

From the fields and barns of America's farms, foodstuffs flow to processor and packer, store and home, aboard a seemingly limitless stream of trains and trucks. There are 21,000 slat-sided livestock cars and 116,000 refrigerated "reefer" cars on the rails, and on the roads produce trucks ranging from quarter-ton farm pickups to 48-foot-long milk tankers.

Each of the trucks shown below parked outside the Campbell Soup Company cannery at Napoleon, Ohio, carries 500 wooden boxes filled with tomatoes. After processing, the tomatoes will emerge from the plant as juices, sauces and tomato soup. The company buys entire fields of crops from local farmers even before the vegetables have been planted.

THE PRODUCTION LINE STARTS

Inside the processing plants, machines and conveyors take over. Some foods, like the apples bobbing along the water-filled flume in the top picture below, may simply get a bath and a preservative coating before being tucked into packages for shipment to market. The tomatoes at bottom are cleaned while moving on conveyor belts under a high-power water spray; then they are cooked. Pumpkins are washed as they are spun and sprayed in a rotating drum *(right),* after they have been split by machine at a cannery in Illinois. The spray both removes the dirt and slushes out seeds. Then the pumpkins are crushed into a paste by a special machine and canned for home use.

How the food is carried from step to step of its processing depends on the food itself: apples are floated, meat hangs on rolling hooks and dried foods, such as flour, may be blown through pneumatic tubes.

THE CREAM OF THE CROP

Amidst the clank and whir of efficient food-processing machines, human help is still needed, most often to watch for spoiled produce. At a soup cannery *(below)* inspectors at the far right pull defective tomatoes from the main conveyor and place them on a smaller belt where their bruised parts are pared away by other workers. The salvaged tomatoes are then returned to the soup-making process.

Eggs are also inspected and graded in a modern-day version of the farmwife's old "candling" process. The eggs *(right)* are rotated while a strong light shines through them. An inspector notices the way the yolk moves as the egg turns; very free motion indicates lower quality.

MACHINES THAT PEEL AND SHELL

Some of the most ingenious machines that speed food processing are those that skin farm produce. Vegetables such as onions, potatoes and carrots are attacked by steam, abrasives or even flames. Fruit is peeled by whirling blades or lye baths. And eggs are deftly separated from their shells by a complicated sequence of maneuvers, shown here at a mayonnaise plant. Blades chop the eggshells and the insides of the eggs drop into conveyor cups. The shells are swept away by mechanical arms. This machine can process 5,760 eggs in an hour.

MEAT MADE READY FOR THE POT

Meat is graded and often smoked, frozen or canned at processing plants. After cattle are slaughtered, the beef is cleaned and graded *(right)* according to Department of Agriculture standards for age, texture and fat content. As for chicken, once a Sunday luxury, it is now one of the most economical foods because of efficient production and processing. A chicken enters the plant alive, moves along a belt past a slaughterer who cuts its throat, is dipped into boiling water to loosen the feathers, then plucked by rubber-fingered rollers. A tongue of flame burns off the pinfeathers and hairs *(above)* after the chicken has been cut open, inspected and cleaned. Then it is refrigerated and shipped to market.

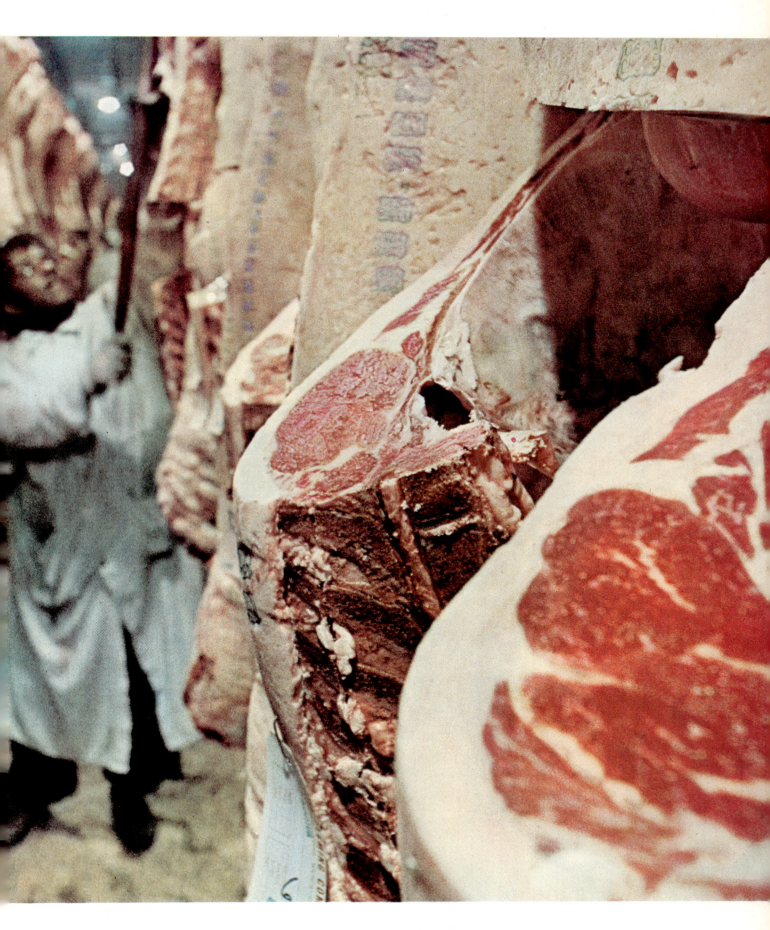

THE FINAL PREPARATION

Preserved, cooked or sliced, food undergoes the last stages of its processing just before it is wrapped in a package, in a form convenient for the housewife to use. Green beans *(below, center)* are frozen in seven minutes inside a rime-encrusted tunnel by 30-mile-per-hour blasts of air that have been chilled to −40° F. American cheese *(left)* is cut into long, thin ribbons that fall in layers; these are then cut crosswise, making blocks of sliced cheese ready for wrapping and marketing. At right, a 115-gallon cart of tomato soup is stirred by a worker with a stainless-steel paddle, on its way to a filling machine *(background)* where it will be sucked up and transferred to cans.

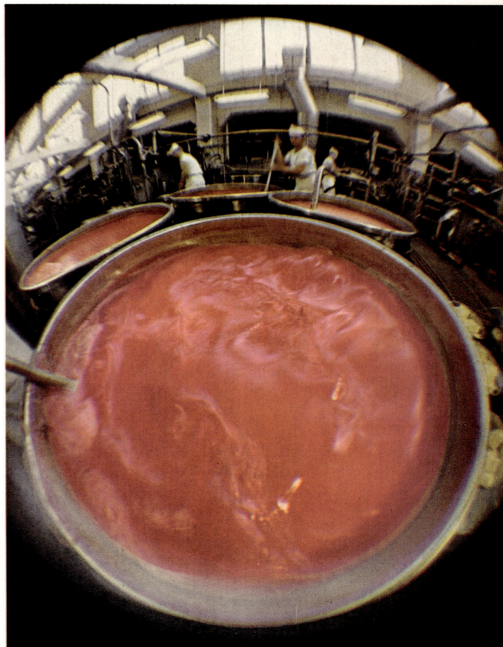

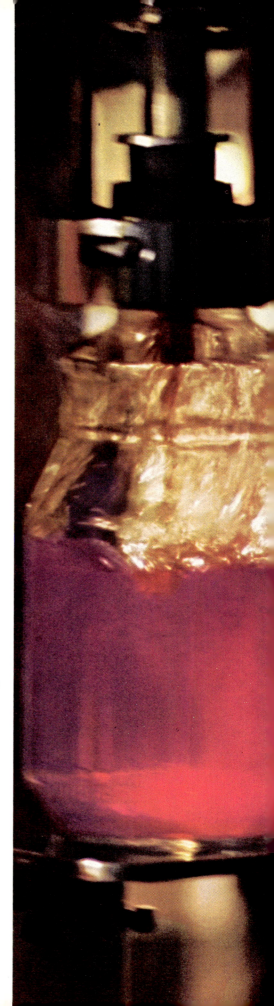

AND INTO THE PACKAGE

Food processing ends when the product is bottled, canned, wrapped or
sealed. The packaging process also rids the food of the bacteria that
ordinarily cause spoilage. The cranberry juice being bottled at right has
been pasteurized beforehand by a quick exposure to intense heat.

A different method is followed for foods that are to be canned; they
are usually sterilized only after they are inside their containers. After the
can is sealed it is placed in a pressure cooker that maintains temperatures
as high as 250° F. for a period lasting, in some cases, as long as three
hours. This intense heat kills the bacteria inside and at the same time
cooks the food, making a foolproof dish for the young bride and a
work-saving ingredient for the experienced cook.

4
Miracle
of Digestion

A man is what he eats; such is the impli-
cation of this painting depicting a man
literally assembled from food. It is one of
several similar works by the 16th Century
artist Giuseppe Arcimboldo, whose technique foreshadowed modern surrealism.

IT IS BARELY 200 YEARS since anyone began to understand what happens to food after it is eaten. In a series of intricate experiments—many of them requiring tests on human volunteers—scientists laboriously learned how to trace (and even how to photograph—*pages 88-101)* the course taken by food as it moves through the body. But only today are the basic chemical processes that go on in the body beginning to be deciphered, and many of the fundamental steps that transform food ingredients into the energy and substance of human life remain the most obdurate mysteries challenging modern science.

The broad outlines of how the body uses food are now clear. Like a chemical factory, the body converts the raw materials supplied by food into usable substances, in this case the 45 essential nutrients that build cells and fuel activity. Food is first digested in the alimentary canal, which extends from the mouth to the anus—that is, meat, fish, grains and vegetables are physically and chemically changed from their original forms into simple, more soluble substances. The nutrients in these substances are absorbed by the tissues that surround part of the canal. They are then transported to the 100 trillion cells that need them. Finally, the nutrients are assimilated to build body tissue or generate energy.

Most steps along the way are clear, and many of the details of these steps are now known, although in some cases their discovery has raised questions subtler than those that were answered. Even before food is eaten, for example, the body prepares to digest it. Everyone has felt his mouth "water" at the sight or smell of food, or at the mere memory or thought of food. What we actually feel on these occasions is the release of saliva by the glands located in the face and neck—glands whose products are indispensable to digestion. Obviously these glands respond not only to the touch of food itself but also to stimulation triggered by the eyes or the nose or the brain itself. This "psychic stimulation" of the glands was first investigated by Ivan Pavlov, the Russian physiologist who laid the foundation for most modern research on digestion.

Pavlov brought to his task the skills of a master technician and the daring imagination of a great innovator. His study of the process of digestion began in 1877 and was carried out mainly at Leningrad's Institute of Experimental Medicine, where he headed the department of physiology for 45 years. To begin with, Pavlov used the surgical technique of cutting an artificial opening, or fistula, into the body of an experimental animal without impairing the normal functioning of its organs. Through a fistula in the salivary glands, stomach or pancreas of a dog, he could actually watch the secretion of digestive juices. With a tube inserted into the opening, he could collect and measure these secretions.

In about 1890 Pavlov began to show how the digestive process could be started by the brain alone, even when an animal was given nothing to eat. Over the next 35 years, in experiments of enormous ingenuity and elegance, he learned to transfer the digestive responses of experimental dogs from the sight or smell of food to completely arbitrary stimulation of the brain. His work culminated in his description of the transference of responses—the "conditioned reflex" or "conditioned response"—now almost synonymous with Pavlov's own name.

To isolate his dogs from all influences except those that he himself introduced, Pavlov took elaborate precautions. His Leningrad laboratory, nicknamed the "tower of silence," was surrounded by a straw-filled moat to prevent vibrations from the outside world from reaching the animals. Within the tower, Pavlov built soundproof testing rooms that had padded walls two feet thick and were sealed by massive steel doors. Each room was subdivided into a concrete cell for one dog and a separate observation chamber from which an experimenter could apply stimuli to the animal. Except for feeding and cleaning periods the dog never saw a human being: the experimenter applied his stimuli by remotely controlled apparatus and collected his data with electrical instruments.

Sounds, sights and saliva

In a typical conditioned-reflex experiment, a dog might hear a metronome beginning to tick in his cell just before he was fed. At every mealtime the association between the ticking and the food would be repeated to strengthen the dog's unconscious connection between the two actions. Eventually—usually after 10 to 20 repetitions—the dog would begin to secrete saliva at the sound of the metronome, before his meal came within sight or smell. At this point a conditioned reflex had been established; the dog would salivate at the tick of the metronome even if his food never arrived at all. Dogs could be conditioned to give a salivary response to an extraordinary range of stimuli: an electric shock, a flashing light, a ringing bell, the blast of a trumpet. And conditioning could be amazingly specific; a dog's digestive juices could be made to flow at the sight of an object rotating clockwise but not counterclockwise, or at the sound made by one organ pipe but not that made by a pipe one semitone higher or lower in pitch.

Pavlov had proved that many different links could be set up between the sensory receptors of the brain, on the one hand, and the digestive system, on the other. He clinched his proof through the surgical removal of the cerebral cortexes of conditioned dogs; deprived of the highly developed parts of their brains, they no longer salivated in response to the conditioning stimuli.

More recent research has found that emotions and other kinds of mental activity influence digestion, and has even identified specific brain sections that control the consumption and use of food. But exactly how these control centers work is one of the unsolved mysteries of the brain that psychologists and physiologists are still studying.

Although most experiments like Pavlov's have used animals as subjects, the results seem to apply equally well to men. In men, who are rarely conditioned by deliberate Pavlovian treatment, the salivary glands normally begin to secrete their juices at the actual sight, smell or thought of food. Then, as food is taken into the mouth, the process of digestion begins. Chewing is a mechanical action that serves two purposes: it

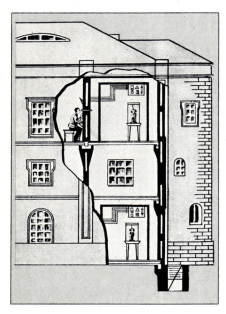

PAVLOV'S LABORATORY, seen in a cutaway view, shows the fortresslike construction that enabled the famous Russian physiologist to isolate dogs for experiments with digestive reflexes without interference from outside noise. Located in Leningrad, the three-story building was called the "tower of silence." Only the top and bottom floors were used for the experiments, so that animals would not be disturbed by hearing one another. An experimenter, also isolated, is shown on the top floor observing his animal through a periscope.

makes food easier to swallow by breaking it into smaller particles and it exposes more surfaces to the saliva and the juices of the lower digestive tract. The saliva itself has a double function. It moistens food for easier swallowing, and it also carries a substance called ptyalin, which begins the chemical action of digestion by starting the breakdown of food starch into simple sugars.

An army of chemical catalysts

Ptyalin is an enzyme, one of some 20,000 to 30,000 in the human body. The figure is no more than an estimate based on the number of bodily processes that seem to require enzyme action. Only about 1,000 enzymes have been identified, but their great importance in nutrition and other living processes has been established beyond any doubt. They are all complex proteins that act as catalysts to speed up chemical reactions.

The action of an enzyme is vital, powerful and more efficient than that of any reagent concocted by chemists. The element iron, for example, will break down hydrogen peroxide, a poisonous by-product of the human body. But an iron-containing enzyme called catalase will break down as much hydrogen peroxide in one second as a similar quantity of iron could handle by itself in 300 years. Chemists can separate proteins into their component amino acids by boiling them at 330° F. for 18 to 24 hours in a strong solution of hydrochloric acid; the enzymes of the small intestine perform the same operation in under three hours, at body temperature, in a neutral or even slightly alkaline medium. And the ptyalin of saliva, mixed with food while it is chewed, converts starch into sugar within minutes after the food reaches the stomach.

Although enzymatic action starts while food is being chewed, digestion does not move into high gear until the chewed food has passed along the 10-inch esophagus, or gullet, and reached the stomach. Like the mouth, the stomach subjects its contents to both physical and chemical processes. In the physical action of peristalsis, waves of contraction and relaxation pass along the walls of a full stomach to churn and knead solid food into a semisolid, amorphous mixture called chyme.

Meanwhile, the chyme undergoes chemical changes initiated by gastric juices secreted by the walls of the stomach. These digestive fluids are among the most potent in the body. They include a number of enzymes, such as rennin, which aids in the digestion of milk, as well as hydrochloric acid, so corrosive that it would eat away the walls of the stomach if they were not protected by a layer of mucus. Most powerful of all is the combination of the enzyme pepsin with hydrochloric acid: the enzyme, which is triggered into action by the acid, starts the breakdown of proteins into absorbable amino acids; the acid also acts upon proteins, but has an additional function, the destruction of the invading bacteria of disease and the putrefying bacteria in food.

Protection against putrefaction is needed because food may remain in the stomach for a considerable length of time. After a full meal the stomach may take from three to more than four and a half hours to process its chyme. The difference in time depends partly upon the kind of food being processed. Carbohydrates pass through the stomach with relative speed. This is why the person who eats a high-carbohydrate Chinese meal—such as rice, bamboo shoots and bean sprouts—may observe that the food "doesn't stay with him" or that he "feels hungry a couple of hours later." High-protein foods, like steak, and high-fat ones, like pork, fried foods and oil-based salad dressing, stay in the stomach longest. When those foods are eaten, the feeling of satiety lasts a long time, and people say that such a meal "sticks to the ribs."

The stomach and the mind

In addition to the effect of the mind on the salivary glands, there is another and more puzzling relationship between psychology and digestion. In ways that are not yet fully understood, the emotional state of a diner affects the length of time that his stomach takes to empty itself, because emotions can alter the rate of peristaltic action. Fear slows the contractions and causes food to move more slowly through the stomach: the cliché about "paralyzing fear" is no mere metaphor. Contrariwise, a person who announces that his stomach is "churning" with anger or hostility is telling the literal truth. These emotions speed up the peristaltic rate and force food through the stomach more rapidly—so rapidly, in fact, that it sometimes reaches the small intestine before it should and adds a case of indigestion to the sufferer's emotional ills.

When chyme leaves the stomach to enter the small intestine, its passage is precisely regulated. A valve—the pyloric sphincter, which connects stomach to intestines—transmits a small amount of chyme into the first section of the intestine, the duodenum. Now the stomach temporarily halts its peristalsis until the chyme that has been admitted to the duodenum continues on its journey through the small intestine—a 22-foot-long coiled tube equipped, like the other parts of the alimentary canal, with both chemical and physical tools for digestion.

As chyme begins this stage of its processing, it contains much food that is still in the form of raw material, not yet ready to be absorbed by the body. Proteins are fragmented but not completely broken down; starches are still becoming simple sugars; fats have not passed the large-globule stage. Inside the small intestine digestion will be completed by hardworking juices. From the liver comes a liquid called bile, which transforms fat globules into a smooth emulsion. The pancreas contributes enzymes that continue the breakdown of proteins and others that help to divide starch into sugars and work with bile in digesting fats. And the small intestine itself secretes enzymes from its inner walls, or mucosa, to complete the reactions.

When all these enzymes have done their work, the food is digested and its nutrients are ready for absorption. The protein molecules have been dismantled into their amino acid components; starches have been split into simple sugars; fats, divided into smaller molecules and emulsified by bile, have formed a fluid resembling colorless cream. (The min-

THE ACTION OF AN ENZYME (green), as it assembles amino acids from food into protein molecules for the body, is similar to the fitting of the interlocking parts of a jigsaw puzzle. In the first step (1), the enzyme accepts certain specific amino acids (notched triangles), which fit precisely into its surface; other types of amino acids (triangles) cannot fit, requiring a different enzyme for their assembly. Once joined, the amino acids are permanently connected by chemical bonds (2); finally the bonded combination floats away (3), leaving the enzyme free to assemble another similar pair.

erals and vitamins, which are used by the body in their original forms, have been ready for absorption all along.) The watery nonnutrient residue will move on to the large intestine, where the water will be absorbed; the remaining solid waste will be eliminated.

Up to this point, none of the material—whether in the form of ingested food or chyme—has actually been inside the body proper. It has been moving through the 30-foot-long alimentary canal, which is separated from the interior of the body by the walls of the mouth, the esophagus, the stomach and the intestines. But in the small intestine, by methods that present one of the many mysteries of nutrition, most of the nutrients in food are absorbed by the body.

The physical instruments of absorption are perfectly plain. They are fingerlike tentacles called villi that line the inner walls of the small intestine like the pile of a carpet. The constantly moving villi somehow pick nutrient molecules out of the chyme, and by the time the chyme has passed through the small intestine, the villi have absorbed nearly 95 per cent of all nutrient molecules.

Osmosis in reverse

It is in this absorption process that the mystery lies. Some nutrient molecules pass through the surface of the villi by so-called osmosis. That is, because there is a greater concentration of these molecules outside the villi cells than inside, the villi soak up the nutrient molecules much as a dry sponge soaks up water. In so doing, the villi are duplicating the mechanics of osmosis as it occurs elsewhere in nature. Here the resemblance ceases, for most nutrient molecules move from *low* concentrations in the intestine to high concentrations inside the villi, in apparent defiance of physical laws. It is almost as if a soaking wet sponge did not dry out in the air, but instead absorbed still more moisture from the atmosphere around it. Scientists who are searching for an explanation of the phenomenon have called it "reverse osmosis" or "active absorption." They speculate that it may involve a process in which "carriers" at the surface of villi cells seize upon nutrient molecules, transport them across the cells, release them and go back for more. "Unfortunately," as one physiologist has remarked, "the precise mechanism of even a single carrier system . . . has not yet been worked out."

The next phase of the nutrients' journey—transport to the individual cells they are to nourish—is better understood. Two routes lead to the destination. Fats move through a series of ducts called lymphatics that run from the villi to the bloodstream, and through the blood to the cells. The creamy form in which fats are transported actually affects the appearance of the blood for a time. A blood sample taken shortly after a person drank a fat-rich milk shake appears creamy because of the tiny droplets of fat the blood carries. A sample taken a few hours later would show clear blood, because the fats would by then have been picked up by the cells of body tissue.

Only fats and fat-soluble vitamins take this route. The other nutrients follow a more circuitous path. They are carried away from the villi by tiny blood vessels called capillaries, which funnel them into the portal vein leading to the liver. If the body is considered as a complex chemical factory, the liver is its main processing and storage plant. Here, many kinds of enzymes help change the nutrient molecules into new forms for new purposes. Unlike earlier changes, which prepared nutrients for absorption and transport, the reactions in the liver produce the products needed by individual cells. Some of the products are used by the liver itself. Part of the rest is held in storage by the liver, to be released into the body as needed. The remainder goes into the bloodstream, from which it is picked up by the cells of the body and put to work.

The "burning" of food fuels

At this point the handling of food within the body has reached its final stage. The cells assimilate the nutrients and, by a process called cell metabolism, use them as fuel for energy or as material for the manufacture of body chemicals and tissues. Within each cell a full complement of enzymes catalyze the metabolic reactions and regulate the rate at which these reactions proceed.

To produce energy, the cells generally call on carbohydrates and fats for fuel, thus putting to use the energy that had originally been derived from the sun. Using the sun's energy, green plants—and only green plants—have the power to combine carbon dioxide and water into a simple sugar called glucose. Plants link such sugars together to form starches; animals that eat the plants store the energy of sugars and starches in the form of fats. The human body reverses the process by which energy was stored. For in assimilating a simple sugar, a cell oxidizes—in effect, "burns"—the nutrient to release energy, leaving carbon dioxide and water to be subsequently eliminated from the body. The process involves more than a score of separate chemical transformations, in each of which some unique enzyme does its job.

Enzymes are even more crucial in deciding how much energy should be generated and when. The instantaneous release of the potential energy in a steak dinner could kill a man; it could raise his temperature roughly 70° F. A regulatory system based upon enzymes prevents this from happening. With remarkable efficiency, the system senses the body's needs and reacts accordingly, doling out energy at a flexible rate that is continuously and automatically adjusted to the demand.

Along with energy, nutrients must provide materials for the growth and repair—or more correctly, replacement—of tissue. Even after the growing time of youth is over, the body must build millions of new cells every day, for cells die off and must be replaced. The red cells of the blood have a lifetime of about three months, while the furiously active cells of the villi last for some 43 hours. To sustain its organs and tissues, the body must create new cells to replace dead or discarded ones.

The major nutrients for the building of new tissue are the amino acids, which the body either manufactures or takes from food proteins

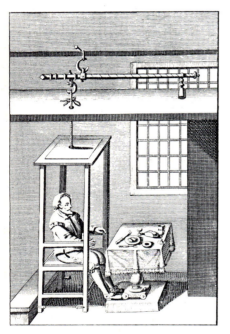

EATING ON A SCALE, a 17th Century Italian physician named Sanctorius tried to find out what happened to the food in his body. He weighed himself and his food on the scale before eating. To his surprise, he noticed a loss in his weight as he digested his food. After considering the problem, Sanctorius attributed the weight loss to the conversion of food into "insensible perspiration," and he was partially right. The loss of weight came with the release of end products of food use—moisture that was partly given off through the skin and lungs, and carbon dioxide that was exhaled.

and then combines to form proteins it needs. Within the cells, enzymes link the amino acids together in the molecular structures required for specific jobs. Manufacturing protein is a complex job: no less than 17 amino acids, for example, are combined in the liver in hundreds of different combinations to synthesize a single protein, albumin, essential for the transport of nutrients in the blood.

With the manufacture of body chemicals and tissue and the production of energy, the body's transformation of food is completed. Though the operations involved are intricate and continue day and night throughout our lives, we need not deliberately control them or, indeed, even be aware of them. But let the machinery falter at any point and the failure soon becomes painfully obvious. The hydrochloric acid in the stomach can, if improperly regulated, burn holes in the stomach lining to produce stomach ulcers. A deficiency in a child's vitamin D intake (.01 milligram per day is usually recommended) so handicaps bone growth that legs become bowed. And the lack of sufficient food causes the major steps of food utilization to fail, until finally life can no longer be maintained.

A strange story of starvation

The progressive deterioration caused by total starvation has been recorded, in dispassionate detail, in one strange case. When the Irish rebellion against England was at its height in 1920, Terence James Mac-Swiney was serving as Lord Mayor of Cork. Imprisoned by the British as a revolutionary, the Lord Mayor went on a hunger strike.

MacSwiney stopped eating on August 12, 1920. After eight days his wife reported that he was able to write a letter only "with great difficulty and he nearly fainted twice while writing it." This was an early sign of starvation. Lacking food for energy, MacSwiney's body began to burn off its own fat tissues, but these energy reserves were limited, and soon failed to supply the needed vitality.

On the 15th day of the hunger strike MacSwiney collapsed; in the days thereafter he became "noticeably thinner and more sunken in the face." He had passed into the second stage of starvation. With his reserves of fat tissue exhausted, his body was extracting energy by consuming muscles and body organs.

During the next month advanced starvation became evident. MacSwiney's body adjusted to the absence of food by slowing down its physical systems. His temperature and blood pressure dropped; his heart slowed; glands became dormant or inactive.

At this point the downward slide could still have been arrested and reversed—but then MacSwiney passed the point of no return. During the 10th week of his hunger strike physicians fed him by force, but it was too late, for the enzymes of his digestive tract were no longer functioning. During the last days of his ordeal MacSwiney lay quietly, usually unconscious, his lips sometimes moving soundlessly, his eyes sometimes opening to stare sightlessly at the ceiling. On the 76th day of his protest, with nothing left in his body to draw upon for energy, he died.

The Human Nutrition Machine

Inside every human being, awake or asleep, a continuous, finely meshed and almost unbelievably complex series of mechanical and chemical processes takes place, constantly adapting food to meet the needs of the body. With little conscious control, the body's delicate organs first digest food to release its nutrient molecules and then use these products to build tissue and generate the energy of life. Many of the actions are still only dimly understood, for until recently these operations could not be seen in detail. But today electron microscopes, color cameras and new X-ray techniques make dramatically visible the steps through which the body processes nutrients.

The route food takes, from the time it first enters the mouth, can be recorded by the color camera. X-rays picture stomach and intestine movements as they churn food with chemicals. Photomicrographs reveal the little projections that absorb nutrients from the intestine, and show that these tiny organs are more complicated than anyone had ever imagined. And pictures of the liver, circulatory system and muscle structure now give the first detailed view of the intricate, efficient machinery that makes the human being function.

A CLEAR VIEW OF BODILY PROCESSES
The long-mysterious progress of food from ingestion to utilization by individual cells is finally being clarified with the aid of new instruments. These aids have made possible the closeup views of the significant areas of the body's organs *(shown on this plastic model)* that appear on the following pages, as indicated by the numbers in the picture at right.

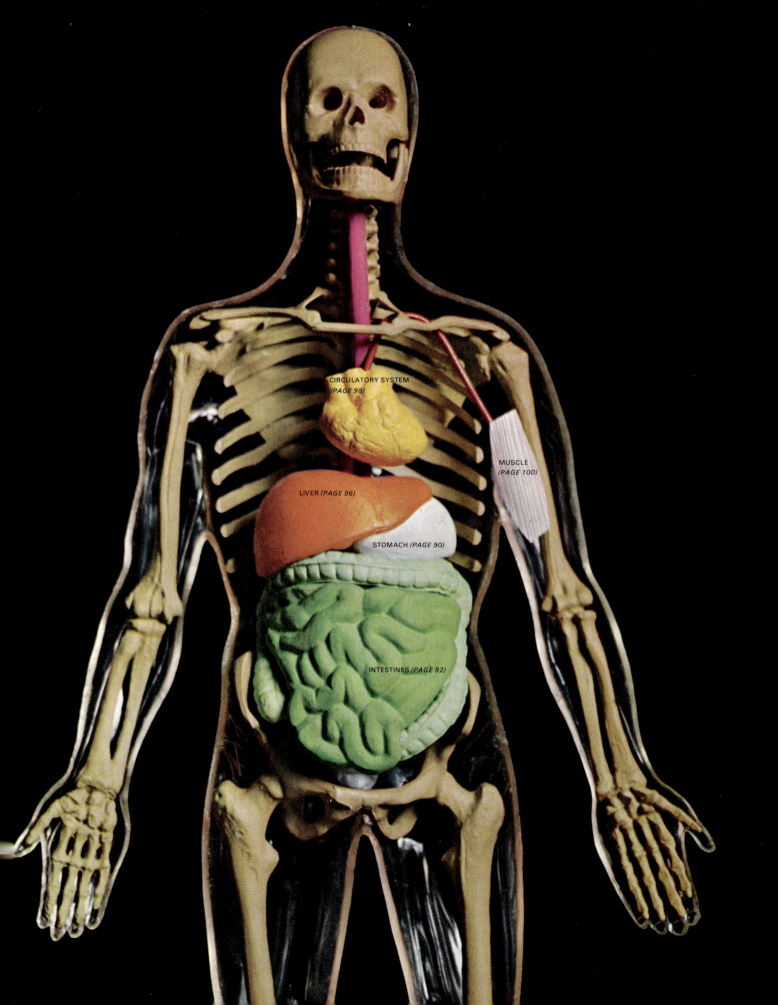

CIRCULATORY SYSTEM
(PAGE 98)

MUSCLE
(PAGE 100)

LIVER *(PAGE 96)*

STOMACH *(PAGE 90)*

INTESTINES *(PAGE 92)*

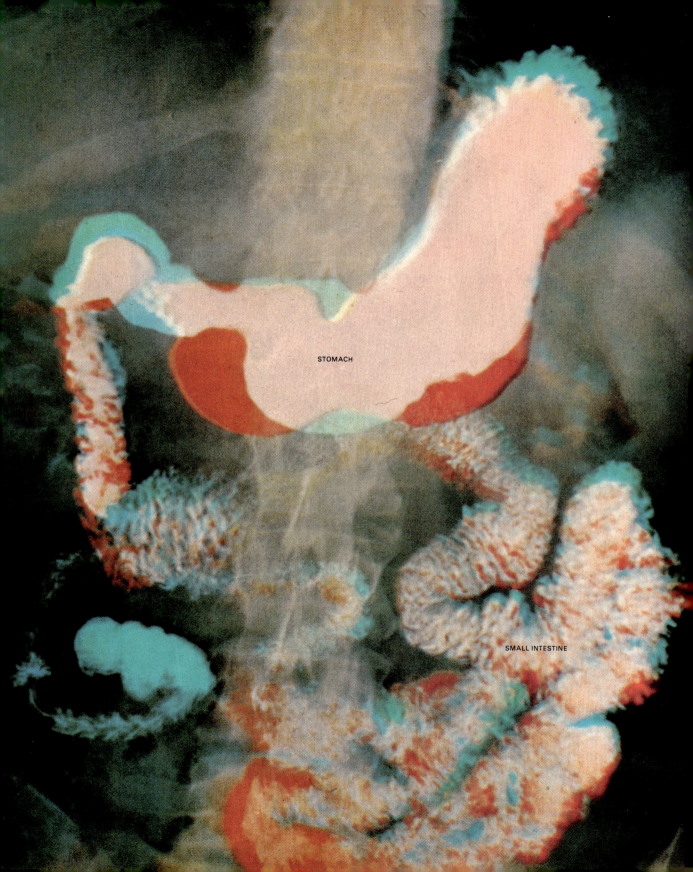

A Human Churn for Digesting Food

By the time food reaches the stomach, it has already begun the series of treatments that will, hours later, enable it to do useful work inside the tissues of the body. The X-rays seen on these pages show the initial steps of the process.

First, the food must be mechanically churned and propelled through stomach and intestine (*opposite and below*) by rhythmic muscular contractions called peristalsis, which build in intensity until they follow one another along the stomach every five to 15 seconds. At the same time, the chemical action of enzymes and acids further breaks down food into usable nutrient molecules.

In the course of this process, the food is transformed into a thick fluid called chyme. Continuing stomach contractions push the chyme into the small intestine, where it is further soaked and agitated. This mixing action brings all the chyme into contact with the walls of the intestine, which are lined with millions of protrusions that absorb the nutrients.

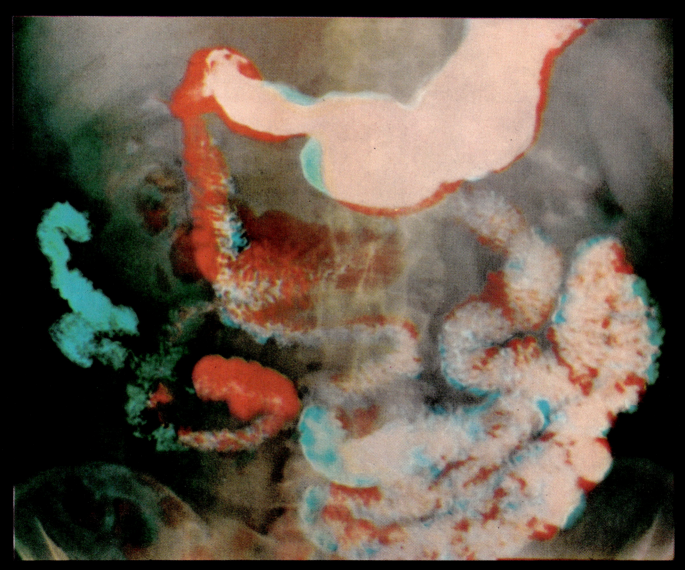

A PULSATING CONVEYOR OF FOOD

These remarkable X-rays, taken a few seconds apart, show how the muscular contractions of peristalsis move food through the stomach and small intestine. Each picture is a composite of two X-rays, the first viewed through a red filter and the next through a blue one. At left, the difference in the red and blue stomach outlines shows the contractions as barium (a chalky substance seen clearly in X-rays) is mixed and pushed into the intestine. In the red phase, the first section of intestine is contracted and empty. In the blue phase, it has expanded to accept barium from the stomach; then it will contract again to force the barium farther along, as shown above. Here the bright red part *(lower center)* occupies the same spot as the bright blue part in the picture opposite—and the new blue area *(far left)* marks the barium's advance.

Velvet for Absorbing Nutrients

Once digestion has freed the essential chemical ingredients contained in food, these nutrients must penetrate living cell walls to enter the body's intricate system of circulating fluids. This transfer is accomplished by the lining of the small intestine, which is peculiarly adapted to the task of absorption.

To present the greatest possible surface area for absorption, the intestinal lining is convoluted and folded, making its surface three times larger in area than that of a straight tube of similar length. An even greater increase in area is provided by the lining's fuzzy covering, which consists of five million small, fingerlike projections called villi, seen below in a highly magnified photograph. When viewed by the naked eye, the villi resemble the nap of a carpet (*villus* is Latin for shaggy hair). Each villus is about the size of a comma on this page, but their great number makes the intestinal lining 10 times larger in area than it would be if it were smooth. This combination of shag-

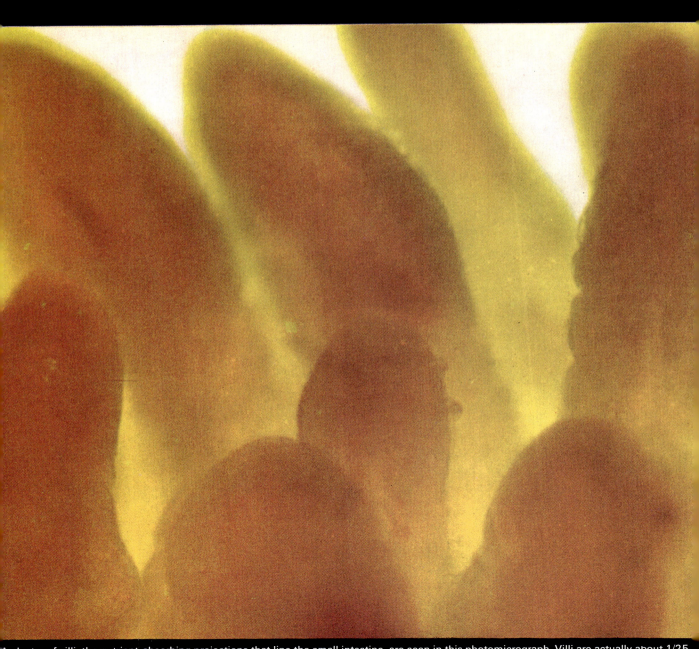

A cluster of villi, the nutrient-absorbing projections that line the small intestine, are seen in this photomicrograph. Villi are actually about 1/25

gy nap, convolutions and folds gives the intestinal wall a total area of about 100 square feet, five times that of the entire human skin.

When the small intestine is empty, the villi are quiet. But as partially digested food, or chyme, reaches them from the stomach the villi become animated. Muscle fibers enable the villi to telescope in and out. This motion helps keep the chyme agitated and exposes the villi to fresh material to be absorbed. The pumping motion also may help the villi push the nutrients into the circulation system.

Vitamins, minerals and simple sugars can be absorbed in their original forms by the villi. But complex carbohydrates first must be chemically changed into simple sugar molecules, protein molecules broken into their constituent amino acid components, and fats emulsified and then converted into fatty acids. In these digested forms, the nutrients are small enough to pass through the villi cell walls—often to be rebuilt later into large molecules needed by the body.

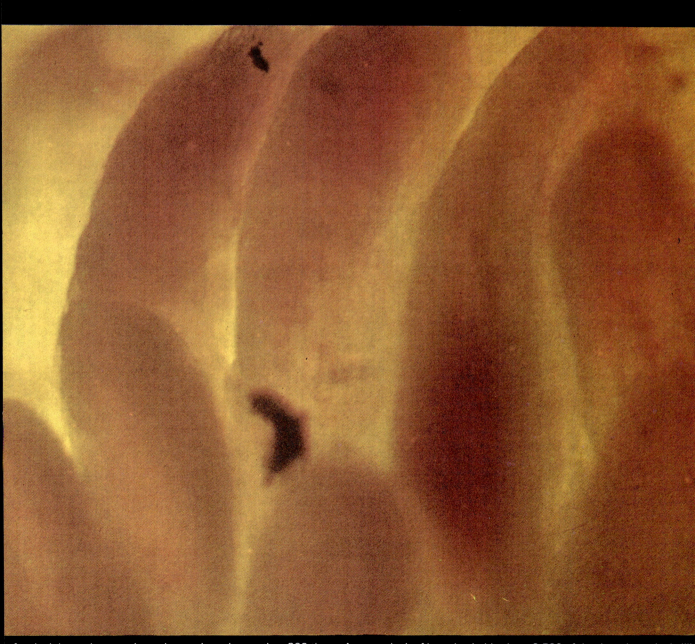

of an inch long; they are shown here enlarged more than 300 times. A square inch of intestine holds about 3,500 of the densely packed villi

A Barrier That Passes Molecules

Exactly how nutrients penetrate the walls of living cells on their passage through the body remains a mystery. But some clues are provided by detailed studies of villi. Photomicrographs like the one at far right reveal that each villus has a covering of cells, called epithelial cells, and these have tiny villi of their own—a nap of "microvilli."

The epithelial cells are the ones that actually absorb nutrient molecules. Some nutrient molecules enter by osmosis, moving from the highly concentrated chyme in the intestine to a lower concentration in the epithelial cells. But a majority of the nutrient molecules are pulled through the epithelial cells by an inexplicable process called active transport.

The hard-working epithelial cells live an average of two days. Fresh cells, manufactured at the base of every villus, migrate up its side to replace the worn-out cells that are sloughed off. Each day, some eight ounces of epithelial cells are used up by the intestine; the old cells are digested and absorbed like food.

Once absorbed by the villi, nutrient molecules are passed along unchanged except for fats. Fats cross the epithelial cell wall as fatty acids, then are immediately transformed back into large fat molecules, forming droplets in the cell. The fat droplets then enter the lymph duct, which will later carry them into the blood. The other nutrient molecules are picked up by the villi's bloodstream, which will take them to the body's most complex organ, the liver.

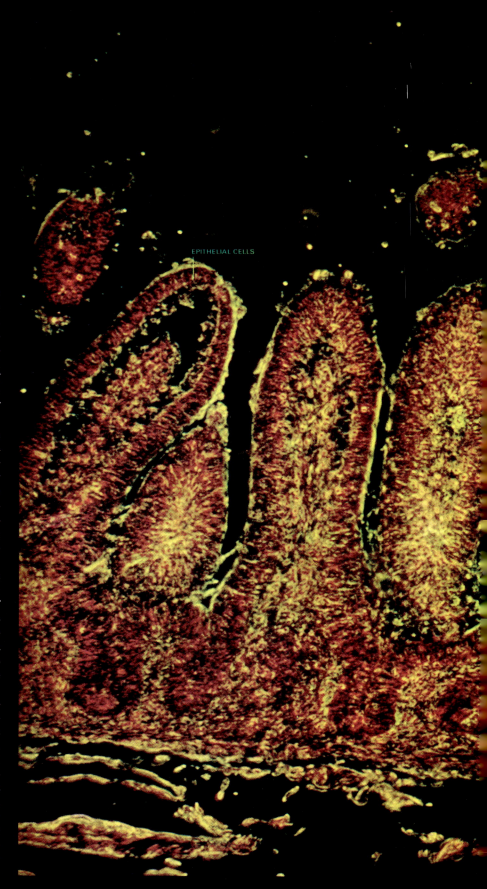

EPITHELIAL CELLS

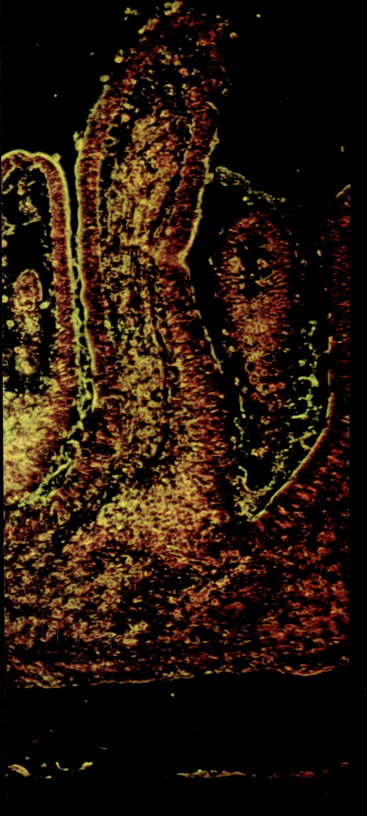

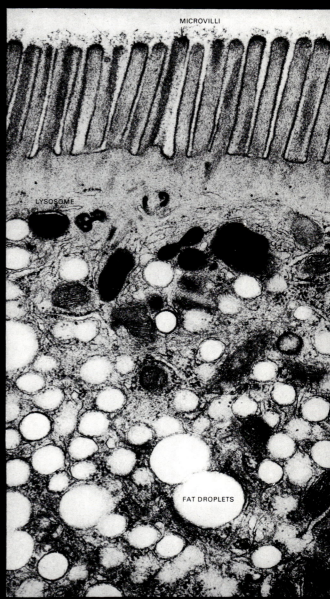

ANATOMY OF THE ABSORBERS

At the left is a section of human villi. Along the outer edges are the epithelial cells, through which nutrient molecules are absorbed. Inside are muscles that give the villi motion and capillaries and lymph ducts that transport nutrients. Above is a section of one epithelial cell, its microvilli on top. The white circles inside are fat that the cell has absorbed, while the black areas are bodies called lysosomes, which dispose of wastes.

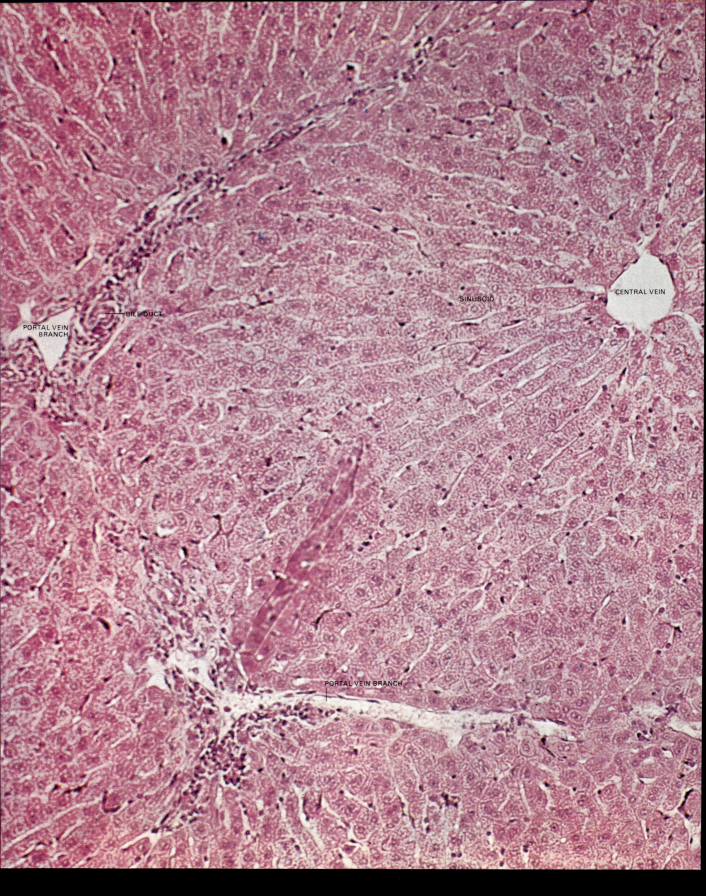

PORTAL VEIN
BRANCH

BILE DUCT

SINUSOID

CENTRAL VEIN

PORTAL VEIN BRANCH

96

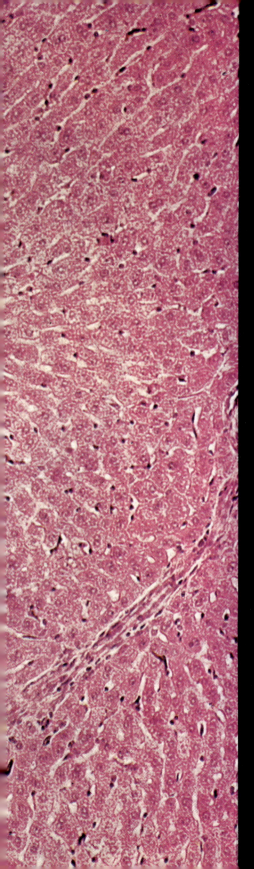

A Unit for Storing and Processing

The liver, largest and most complicated organ in the body, is the key unit in the processing of food nutrients. To its spongelike tissue (shown here in photomicrographs of animal livers similar to human ones) comes blood with nutrients. Some nutrients move directly from the intestine, some indirectly by way of the lymph system. The liver serves numerous functions. Among others, it is (1) a manufacturing center, making body chemicals such as the bile needed for digestion; (2) a storehouse for nutrients; and (3) a filter, neutralizing waste products.

Its cells are clustered in groups called lobules, each about 1/25 inch in diameter. A lobule receives nutrient-laden blood from the intestine via branches of the portal vein. A the lobule the vein branches connec with a labyrinth of minuscule chan nels known as sinusoids, which carr blood into contact with each cell.

During this trip, the cells cleans the blood of such noxious compound as ammonia, which is a by-produc of protein processing. They also re move some nutrient molecules to b held in reserve for the body's futur use: sugar (which is stored as th compound glycogen), protein and vi tamins (95 per cent of all the body' vitamin A is stockpiled in the live cells). After these filtering process es, the remaining nutrients travel i the blood to a central vein that wi then carry them to the heart for dis tribution throughout the entire body

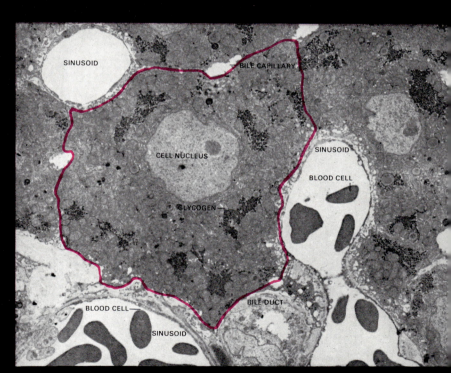

AN EFFICIENT CELL GROUPING

A section of a rabbit's liver *(left)* shows cells clustered in groups called lobules; the hub of each lobule is a central vein *(upper center)*. Blood is taken into the liver by portal vein branches *(far left and lower left)* and is then fed into thousands of sinusoids—tiny channels that weave through the lobules and drain into the central veins that return blood to the heart

A BUSY CELL AT WORK

Around one cell of a mouse's liver *(in outlin above)* can be seen the blood cells seepir through the sinusoids. The bile capillaries car freshly manufactured bile from the liver cell the bile duct. The liver cell also stockpiles nutr ents that will later be used by the body; th darkest blotches contain sugar that has bee made into the compound glycogen for storag

Tiny Tubes to Deliver Blood

Nutrients are transported to every part of the body by minuscule vessels called capillaries (below), which deliver blood to its ultimate destination, the individual cells. The route of transport is complicated. Nutrient-laden blood moves from the liver to the heart, crosses to the lungs for oxygen, then returns to the heart and is pumped to the aorta, the largest artery, for circulation throughout the body. The aorta branches out and then spreads into smaller and smaller ducts. The smallest of these ducts are the capillaries, which crisscross through the body in an intricate web.

The capillaries are so narrow that they can be studied only with a powerful microscope. The average diameter is 7/10,000 inch—⅕ the diameter of a human hair—just wide enough for blood cells to squeeze through, slowly; it takes two hours for 1/100 ounce of blood to travel the length of a single capillary. Yet there are so many capillaries—some 60,000 miles

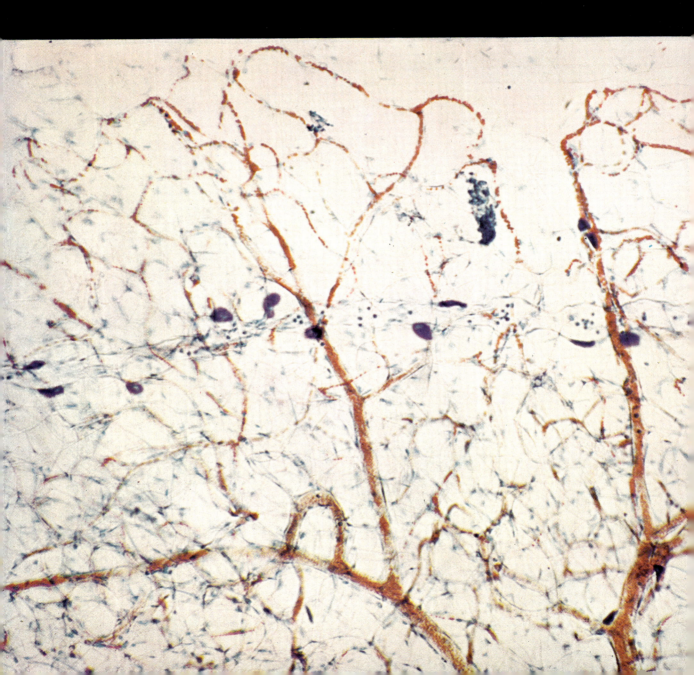

of them—that all the blood in the body can be pumped through the system in only a few minutes.

As the blood trickles through the capillaries, it deposits oxygen and nutrient molecules in each adjacent cell, while cell wastes, such as carbon dioxide, are carried away. Molecules moving to and from the blood travel through the capillary wall, which is exactly one cell thick *(below, right)*—about 1/25,000 inch. Nutrients and wastes diffuse through this wispy barrier, squeezing past unimaginably tiny openings under the pressure of similar molecules backed up behind them. This diffusion process can be extremely swift; some smaller molecules cross the wall several thousand times faster than blood travels along the capillaries themselves. And so efficient is diffusion that 80 to 90 per cent of the smaller molecules carried by the blood are delivered to body cells during a single trip through the capillary system.

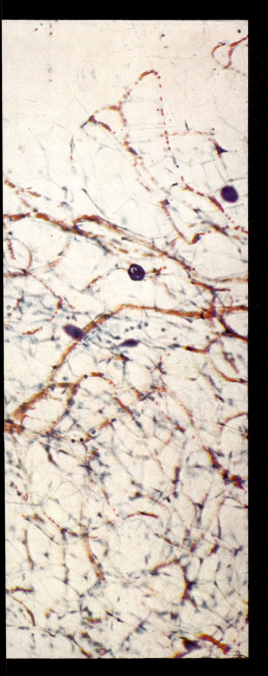

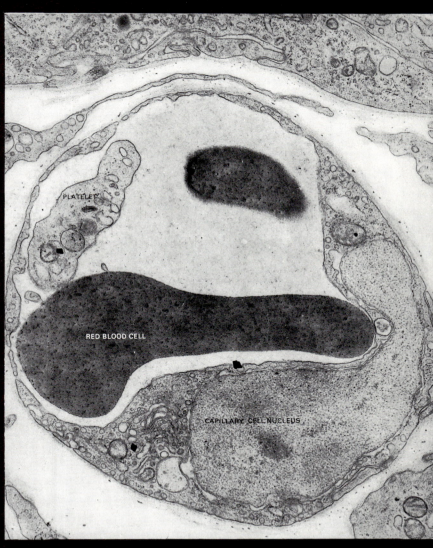

A WEB OF VESSELS

The capillary network of rabbit tissue *(left)*, magnified 275 times, branches out from the arteries to bring nutrients to every cell, just like its human counterpart. Each capillary is only large enough to pass one red blood cell at a time, seen here as rows of beads filing through the vessels. The blue coloring indicates lymph ducts.

INSIDE A CAPILLARY

A segment of a rabbit capillary, seen in cross-section above, consists of a single cell rolled into a tube barely wide enough for a bit of clotting material called a platelet and a single red blood cell. One such cell occupies the full width at center while above it can be observed the front of another cell following closely behind.

Food at Work in Cells

Food finally carries out its functions —the building, the maintenance and powering of the body—in individual cells like those of the muscle shown here. To these cells come carbohydrates to provide the energy for life and work. The fats are accumulated as a reserve energy source and also as padding and insulation. The proteins become building materials.

How proteins make up body tissue can be seen in these photomicrographs. In the voluntary muscle (one under conscious control) like the one at right, the striped effect is caused by the arrangement of two proteins, actin and myosin. Their long filaments interweave with each other. The filaments are grouped in sheaves called myofibrils, each of which runs the length of the muscle cell. When the muscle contracts, the protein filaments inside the sheaves overlap even more, bunching up and "making a muscle."

Actually, muscles cannot be made; nearly all their cells are formed before birth. Muscles grow bigger by adding protein to the original cells.

THE VITAL STRIPES OF MUSCLE
A magnified section of leg muscle *(opposite)* shows the striations caused by the arrangement of the protein filaments in each cell. On this page, a close-up shows how their pattern is formed. Each long, wide band is a sheaf of filaments of actin and myosin protein. Actin and myosin filaments are different in thickness; where they overlap, they appear as wide dark bands. The narrow, dark transverse bands are the joints between groups of actin filaments; the clear circles are tubules that carry nutrients and take away wastes from inside the cell.

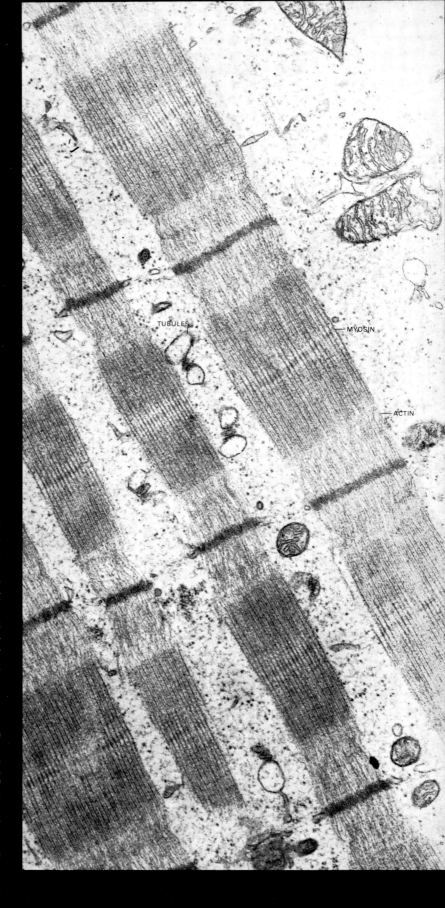

TUBULES

MYOSIN

ACTIN

100

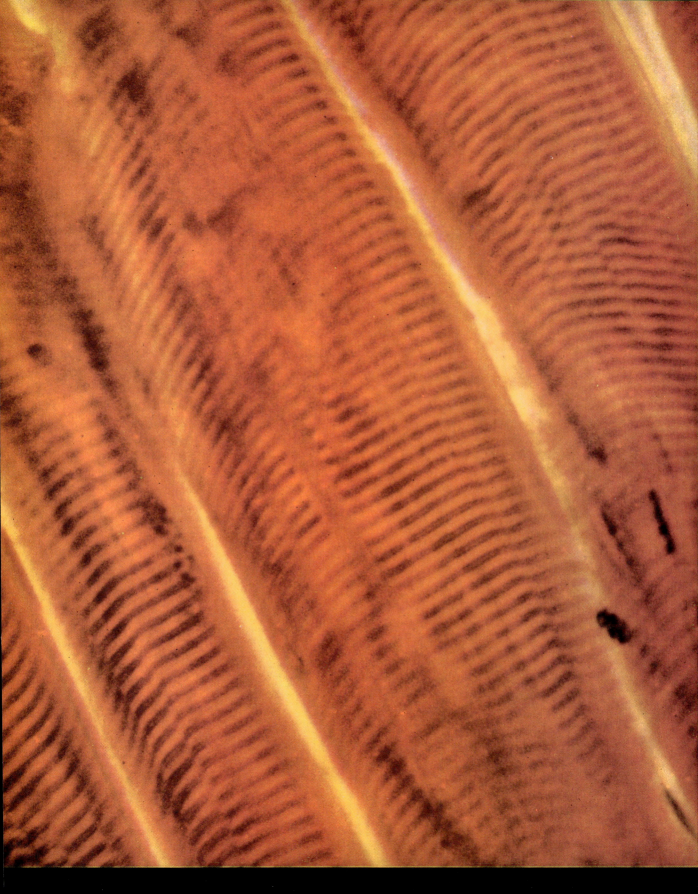

5
The Great Vitamin Mystery

The first man to identify a vitamin was Elmer McCollum. Scientists had suspected that certain ingredients in food could prevent a number of puzzling diseases, but what they were was unknown until McCollum discovered vitamin A in 1912.

THE IDEA THAT illness might be caused by the absence of something that belonged in the diet was a long time gaining credence. It was easy enough to understand how a man could be poisoned by a toxic substance in the food he ate, but to accept that he could be as seriously harmed by a substance *not* in the food—by a deficiency—seemed alien to common sense and experience. Not until the 20th Century, when refined methods of research revealed the crucial role in human nutrition of such complex and elusive food compounds as vitamins, were deficiency diseases recognized for what they were. Only then could the missing substances, which are needed in extremely small amounts, be identified and established as causes of illnesses.

Yet long before the causes of deficiency diseases were even guessed at, their cures were occasionally found by lucky accident or patient trial and error. In 1535, when French explorer Jacques Cartier attempted to colonize the coast of Newfoundland, 100 of his 110 men came down with scurvy, an incapacitating and sometimes fatal ailment that is now known to arise from a lack of vitamin C. Cartier's expedition was saved by the Indians of the region, whose medicine men knew the symptoms—and the cure: an extract of spruce needles, which are rich in vitamin C. During the 18th Century the Scots somehow came to realize that their children could be protected against rickets, a bone-deforming disease caused by a vitamin D deficiency, if they were given cod-liver oil, which is one of the few foodstuffs naturally rich in vitamin D. And in 18th Century Italy pellagra (caused by a lack of the vitamin niacin) was successfully treated by blind accident. The disease was so widespread that the government built special pellagra hospitals—where the victims mysteriously recovered, to the bewilderment of their physicians. The reason, of course, was that the hospital food—which very likely included more meat than the patients were used to—contained the niacin that was missing from their everyday diets.

At about the same time that Italian doctors were curing one deficiency disease by chance, without ever learning what they had done right, a Scottish physician made the first truly scientific attack on another such ailment. And he succeeded in identifying its cure—even though he had no more understanding of the true nature of the ailment than anyone else of the day.

The disease was again, scurvy. For centuries this ailment plagued sailors so severely that the British navy's fighting strength was often seriously reduced. Few illnesses could have interfered more with the performance of duty. A victim of scurvy is depressed, weak and often anemic. He loses blood by internal hemorrhages and by seepage at the bases of his body hairs; a wound—even a mere scratch on the surface of his skin—stubbornly refuses to heal. From its onset, scurvy incapacitates its victim; if prolonged, it kills him.

In 1747 James Lind, Physician to the Royal Navy, undertook an experiment that one modern textbook has called a "remarkable piece of well-controlled clinical investigation." Lind isolated 12 scurvy victims whose cases, as he put it, "were similar as I could have them." All received an identical diet: "water-gruel sweetened with sugar in the morning; fresh mutton-broth often times for dinner; at other times puddings, boiled biscuit with sugar, etc.; and for supper, barley and raisins, rice and currants, sago and wine, or the like." It was, as any 20th Century physician would realize, an ideal regime for bringing on or perpetuating a case of scurvy.

"Sudden and visible good effects"

But then Lind divided his patients into six pairs of men, and fed them six different remedies. Four of the teams received liquid additives: cider, vinegar, a dilute sulfuric acid mixture and ordinary seawater. The fifth received a remedy "recommended by a hospital-surgeon": an "electuary," or paste, that contained (among other things) garlic, mustard seed, balsam of Peru and gum myrrh. The men in the last team were each given two oranges and a lemon every day. "These they eat with greediness," Lind noted—and he also observed the "sudden and visible good effects" that resulted. One of the two men who took this remedy was fit for active duty six days after the beginning of the treatment; the other was well enough to nurse the remaining patients.

The experiments of Lind and his successors were eventually to establish citrus fruits and green vegetables—two rich sources of vitamin C—as essential ingredients in the well-regulated diet. But the wheels of the British Admiralty Office turn slowly. Nearly 50 years passed before James Lind's discovery was officially recognized; when recognition did come it was total. In 1795 the Admiralty ordered that every British seaman be provided with a daily dose of fresh citrus juice. As a consequence the Royal Navy's fighting force was doubled at the start of the Napoleonic wars; it has been said that "Lind as much as Nelson broke the power of Napoleon." (The order also had a less portentous, if equally lasting, effect on the language. At that time the British called lemons "limes," the warehouse area along the east London docks became known as "Limehouse," and British sailors acquired the nickname "Limeys.")

The real significance of Lind's discovery, however, escaped attention. His citrus juices were thought of as medicinal drugs rather than as the sources of an essential food substance, and physicians failed to see that the disease was caused by the absence of some nutrient that was contained in the fruit. Their misunderstanding is not surprising. Dietary deficiencies—unlike starvation, which is accompanied by obvious weakness and severe loss of weight—give no immediate evidence of their existence. The victim may never know that he lacks a specific food, even when the symptoms of advanced disease become obvious.

In the past, deficiency diseases were often diagnosed as infections.

A DIET DETECTIVE, Joseph Goldberger, discovered the food deficiency responsible for the often-fatal disease pellagra. Until then many authorities believed the disease stemmed from an infection. After experimenting with a special diet on convicts in Mississippi, he concluded that the problem was a lack of meat, milk and eggs in the diets of the victims. In 1937 the essential nutrient supplied by these foods was identified as the vitamin niacin.

Weather was another suspect: lack of sunlight, too much sunlight, fog, or changes in temperature or humidity were blamed. Even when the mysterious afflictions were associated with food, the trouble was invariably thought to be some debilitating substance *in* the food.

Not until the early years of the 20th Century did medical science begin to make inroads on deficiency disease. Armed with a mounting fund of nutritional information and powerful new research techniques, dedicated researchers took up the quest for cause and prevention. They found their goals by three different routes: by fundamental research, or the attempt to isolate those substances that were essential to life but that were still unknown; by the medical approach, which sought to identify the cause of a disease and then to produce a method of curing or preventing it without particular regard for the chemistry involved; and by the biochemical approach, determining the chemical components of a curative substance so that it could be synthesized.

The conquest of deficiency disease, which has saved millions of lives, was the work of a great many men of medicine. How they went about it can best be told by focusing on a trio of brilliant scientists who exemplify the three basic approaches: Elmer Verner McCollum, pathfinder in the discovery of the family of vitamins; Joseph Goldberger, who found the cure and preventive for pellagra; and Robert R. Williams, who synthesized a substance capable of eradicating beriberi. The efforts of these men constitute three of the most unusual detective stories in the annals of nutritional science.

Apple scrapings for scurvy

It is a curious fact that the man who was to lead the way in vitamin research almost died in infancy from a vitamin-deficiency disease, scurvy. It is even more curious that his mother instinctively found the cure.

Elmer Verner McCollum was born in 1879 near Fort Scott, Kansas. By the time he was a year old the family had all but given up hope for his survival. Then one day, when his mother was peeling apples with the sickly child on her lap, she fed him some of the apple scrapings to quiet his whimpering. He seemed to like them. Martha Kidwell McCollum had long believed that "what the appetite called for, the system needed," so she continued to feed the child apple scrapings every day. Within a few days she noted an improvement in young Elmer's health; again displaying an instinct for nutrition, she further supplemented his diet with raw vegetables and the juice of wild strawberries. She had intuitively hit upon a diet strong in the antiscurvy nutrient, vitamin C— although the vitamin itself was not isolated until 50 years later.

McCollum grew up to work his way through the University of Kansas, achieve his Ph.D. degree at Yale and, in 1907, win a post as an instructor

A VITAMIN DISCOVERER, Robert R. Williams, first identified and synthesized the essential nutrient thiamine. In 1911, while Williams was working as a chemist in the Bureau of Science laboratory in Manila *(left)*, the diet-deficiency disease, beriberi, was widespread in the Philippines. The victims ate mostly polished rice, and scientists suspected that this rice lacked a vital anti-beriberi nutrient. Williams worked on the problem until 1936, before positively identifying the missing ingredient as the vitamin thiamine.

at the College of Agriculture at the University of Wisconsin in Madison. Almost immediately he was plunged into an experiment in nutrition. The college's researchers were attempting to find out whether the chemical composition of a food was a reliable index of its nutritional value. To do so, they were feeding three different groups of cows on three cereals having the same general chemical content—wheat, oats and corn. They were watching to see if one cereal proved superior to the other in its influence on the animals' health. For that would indicate that the food contained "something else," a nutritional factor not apparent in the chemical structure then known.

The search for "something else"

The experiment was well along when McCollum arrived and it was obvious that there were great differences in the three rations. "The wheat-fed cows were small of girth and rough-coated," McCollum later wrote. "They were all blind, as shown by the lead color of the eyes and by their inability to find their way about. Each had recently given birth to a greatly undersized premature calf and all calves were dead when born. The oat-fed cows carried their young to full term. Though the calves were of normal weight at birth, all but one were dead then. . . . The corn-fed cows were, by standards of animal husbandry, in excellent condition. They bore calves that were vigorous and got about well during the first day of post-natal life. Though all the cows had had feed of the same chemical composition, they differed enormously in physiological status. I was employed to discover why this was so. It was a man-sized job for a beginner." McCollum at the time was a skilled biochemist, but he knew little about nutrition and had never analyzed a food by chemical methods or conducted an experiment with animals. But the cow project clearly showed that "something fundamental remained to be discovered. I went to work with the enthusiasm of youth and inexperience."

The enthusiasm waned with time, as McCollum tried one laboratory approach after another in an unavailing search for the "why" behind the variations in the healthfulness of the different feeds. In the meantime, however, he struck upon a new idea—one that was to set a lasting pattern for research in all of biology and psychology. The principal problem with the cow as a test subject was the fact that it was such a long-lived animal; results of the experiments were slow to show up. Why not, McCollum argued, use small animals, which "grow rapidly to maturity, reproduce at an early age, and have a short span of life." He selected the rat, later to become a universally employed laboratory subject, because it could eat just about anything.

For several years, McCollum continued his animal experiments. He fed young rats a test diet and, with the help of his laboratory assistant, Marguerite Davis, carefully observed its effect on the rodents' growth and health. Then he varied the combination of substances, but maintained the same chemical composition. On some combinations the rats thrived, on others they failed. But the "why," the missing dietary link, remained elusive. Then, in 1912, came the answer—and one of the greatest advances ever made in nutritional science.

At that time McCollum was feeding his rats milk, sugar and a combination of pure protein, carbohydrates and minerals together with a fat substance. He noted that the rats grew and remained healthy when the fat source was butter or egg yolk. But when he substituted lard or olive oil for the fat, without changing any other component of the diet, the rats declined and eventually died. This was a discovery of paramount importance. The prevailing belief of the day was that all fats had the same nutritive values; quite obviously they did not. There was a vital something in butter fat and egg yolk that was not present in olive oil.

Over and over McCollum and Davis repeated the experiment, but with a number of modifications. The results were the same; there *did* exist a previously unknown nutrient in certain fats and, as later research showed, in such substances as alfalfa leaves and the livers and kidneys of animals. As final proof, McCollum managed by a complicated laboratory process to extract the mysterious substance from butter and transfer it to olive oil. The resultant product, a yellow-colored oil, was fed to the rats; they thrived. This was absolute evidence of the existence of the new nutrient, which McCollum called "fat-soluble A." It later became known as vitamin A. McCollum had established that previously unrecognized chemical compounds, now widely known as vitamins, are absolutely essential to life. The quantities required are very small (the daily allotment of vitamin A for an average man is about .0001 ounce), but if those small amounts are not present in the diet, illness follows. To forestall possible shortages of vitamin A in the American diet, the substance is today manufactured synthetically and added to some foodstuffs that do not naturally contain it. One rich natural source of vitamin A is, as McCollum had discovered, butter; margarine, the less expensive substitute used by many people, does not naturally have vitamin A, but it is now made the nutritional equal of butter by the addition of the vitamin.

McCollum's discovery launched a new campaign in the war on deficiency diseases. Hundreds of investigators took up the search for other members of the vitamin family of nutrients. In 1922, McCollum himself added vitamin D to the growing list and by 1948 all 13 of the vitamins needed for human nutrition had been isolated.

A health detective on the hunt

Two years after McCollum found vitamin A, Hungarian-born Joseph Goldberger initiated a different type of research that was to lead to another great victory over deficiency disease. Goldberger, a physician with the U.S. Public Health Service, had already acquired a considerable reputation as a health detective skillful in tracking down the origins of various epidemics. In 1914, he was ordered to investigate pellagra in the southern United States.

Pellagra had first been recognized as an important disease in the United States in 1907. In the early years of this century there were an

A MADONNA WITH A GOITER, a neck swelling caused by a diet deficiency, was painted by the 15th Century artist Giovanni Francesco da Rimini. Goiters were common in Giovanni's time, but not until the 20th Century was their cause traced to a shortage of iodine in the diet. The lack of this essential element affects the thyroid gland in the neck, which becomes enlarged. Today, table salt is enriched with iodine to supply this dietary need.

estimated 100,000 cases among poor people in the South; thousands of persons were dying of it each year. Two investigative commissions arrived at the same conclusion: pellagra was, to quote one of them, "in all probability a specific infectious disease communicable from person to person by means at present unknown."

The disease, which took its name from the Italian *pelle* (skin) and *agra* (rough), is characterized by reddish skin lesions, a red tongue and a sore mouth, indigestion and nausea, weakness and nervousness, and, in the advanced stage, by severe diarrhea and mental disturbances. Widespread in Europe, particularly in Italy and Spain, it had baffled the best medical minds of the Continent for almost two hundred years. Some European experts thought the cause was infection, but others attributed it to the consumption of spoiled corn.

By 1914, several able men of the Public Health Service had spent five years attempting to isolate the cause, but they remained as much in the dark as their European colleagues. The incidence of the disease in the South had mounted to alarming proportions. Under pressure from the Congress and the public, Surgeon General Rupert Blue assigned his No. 1 epidemic sleuth, Goldberger, to unravel "one of the knottiest and most urgent problems facing the Service at the present time."

To the 40-year-old Goldberger, the assignment posed a tough decision. After years of struggling to make ends meet on the government physician's meager income, he had just been offered a medical research plum: the directorship of a large, modern, well-staffed laboratory dedicated to research on diphtheria, a field in which he was well versed. The offer was tempting but the challenge of tackling the massive problem of pellagra, which had defied the best efforts of so many medical scientists, was irresistible. He turned down the directorship.

Goldberger started his investigation by reading some of the available literature on pellagra; he soon gave up, for it told him nothing. Next he made a seven-state tour of the areas where pellagra was most widespread, scribbling notes by the ream. At the Georgia State Sanitarium for the Insane, he found his first clue: there were several hundred cases of pellagra among the patients but not a single case among the doctors, nurses or other attendants. Following this lead, Goldberger visited other asylums, orphanages and similar institutions where the disease was prevalent. The situation was the same in each place: pellagra attacked the inmates, but never the staffs. To Goldberger, this was clear proof that the infection theory was invalid; if it were true, some staff people would be getting infected.

Clues in carbohydrates

But why should pellagra so discriminate? There must, Goldberger reasoned, be some difference in living conditions between the pellagra victims and their immune attendants. Eating habits made a likely starting point. With two assistants, Goldberger started a thorough study of the diets of the two types of residents at the various institutions. Both groups, he found, were fed ample quantities of food. But the attendants were getting animal products like milk, butter, eggs and meat, while these items were rarely if ever served the pellagra sufferers. For them, meals were a monotonous succession of grits, corn mush, molasses, syrup, sowbelly and gravy—a diet heavy in carbohydrates but almost entirely devoid of high-quality protein foods.

Goldberger next decided to focus his attention on one particular institution, the Methodist Orphan Asylum at Jackson, Mississippi. A third of the children there had pellagra—but the cases were strangely concentrated among one particular age group. Few victims were very young children or teenagers. Practically all the pellagrous children were in the age bracket from six to 12 years old, a relationship between age and disease that could not be found outside the institution. How did the older and younger inmates escape the disease, when apparently all subsisted on the same grits, mush and sowbelly?

A difference of diets

Taking a closer look at the orphanage fare, Goldberger found some crucial differences in the children's diets. Although all the orphans received an occasional ration of fresh meat—usually about once a week—the children who were over 12 got a substantially larger share, and in this group pellagra was rare. (Actually, the diet of the children over 12 was even better than the asylum officials realized, for as one record of the study points out, "The older children found ways of supplementing their allowed ration. They were hungry. They grabbed food and they stole it.") The youngest children, under six, were the only ones who received much milk, and this group, too, was relatively free of the disease. The six to 12 group received scant meat and milk, and they suffered nearly all the pellagra.

Goldberger quickly put his findings to a test in a controlled experiment. Obtaining funds from the government, he radically changed the diet at the Methodist orphanage and also at a Baptist orphanage in the same city. Meat was served four days a week, milk daily, and eggs—hitherto an unknown item at the orphans' tables—were added to the menu.

The results, evident after only a few weeks, were almost miraculous: there was marked improvement among the pellagra victims at both institutions and no new cases had appeared. Goldberger was elated. But, never one to jump at a conclusion, he decided to wait before publishing his findings. In the meantime he started a similar experiment among adult patients of the Georgia insane asylum.

Within a few months, even the cautious Goldberger was convinced. Practically all of the victims had recovered, and there were no new occurrences of pellagra. But Goldberger was far from satisfied. He had demonstrated that milk, eggs and meat contained some substance that would cure or prevent pellagra. But if his results were to be absolutely conclusive, he must not only be able to cure the disease by proper diet but also to induce it by faulty diet.

Inducing the disease posed a large problem. Obviously he could not subject his orphans and mental patients to a deliberately inadequate diet in order to prove his point. To find a group of volunteers willing to give up time and health, Goldberger turned to a prison. Convicts had all the time in the world, and as for remuneration for their suffering, pardons were considered more than adequate.

Goldberger sought approval from Earl Brewer, governor of Mississippi. A broad-minded, intelligent man, Brewer immediately saw the importance of the experiment and, after gaining assurance that no convict would die, he approved the test early in 1915.

At the prison farm near Jackson, Goldberger found 12 volunteers, all long-termers, all healthy, since the prison fare was remarkably good. Each was to be pardoned at the end of the six-month experiment if he met all the conditions imposed by Goldberger. A special "diet camp" was set up within the prison compound and at noon on April 19, 1915, the experiment got underway.

Mush, bread, grits and gravy

The diet prescribed by Goldberger was typical of that eaten by many poor people in the South. The convict volunteers were fed varying combinations of biscuits, fried mush, grits and gravy, syrup, corn bread, collards, turnip greens, sweet potatoes, rice, and coffee with sugar. They could have all they wanted of these foods, but nothing more.

To the convicts, the experiment was at first a great lark: all they could eat, clean quarters, a light work load and a promise of a pardon in six months. Their delight became concern in a very short time. Within a few weeks, all were complaining of the early symptoms of pellagra—backache, stomach-ache, dizziness and "red-tongue." But no skin lesions, the critical mark of the disease, appeared.

The experiment dragged on. At the start of the fifth month the men were weak and haggard. But there were still no lesions. Goldberger was worried; time was running out and the appearance of skin rash was absolutely essential for a positive diagnosis of pellagra.

Then, during the daily inspection on September 12, Goldberger's assistant, G. A. Wheeler, found what the researchers had been waiting for: a skin rash on one of the subjects. Within two weeks, four more convicts had the rash. Now there was no doubt that this was pellagra, but Goldberger bolstered his own diagnosis by calling for opinions from four prominent physicians. Their verdict was unanimous; Goldberger had induced pellagra by faulty diet. He had no opportunity to cure all his afflicted guinea pigs. Pardoned, they fled the premises, having had enough of the prison farm, grits-and-gravy, and Goldberger.

Goldberger's elation was short-lived. The results of the Jackson tests were published in a scientific journal and although many of the ablest men of medicine accepted his findings, many more did not. Proponents of the infection theory died hard. A highly vocal group of them publicly challenged Goldberger's conclusions, although they could offer little in the way of scientific contradiction. Goldberger was angered; in a letter to his wife he called his critics "blind, selfish, jealous, prejudiced asses."

More than Goldberger's personal sensitivity was at stake. Fearful that publicized criticism might delay wide adoption of preventive measures, he decided on one more experiment, designed to convince even the "asses" that pellagra was not contagious.

From a group of volunteer friends, he selected 16 subjects, including himself and his wife, who were to be given every opportunity to contract pellagra by infection. He used a variety of tests, one being the injection of blood from a known pellagra sufferer into the systems of the volunteers. A second test involved applying secretions from a pellagra victim's nose and throat to the same areas of the human guinea pigs. A third was a particularly revolting measure; it required the swallowing of a small dough ball compounded of flour together with urine, feces and lesion scales from a person with the disease.

In April, May and June of 1916, Goldberger conducted six series of these tests. After the last one he wrote: "We had our final 'filth party'— Wheeler, Sydenstricker [another assistant] and I—this noon. If anyone can get pellagra that way, we three should certainly have it good and hard. It's the last time. Never again." None of the "fifteen men and a housewife," as they were identified in the published report, contracted pellagra. The experiment served its purpose; the report helped to still the braying of the critics.

The scientist-salesmen

A host of questions remained to be answered, and the best way to get the answers was by the patient accumulation of statistical data. In his definitive history, *The United States Public Health Service 1798-1950,* Ralph Chester Williams describes the next stage of work:

"It was not enough for [Goldberger's laboratory] to know that diet was the controlling factor in pellagra. It needed facts—hundreds of them —on which the Public Health Service could build a control program to wipe out the disease. The laboratory wanted to know: Do age and sex have anything to do with contracting the disease? Does it run in families? What about seasonal incidence? Do living conditions, particularly sanitation, make a difference? What is the relation to family incomes? To get the answers, the laboratory set up a field survey in 1916 of 24 South Carolina cotton-mill towns. . . . For five and one-half years every family in the 24 towns was under close scrutiny."

OVER 500
UNDER 500
NOT REPORTING

A REGIONAL DIET PROBLEM is clearly indicated by this map showing the distribution of the deficiency disease, pellagra, in the United States in 1911. The states shown in green reported more than 500 cases during the year; those in gray reported fewer than 500; those in white did not report any cases. Later, research supplied the reason why the problem was concentrated in the South; many Southerners lived on a corn-based diet deficient in the vitamin niacin, needed to prevent pellagra.

Under Goldberger's direction, a corps of doctors, statisticians and sanitary engineers fanned out over the 24 towns. "These doctors were scientists turned house-to-house salesmen. Getting their feet in the door was not the least of their problems, but once in, the job was still ticklish. Tact and patience were required to find out exactly what items were on the weekly market list, and to permit on-the-spot examinations for signs of the red-skinned trouble. Equipped with candy and chewing gum, the doctors first made allies of the children, and proceeded from them to their mothers."

By the end of the survey, the Public Health Service had amassed the largest body of facts on pellagra ever available to researchers. The disease had been studied in terms of its incidence, its death rate, the age and sex and income of its victims. One set of tables showed that the majority of cases occurred between April and August—because "consumption of fresh meat, milk and butter declined in the early months of the year, setting the stage for pellagra." Most important of all, the survey proved once for all that "insanitary conditions had nothing to do with pellagra, but economics did. Pellagra rates went up in hard times, when there was little or no money for even the cheapest foods."

The P-P factor for poor people

Meanwhile, in 1918, Goldberger embarked on the final phase of his pellagra work. He had shown that pellagra was a deficiency disease and that certain foods had preventive value. But those foods were expensive, and Goldberger felt it was essential to find a pellagra-preventing diet within the means of the poor people most susceptible to the disease. To do this he would have to isolate the particular substance in food that was capable of controlling the disease, the "pellagra-preventive factor," or "P-P factor," as he later called it.

After six years of painstaking work Goldberger found that yeast contained the P-P factor. But was it one of the known vitamins in yeast or an undiscovered substance? There was a way to find out, because earlier research had disclosed that the known vitamins in yeast could be destroyed by heating under pressure. Goldberger ran a batch of yeast through a steam chamber, tested it on dogs and humans and found that it still cured pellagra. This was a big discovery; the curative was obviously some new substance. Going a step further, Goldberger and his associates managed to separate the substance from the yeast by adsorbing it onto fuller's earth, a form of clay used in chemical analysis. Thus they concentrated the P-P factor.

One final step remained: identification of the specific chemical nature of the P-P factor. But Goldberger did not live to achieve it. The man who made possible the eradication of one disease fell victim to another, cancer, and died on January 17, 1929. Years after Goldberger's death, in 1937, the P-P factor was identified as a member of the vitamin B complex. It would not have surprised Goldberger, who, in a posthumously published paper, said his studies showed that what had long been known as vitamin B was really at least two distinct factors, one of them "a heat-resistant factor indistinguishable from the pellagra preventive."

Today that "heat-resistant factor" is known as niacin. It is made synthetically and added to bread, spaghetti and other wheat products; thus, in fulfillment of Goldberger's hope, it is readily available in inexpensive foods. This artificial enrichment of the U.S. diet has been only one factor, however, in eradicating pellagra; the disease is now rare mainly because improved economic and social conditions enable Americans to afford high-quality, niacin-rich foods like meat, milk and eggs.

Synthesis, the ultimate answer

The work of Robert R. Williams, representing the third part of the antideficiency story, involved synthesis, or chemical manufacture of a nutrient. Synthesis is the ultimate answer to Goldberger's dream of a disease-preventing diet available to all regardless of means. For when an essential substance can be synthesized, it can usually be produced in large quantities at very low cost.

Williams' predecessors had discovered a compound that would cure or prevent beriberi, a deficiency disease characterized by disorders of the nervous system. The compound, however, was a complex mixture of many chemicals, and no one knew what specific substance within the compound was responsible for its effect. Williams' aim was to isolate the curative, to establish its structure and to synthesize it. This seems like a relatively straightforward problem of chemical analysis. Actually it proved a maddeningly elusive task, one that was to occupy Williams for more than a quarter of a century. That he succeeded is all the more remarkable because he pursued his research not as a primary occupation but as an avocation, at the same time building his reputation in a completely different branch of chemistry.

The son of missionaries, Williams was born in India in 1886, and the poverty and misery he observed as a child impressed him deeply and moved him to commit himself to the fight against deficiency diseases. He obtained a degree in chemistry at the University of Chicago, then returned to the East to start his professional career with the Philippine Bureau of Science in Manila. It was a Manila meeting in 1910 with a U.S. Army doctor, Captain Edward B. Vedder, that started Williams on what was to be his life work. Vedder, conducting an experimental study on beriberi, had asked the Bureau of Science for the help of a chemist. Williams, newest and greenest of the staff, was assigned.

About a decade earlier, the cause of beriberi had been established by two Dutch physicians in Java, Christiaan Eijkman and Gerrit Grijns. Their experiments had shown that the widespread existence of beriberi in the Orient was due to the common diet based on polished rice, that is, rice from which the hull has been removed by milling. Eijkman had started his research by feeding two groups of chickens polished and unpolished rice. He found that the group subsisting on polished rice developed paralytic symptoms similar to those found in human beriberi;

VITAMIN	DISCOVERER	DATE OF DISCOVERY	RECOMMENDED DAILY ALLOWANCE
A (Retinol)	E. McCollum M. Davis	1913	.0003 mg.
D (Calciferol)	E. McCollum	1922	1 mg.
E (Tocopherol)	H. Evans K. Bishop	1923	25-30 mg.
C (Ascorbic acid)	A. Szent-Györgyi G. King	1932	55-60 mg.
B2 (Riboflavin)	P. Gyorgy R. Kuhn	1933	1.5-1.7 mg.
K	H. Dam	1935	unknown
B1 (Thiamine)	R. R. Williams	1936	1.0-1.4 mg.
B6 (Pyridoxine)	T. Birch P. Gyorgy	1936	2.0 mg.
Niacin	C. Elvehjem	1937	13-18 mg. equiv.
Pantothenic acid	R. J. Williams	1938	5-10 mg.
Biotin	P. Gyorgy, et al.	1940	.15-.3 mg.
Folic acid	H. Mitchell E. Snell R. J. Williams	1944	.4 mg.
B12 (Cyanocobalamin)	M. Shorb E. Rickes, et al.	1948	.005 mg.

THE 13 VITAMINS listed above with their discoverers were unusually difficult to recognize as essential food ingredients because the average person's daily required intake of each (above, right) is so very small. The recommended allowance of vitamin B12, the vitamin most recently discovered, is .005 milligrams—only about .00000016 ounce. One scientist—the Hungarian-born professor of pediatrics, Paul Gyorgy—played a key role in the recognition of three different vitamins, although in these cases, as in the others listed, a number of researchers made important contributions to identification of the substances.

the other group remained unaffected. Later, Eijkman was able to induce and then cure the beriberi by feeding chickens and pigeons first polished, then unpolished, rice—a clear indication that something in the rice hull could cure the disease. Grijns took over the experiments when Eijkman left Java, and it was Grijns who first correctly interpreted the results of the research. In a 1901 report, one of the first to explain how a food deficiency could lead to disease, he concluded that the rice hull contained an essential nutrient that was lost in the process of milling.

But Grijns had no idea what that nutrient was. Its isolation, identification and synthesis were to be Williams' task. When he first met Captain Vedder in Manila, Williams was shown a quart bottle of a brown liquid. It was an alcoholic extract of rice hulls with demonstrated ability to cure beriberi; Vedder had already tested it on human patients with excellent results. He wanted Williams to break down the constituents of the extract, to isolate the single ingredient responsible for the curative effect, and then to synthesize it.

An invisible needle in a liquid haystack

Since the extract was a mixture of many different compounds, Williams' job was comparable to the proverbial one of looking for a needle in a haystack—except that a needle, once found in a haystack, can be recognized as a needle. The object of Williams' search was really only another shred of hay, distinguishable from the rest of the stack only in that it had the power to cure beriberi. So he had to separate his haystack —the extract—into chemical components, testing each substance on animals to see if it contained the curative; then he had to break down the major components into subcompounds and test again, hoping eventually to isolate the curative substance in pure form.

Williams followed this procedure for the five remaining years of his tour of duty in the Philippines, making only minor progress. In 1915, he returned to the United States, where he went to work with the government bureau now known as the U.S. Food and Drug Administration. He managed to devote some effort to beriberi research, but with the advent of World War I he was forced to spend practically all of his time in chemical warfare experimentation.

In 1919, unable to support himself, his wife and his experiments on his $2,500 a year salary, Williams left government service. He joined the scientific laboratory of the Bell Telephone Company as a research chemist, became chemical director in 1925, and continued in that post until his retirement in 1946. In the telephone laboratory he was concerned with such matters as the chemistry of cable insulators and other problems very remote from beriberi research. But his interest never waned. Using his own funds for the most part (until years later when he received a grant from the Carnegie Corporation), keeping his experimental animals in the garage of his house, he doggedly continued his search for the structure of the curative factor, a quest which had by now excited the interest of hundreds of other researchers all over the world.

The solution had eluded all of them, and it eluded Williams, too—until the years of the Great Depression in the 1930s.

If any benefit accrued to mankind from those hard times, it was the fact that economic collapse forced the telephone laboratory to shorten its work week to three days. Williams was able to devote a greater portion of his time to the search for the anti-beriberi factor, which he now believed to be an unknown vitamin. Working at Columbia University as well as at home, and aided by skillful volunteers (chief among them Robert E. Waterman, who was to become his son-in-law), Williams produced ever-larger amounts of the basic extract. In 1933, by a laborious multistep process, Williams and his associates succeeded in isolating large amounts of the pure crystalline vitamin.

Building the B₁ molecule

This was a great advance, but Williams had not yet reached his goal. He still had to learn the structure of the molecule—and then to build that molecule himself in a test tube. This was a task almost as great as the isolation of the substance. By chemical methods, the Williams group had to examine the vitamin and identify every element contained within it. Then they had to measure the amounts of each element. But knowledge of the elements and their amounts was not enough for synthesis; the chemists had yet to learn how each atom was attached to another—a puzzle that was solved by splitting the molecule apart and deducing from the fragments how they had been joined.

Breaking down the components and finding the chemical connections was an extremely complicated process of trial, failure and retrial. It took three years. At last, in 1936, the Williams team was rewarded by the final triumph. They were able to determine the structure of the vitamin and to produce it synthetically. Tests proved the synthetic compound identical with the natural substance earlier isolated and confirmatory trials on rats demonstrated the curative effect. Vitamin B₁, as it was first called, had been synthesized; Williams gave it the name by which it is better known today—thiamine.

Synthetic thiamine is a certain and fast cure for beriberi. It is also used as a preventive, being added to rice and wheat products to forestall any shortage in the everyday diet. But it has still to eradicate the disease, which remains a problem in the Orient, where many people can obtain neither enriched foodstuffs to prevent beriberi nor medical treatment to cure it.

Economic and social conditions such as those that block the elimination of beriberi also stand in the way of efforts to cure many other deficiency diseases that continue to plague the world. In underdeveloped nations, the lack, not of minute quantities of vitamins, but of substantial proteins and calories causes tragic harm to millions of men, women and children. Nutritional science knows how, technically, to remedy these deficiencies; it must still find economic and social methods that will enable the cures to be successfully applied.

Campaign against
a Child Killer

The emaciated girl at right, her skin wrinkled, her eyes staring, was a plump and jolly infant until she was weaned. Now, after a few months without milk, she is close to death. Like millions of children the world over, she is wasting away from the insidious form of starvation called protein-calorie malnutrition. Its cause is not famine but ignorance and poverty. It typically strikes when babies are deprived of their mother's milk—usually by the arrival of a new infant—and are put on a diet that contains too little protein for normal development, and, beyond that, often provides too few energy-giving calories to sustain life.

Campaigns to combat malnutrition are underway in several countries, and one pilot program, based at the American University of Beirut, Lebanon, has already achieved notable results. Doctors there are treating severely malnourished children, tackling the problem from all angles. For less seriously ill children, the Beirut scientists have developed a cheap food supplement that quickly restores vigor. But the program looks beyond emergency relief. If the poor families now being helped can be taught how to enrich children's meals, malnutrition can be prevented from ever occurring.

A TINY VICTIM OF MALNUTRITION
Weak, frightened, her decorative gold earrings adding a pathetic note, this child lies in a hospital in Jordan where she is being treated for protein-calorie malnutrition. An unusually scanty diet and infection have so damaged her digestive processes that, although five months old, she weighs only seven pounds —about as much as she weighed at birth.

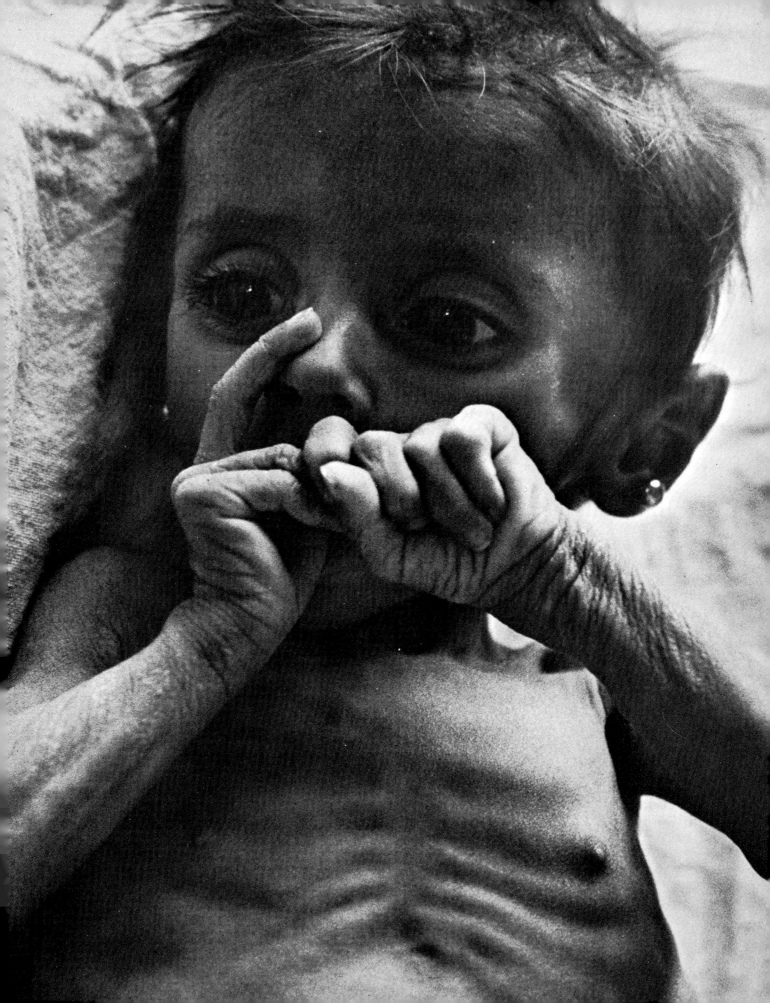

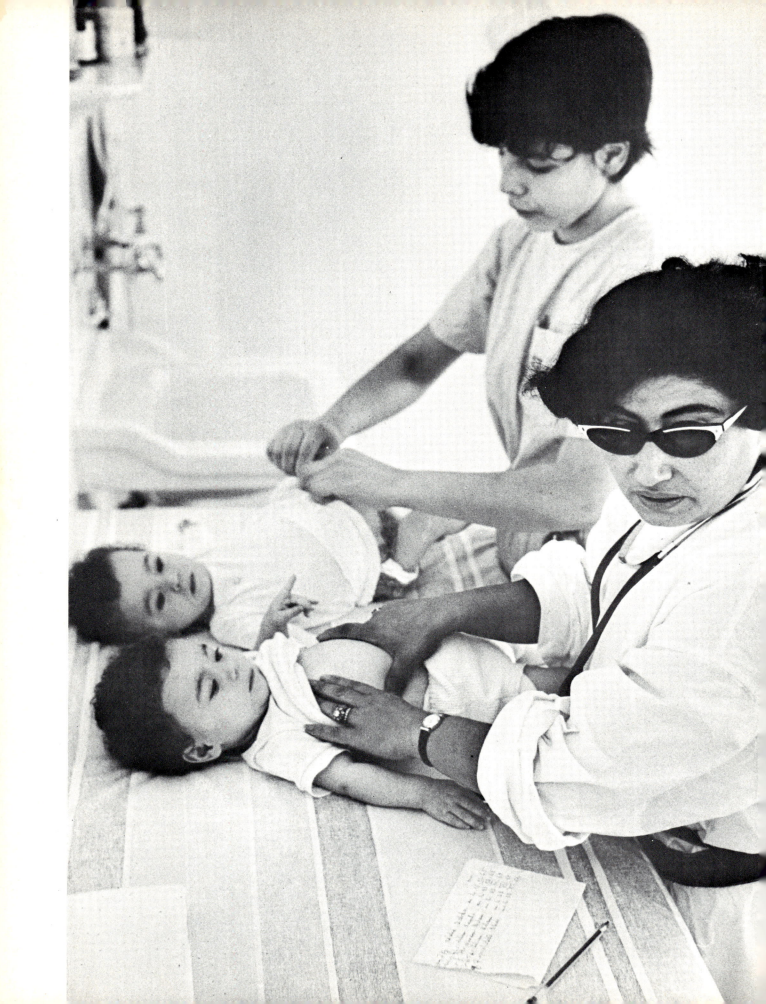

The Vulnerable Years

Like a beast of prey, malnutrition attacks the weakest members of human society: the babies of the poor and uneducated. Ignorance often invites the disease. Symptoms are not easily recognized, because they may suggest other illnesses and they vary from case to case *(below)*, depending on the respect in which the child's diet is faulty.

In Lebanon, where protein-rich and calorie-rich foods are both fairly plentiful, the most serious problem is the inadequate diets of newly weaned infants. Weaning comes at a time when the child needs twice as much protein, in relation to body weight, as do adults. Yet the child's allotment of protein may be exceedingly low. Most of the protein foods, like meat and fish, are usually given to the men in the family, who must work; the women and children fill up on whatever is left—mainly thin soup and mashed vegetables.

Weakened by such meager meals, the child may fall victim to a severe case of diarrhea, and the mother, misled by this symptom, often makes matters worse by applying one of the traditional remedies for diarrhea: rice water or tea, which contain still fewer calories and no protein whatever. Soon his skin peels, his body swells and he may die.

When a child suffers from a severe lack of calories, as well as protein shortage, his symptoms are different —he wastes away to skin and bones, like the youngster below—but his future is equally grim: he is practically defenseless against fatal infections.

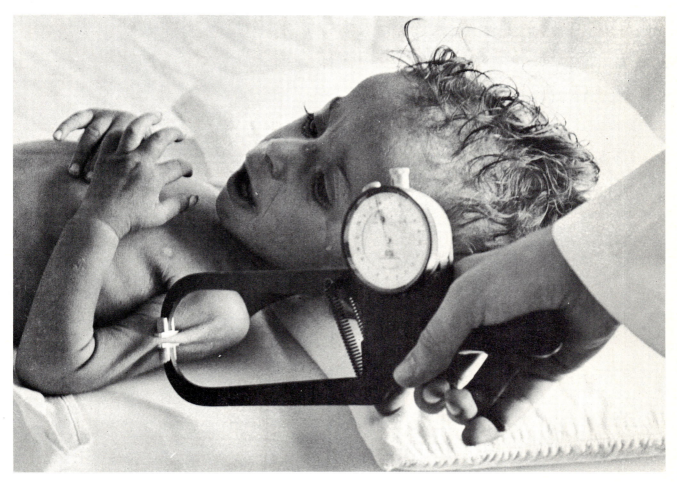

DETECTING THE DISEASE
Dr. Suad Azhari Abu-Khadra, a researcher at the American University of Beirut, touches the abdomen of a child to see whether the liver is enlarged, one sign that betrays a deficiency of protein in the diet. An assistant *(background)* gets another child ready for the examination.

DIAGNOSING THE DEFICIENCY
A measuring instrument called the skin-fold caliper indicates on its dial the thinness of the layer of fat beneath this girl's skin. The reading helps doctors to diagnose the exact nature of her dangerous malnutrition. The scanty fat reveals that her diet has lacked calories as well as protein (symptoms of both deficiencies generally occur together). A diet severely deficient in calories causes emaciation, dry hair and wrinkled skin. But if the principal deficiency is lack of protein, the characteristic symptoms are a swollen body, discolored hair and peeling skin.

A Food Cooked Up by Doctors

"A land of milk and honey" is what the Bible called Canaan, which included present-day Lebanon. While Lebanon's fruitfulness has never quite lived up to this praise, the land is capable of providing an adequate diet for its population. Yet malnutrition afflicts as many as 10 per cent of Lebanese children because many high-protein foods—notably meat, fish and cheese—are too expensive for low-income families.

Doctors at the American University of Beirut concluded that the children in these impoverished families could be restored to health with a diet supplement concocted largely of inexpensive local products. This approach had worked well elsewhere; among the diet supplements made from indigenous foods were protein-rich peanut flour in India, cottonseed flour in Central America and soybean flour in Turkey.

In Lebanon, the best supplement proved to be a blend of locally grown chick-peas and boiled wheat mixed with dried skimmed milk from America. Made into a powder called L'aubina—a name derived from the initials of the American University of Beirut—the high-protein substance can be manufactured in volume to feed a child for about 10 cents a day.

THE LABORATORY AS A KITCHEN
Doctors in the nutrition laboratory of the American University of Beirut blend L'aubina powder from the three principal ingredients shown in the jars on the table. The bulk of the mixture consists of 10 per cent skimmed milk, 25 per cent chick-peas, and 62 per cent boiled wheat.

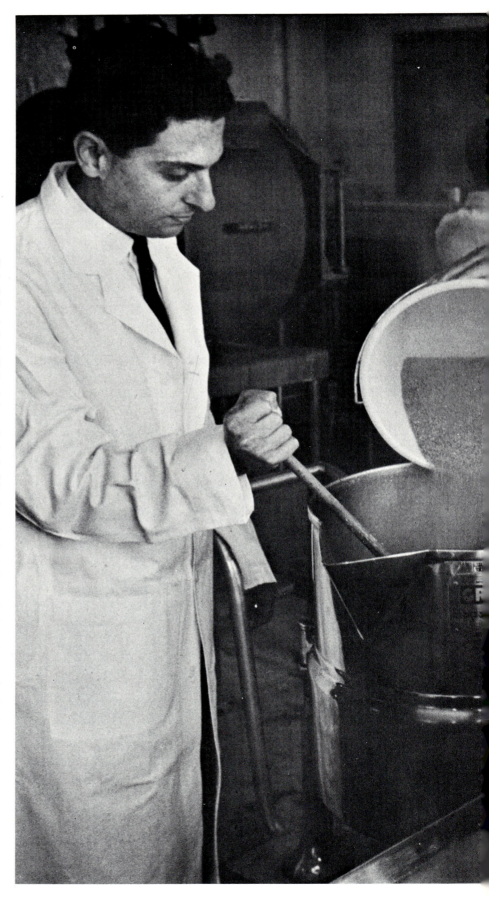

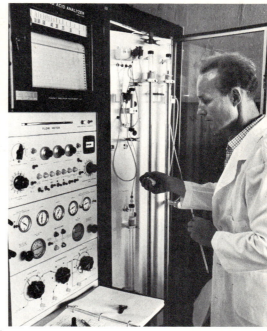

ANALYZING THE MIXTURE

With an instrument called an amino acid analyzer, a doctor measures the composition of protein in a sample of L'aubina to make sure that its major ingredients are correctly proportioned. In addition to protein, the diet supplement contains small amounts of vitamins A and D, citric acid for flavor, and bone ash to provide calcium for growing teeth and bones.

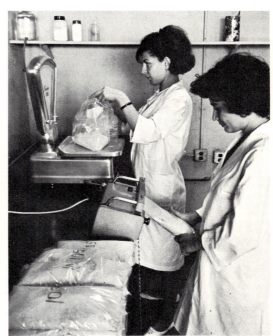

PACKAGING THE PRODUCT

Preparing the diet supplement for use, technicians in the nutrition laboratory package L'aubina in plastic bags and weigh each batch. The bags must be carefully marked before distribution, for the doctors in the project periodically change the mixture to see if another formula will taste better while still remaining effective against protein-calorie malnutrition.

A Tasty Dish for Hungry Children

Will it stop malnutrition? Will the children eat it? Both questions had to be answered before L'aubina could be considered a useful weapon in the campaign against malnutrition. And the only way to get answers to these questions was by feeding the supplement, in a controlled test, to malnourished children.

The first studies were made at a Beirut orphanage where the meals were known to be poor in protein. To suit the needs and palates of 130 children of several different age groups,

doctors worked out several L'aubina-enriched recipes.

To their delight, the doctors found that the diets not only wiped out all signs of malnutrition but that the orphans ate the new food with gusto. (Some diet supplements, tried out in other areas, had proved so distasteful that they could not be used.)

Encouraged by this success with mild cases of malnutrition, the Lebanon project extended its study to include infants who were recovering from severe attacks. At the end of

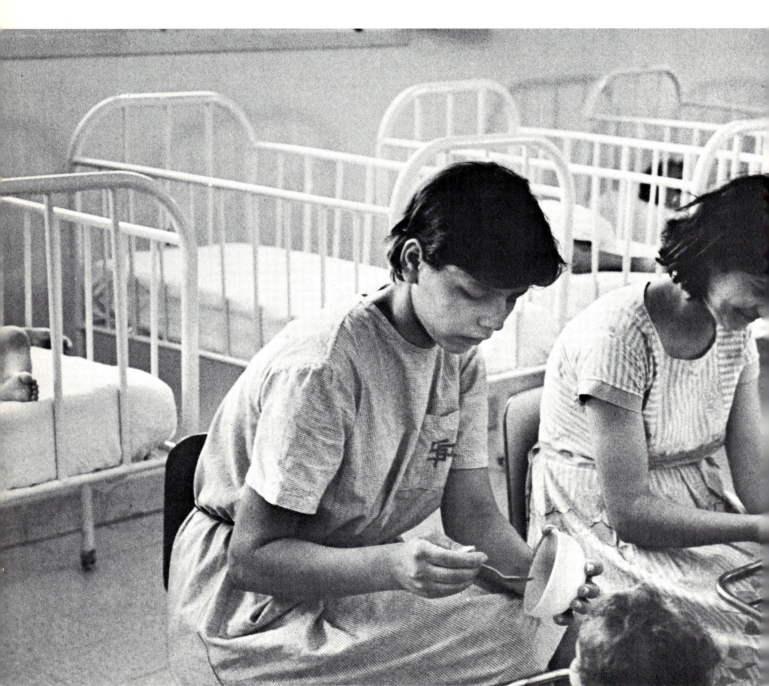

four months of treatment with L'aubina and other foods, the babies were bright-eyed, plump and normal. The doctors in the project then began juggling the formula for L'aubina in an effort to reduce the time required for complete cure. This is a deliberately slow process, for each time the mixture is changed, the new L'aubina must be put through a long series of laboratory tests to make certain it will serve both of its functions: to cure sick children, and to keep normal ones in the full flush of health.

MEALTIME AT THE ORPHANAGE
Twice a day, the children in the six-month-to-one-year age group at the orphanage receive a thick, heated mixture of milk, cereal, sugar and L'aubina *(below, left)*. The children in the two-to-three-year age group are fed three times a day *(below)* and thrive on a diet of vegetables and a little meat supplemented with L'aubina.

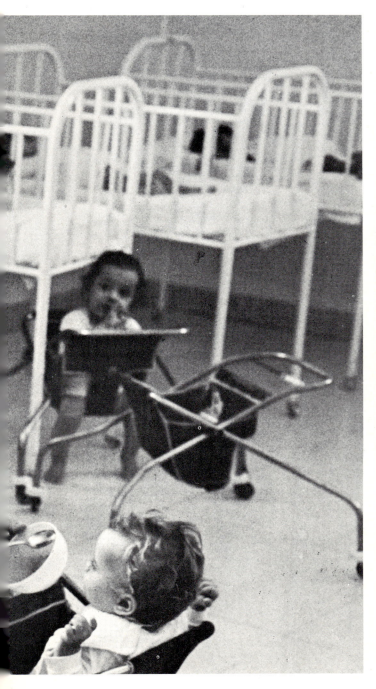

Ending the Dietary Dark Ages

Many Lebanese mothers whose young children have been cured of malnutrition by L'aubina regard the diet supplement as a miracle 'potion. But magic cannot eliminate the disease. It will recur until people learn how it is related to their everyday diet and how it can be prevented by the proper choice of food.

Disseminating the gospel of the balanced diet was an indispensable part of the American University test program. Mothers were given recipes for increasing their children's intake of proteins and calories. They were shown the correct way to prepare skimmed-milk powder for their babies, and were urged to feed the older children in the family the protein-rich Lebanese staples, chick-peas and wheat products.

Instruction at this elementary level is crucial: If a mother is taught how to mix a high-protein food herself, and then watches her sick child improve after he has eaten the food, she will no longer doubt the importance of a properly balanced diet—and she will almost certainly become a dedicated missionary among her friends and neighbors, preaching the nutritional wisdom that can help to save the lives of their ill-fed children.

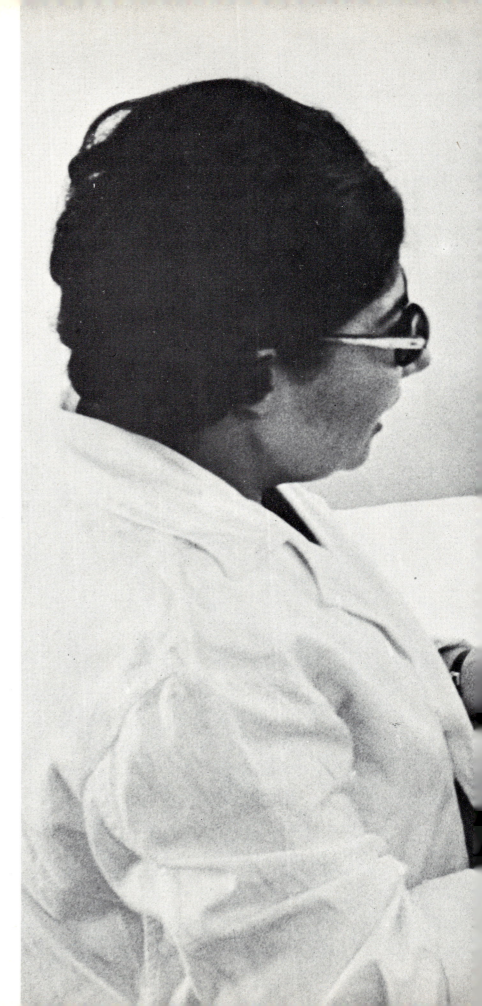

PROTEIN FOR AN OUTPATIENT
A Lebanese mother, whose baby, now plump and healthy, had nearly died of malnutrition, gets detailed instructions on the correct use of L'aubina—and a brief lecture on the diet rules that she must follow to keep her child well.

6

Diseases
of Feast

Indulging in a snack at a Munich delicatessen, a 277-pound gourmand downs one of his six daily meals. Overeating is commonplace and obesity a serious health problem in West Germany, one of Europe's most affluent nations.

UNTIL THE 20TH CENTURY, there was no country in the world in which everyone could be guaranteed enough to eat. Hunger was common and starvation a familiar threat everywhere. In Ireland between 1846 and 1849, over a million people died and more than two million were forced to leave the country where blight repeatedly destroyed the potato crops. In California during the great 1849 Gold Rush, 10,000 Americans, cut off from a normal supply of fresh vegetables, died of scurvy.

Today, for the first time in human history, large parts of the world are free of such terrors. Shortages, particularly of the right kinds of food, still plague the underdeveloped nations. But in Western Europe and most of North America, modern agriculture, improvements in distribution systems and high levels of general prosperity have made it possible to provide ample quantities of nutritious food for everyone. Yet the very advances that ended one danger have created others almost as serious. Many persons now damage their health by eating too much food and, it appears, too much of certain favored foods.

Because so many people are eating more than they should, increasing numbers of them have become overweight; their excess poundage is clearly a cause of their increased susceptibility to such ailments as diabetes, heart disease and kidney disease. Because they eat more fatty meat and dairy products than in the past they may be increasing their chances of developing atherosclerosis—one form of hardening of the arteries. And atherosclerosis can lead to heart attacks or strokes.

The "diseases of feast" have posed two of the most intricate puzzles occupying medical science today. The first concerns excess weight. Its harm is indisputable and its cause is obviously overeating, but an easy cure probably will continue to elude researchers until the reasons for overeating are better understood. The second puzzle concerns the connection between eating habits and arterial disease. Mounting evidence indicates that certain animal foods are the principal causes of such disease, yet contradictory facts muddle the case and provoke bitter arguments among the experts. The two problems are interrelated in very complex ways, for both touch on all the processes involved in human nutrition. The search for answers has sent scientists off on pioneering explorations of the factors—psychological, biochemical and social—that link the foods people eat with health and disease.

The dangers of overeating were recognized more than half a century ago, when actuarial studies by life-insurance companies indicated that their fat policyholders were poor risks. By now there are mountains of statistics that establish beyond any question that overweight people do not live as long, on the average, as slimmer ones. A table prepared by the Metropolitan Life Insurance Company, showing the mortality rate among men, indicates that as little as 10 per cent in excess poundage increases the likelihood of death by 13 per cent. And the risk increases with every additional pound of weight. Men who are 20 per cent overweight have a 25 per cent greater chance of dying prematurely than do those of normal weight; those who are 30 per cent overweight have a 42 per cent greater chance. The figures for women are not quite so dramatic, but they are equally disturbing.

In the United States the risk of premature death from overweight is especially widespread because so many Americans weigh more than they should—that is, more than a so-called "normal weight" determined by age, height and body build. A person who weighs from 10 to 19 per cent more than the norm is considered overweight; one whose weight exceeds the norm by 20 per cent or more is considered obese. About one third of all Americans are obese, and many more are overweight.

A person becomes fat simply because he takes in more calories in his food than are used up by his daily activities. No single optimum figure can be set for calorie intake because the number of calories a person needs depends on the amount of energy he expends: a farmer's requirements are higher than a clerk's. However, once particular requirements have been satisfied, the excess calories, in the form of fats, are carried by the bloodstream to special storage depots in the body, the fat cells, and deposited there as the fat compounds called triglycerides. If at any time the body needs additional energy, it calls upon these depots for a supply of fuel. But when intake consistently exceeds requirement, the storage of triglyceride increases, the fat cells increase in size and number, and ever-larger deposits of fat are left under the skin, around the heart and kidneys and near the organs of the intestinal tract.

Training children to be fat

An excess intake of calories can result either from the kind or from the amount of food that is consumed. Some foods are higher in calories than others, and any number of factors encourage people to take in more calories than their bodies need. For example, certain eating patterns, handed down from one generation to the next, involve regular servings of such high-calorie dishes as spaghetti, apple pie à la mode, and beans and greens cooked in bacon fat. And family traditions such as "wasting food is sinful" and "a fat child is a healthy child" also encourage youngsters to overeat. The habit, once established, is likely to persist.

Psychological factors can also influence weight. For some people, food is a remedy for tension, worry, frustration, boredom or the feeling of being rejected: through indulgence in the pleasures of the table they try to compensate for general unhappiness.

Social customs, too, play an important role. Candy and other sweets are standard gifts. In preparing dinner for guests, most hostesses serve their most elaborate menus—and these are generally highest in caloric content. Certainly that staple of modern social life, the cocktail party, has contributed its share of bulging figures. Not only is alcohol itself high in calories, but so are the cheese dips, peanuts and potato chips that so often accompany it.

In addition to these factors, there are certain physiological explanations of obesity. Some metabolic disorders, such as thyroid ailments, produce a tendency to overweight. The changes in function that accompany injury to the hypothalamus gland create an increased appetite. Although these problems are serious, they are rare.

Another physiological factor that may be at work is the genetic one—the hereditary disposition to take on weight. A number of studies show a definite relationship between the weight levels of heavy children and their parents. Since this pattern is not always as clear in the case of children adopted by obese parents, it is possible that the tendency to overweight may be communicated by the genes.

The drawbacks of progress

All of these forces have for centuries helped make people gain weight. But their effect has been heightened by the technological changes of the last 100 years. As machines have taken over the tasks once performed by muscles, the need for physical exercise has lessened. Sedentary work, not manual labor, is the rule today, and the automobile has almost eliminated walking. This decrease in exercise, which reduces the requirement for calories, has not always been accompanied by a corresponding decrease in appetite. And overeating is triggered by appetite, which is the desire to eat, rather than by hunger, which signals the body's need for fuel. Therefore the answer to the question of why people get fat must be sought in an analysis of appetite itself. Since appetite involves both psychological and physiological processes, the investigation must include an examination of the way the brain controls appetite.

The appetite regulator, often called the "appestat," is now known to be housed in an area at the base of the brain known as the hypothalamus. Within the appestat are two distinct groups of cells, or control centers. One, known as the "feeding center," initiates the urge to eat. The other, called the "satiety center," counteracts this urge. In a normal person, when the demand of the body for energy-producing food has been satisfied the satiety center signals the feeding center to halt further intake. But in some people the satiety center apparently fails to operate properly and the victim literally "doesn't know when to stop eating."

The key role of the appestat has been dramatically demonstrated in a series of experiments with rats performed by Philip Teitelbaum of the University of Pennsylvania, who confirmed and extended similar work done by John Brobeck of the same institution and many other investigators. Teitelbaum, employing delicate surgical techniques, deliberately damaged the feeding centers of some rats, and the satiety centers of others. He then compared the eating habits of the altered animals with those of normal rats. Although all the rats were allowed to eat as much —or as little—as they liked, their actual food consumption showed striking contrasts. The animals having damaged satiety centers ate two to three times as much as the normal animals did, and within 6 to 12 months some exceptional animals grew to nearly five times normal weight. The rats having damaged feeding centers ate little or nothing, and many of them starved to death despite the availability of food.

The regulating action of the appestat seems to be only the last link in

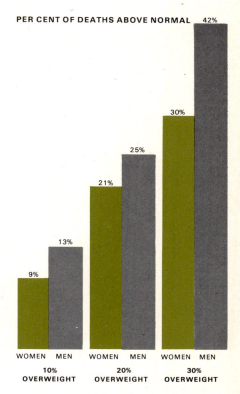

PER CENT OF DEATHS ABOVE NORMAL

					42%
				30%	
			25%		
		21%			
	13%				
9%					
WOMEN	MEN	WOMEN	MEN	WOMEN	MEN
10% OVERWEIGHT		20% OVERWEIGHT		30% OVERWEIGHT	

THE RISK OF BEING FAT, as this graph shows, is greater for men than for women and it increases with the amount of overweight. Thus, there are 13 per cent more deaths among men and 9 per cent more among women who are 10 per cent overweight than among normal-weight people in the same 15 to 69 age group. For the 20 per cent overweight, the figures go up to 25 per cent more deaths for men and 21 per cent for women. For the 30 per cent overweight, there are 42 per cent more deaths among men, 30 per cent among women.

a long chain of control mechanisms. Even the "hyperphagic" rats—those that overate after hypothalamic damage—gained weight only up to a certain point; having reached that plateau, they reverted to a food intake close to normal. This suggests that their weight controls had been "reset." Moreover, as Teitelbaum discovered, another factor was at work: the pleasure the eater takes in the food set before him also affects the appetite. The hyperphagic rats could be made to stop eating and start losing weight if certain distasteful substances, such as cellulose or quinine, were added to their food, while pleasant-tasting chemicals—like dextrose—made them ravenous once again. If food was pumped directly into the animals' stomachs so that the taste centers were bypassed and the rats could not taste the food at all, the hyperphagic animals promptly lost interest in food entirely; however, normal rats, who were responding to hunger rather than appetite, were little affected by this method of feeding and continued to consume their usual rations.

The appetite computer

To account for the responses recorded by these experiments with normal and altered rats, some experts have compared the hypothalamus to a computer which is very efficient at handling information it has received but which cannot initiate the information itself. Just as the computer must be supplied with data from the outside, so the hypothalamus operates largely on the basis of data that are originated elsewhere. A damaged computer can no longer give correct answers; the rat whose hypothalamus has been altered is similarly handicapped.

Years of experimentation have produced a number of tentative ideas about the sources and the nature of the data that must come into the hypothalamus. According to one theory the input signal reports body temperature, which normally rises after food ingestion; defective transmission of the temperature readings leads to overeating. Another proposal suggests that the rate at which the body uses blood sugar signals "eat" or "don't eat." Still another holds that the signals come from hormones responding to changes in fat reserves. And the pleasures of eating must also be involved, as Teitelbaum's experiments suggest.

If the specific agent or agents that regulate appetite could be isolated, medicine would gain a tool of immense value. If doctors knew which substance makes the hypothalamus order "don't eat," they might inject it directly into the bloodstream to stop overeating and restore a balance between food intake and consumption, much as insulin is injected to control sugar metabolism. The appestat would be as repairable as a furnace thermostat, and obesity would become easy to cure.

Until that hope is realized, there is only one remedy for excess weight: a low-calorie diet combined with exercise. This combination, by supplying less energy-producing food than the body uses, reverses the process by which the fat was acquired in the first place. For once the body has used the energy that has been made available by eating, it will then turn to its fat storehouse, making gradual withdrawals until all of the excess

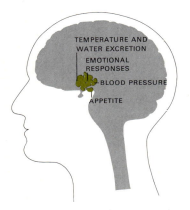

THE APPETITE'S REGULATOR is a part of the walnut-sized control center known as the hypothalamus, located in the lower-middle region of the brain. This center contains several groups of nerve cells, which govern body temperature, emotional responses, blood pressure and water excretion as well as appetite. The cell group that influences appetite, the "appestat," is itself made up of two parts; one sends signals to stimulate the desire to eat, the other sends contrary signals to depress appetite.

has been burned off, and body weight has returned to normal.

Any diet is a good reducing diet provided it is low in caloric value and nutritionally balanced. A menu typical of those prescribed by doctors is shown at right.

This is nutritionally balanced: it contains proper proportions of all the 45 necessary nutrients. And it assures a loss of weight because it contains about 1,400 fewer calories than the average man requires per day. It will cause him to lose two or more pounds per week, a slow and steady reduction that is less painful than a crash program, and much more likely to achieve lasting results.

Diet alone is not enough, however. Fat people generally exercise too little, and unless they alter both eating and exercising habits, they cannot attain healthful slimness. Most doctors now insist that their overweight patients make a practice of moderate but regular exercise rather than occasional violent activity. By walking three miles at a reasonable pace an average-sized man can burn roughly 140 calories more than he would sitting still. Jogging, an increasingly popular prescription, consumes about 400 extra calories per hour, and swimming better than 550. Even the housewife's chores can help: a half-hour stint with the vacuum cleaner uses almost 100 calories. These energy expenditures are hardly dramatic. But for the dieter, every little bit helps. Moreover, exercise produces important corollary benefits: it stimulates the blood circulation, promotes mental relaxation and, in general, induces a feeling of well-being. These psychological effects may be of critical importance, for the improvement the dieter feels in his physical condition can inspire a determination to maintain the diet and exercise he has begun.

Reducing for love

Determination is crucial to weight reduction. People lose weight only when they are motivated to. The motivating factor may be the desire for better health, improvement of appearance or a simple matter of economics, like slimming back into an expensive wardrobe. Love is a great motivator. It drove one young man to seek help in a New York hospital. He was only 26, of average height but of startling girth; he weighed over 400 pounds. So obese was he that he could not walk the length of a city block without stopping several times to lean against a building and catch his breath. His weight had cost him several jobs; he could not meet their physical demands. Still, he continued to gain—until, at last, he met the girl who apparently felt she could love him more if there were considerably less of him. With this motivation, he put himself under the care of nutritional specialists, to whom he soon became known as the "vanishing American." In the course of 37 weeks on a diet that averaged about 400 calories a day, he lost about half his weight, regained his physical vigor and won the lady of his heart.

Whatever the motivation that inspires a fat man to lose weight, it must be powerful enough to overcome his powerful appetite, and it must be of indefinite duration. There is no point in enduring the agony

BREAKFAST
½ LARGE GRAPEFRUIT
¾ CUP DRY CEREAL
1 POACHED EGG
1 CUP WHOLE MILK
1 TEASPOON BUTTER
TEA OR COFFEE

LUNCH

1 SLICE WHITE BREAD
¾ CUP TUNAFISH WITH 1 TEASPOON MAYONNAISE
    AND SALAD GREENS
½ CUP BEETS
2 SMALL APPLES
½ CUP WHOLE MILK

DINNER

CLEAR BROTH
3 SLICES ROAST BEEF
½ CUP MASHED POTATOES
TOSSED SALAD
½ CUP COOKED CARROTS
1 TEASPOON BUTTER
½ CUP WHOLE MILK
½ SMALL BANANA COMBINED WITH 1 MEDIUM PEACH

A SENSIBLE REDUCING DIET, typical of those prescribed by physicians, includes daily menus like this one developed at the Nutrition Clinic of Philadelphia General Hospital. It contains all the nutrients—proteins, fats, carbohydrates, minerals and vitamins—needed for maintaining good health, but provides only 1,500 calories, a daily intake that will cause a man who is 25 pounds overweight to lose about two and a half pounds per week.

of losing 50 to 100 pounds if the dieter then slips back into his former eating pattern. The influences that made him overweight in the first place are, in all probability, still present, and he will soon reacquire his avoirdupois. If the dieter is to be successful, he must reconcile himself to a decided change in his mode of life, and a permanent one. He needs willpower strong enough to defeat the habits of a lifetime. Given such motivation, a nutritionally balanced diet and a program of moderate exercise will cure the disease of obesity.

No such clear-cut remedy exists for the second "disease of feast," atherosclerosis. In this ailment of the arteries, which is a severe health problem in all the world's overnourished countries, the walls of the blood vessels become lined with fatty deposits called plaques. As the plaques build up they weaken the artery and narrow the tubes, sometimes so impeding the flow of blood that angina pectoris, a painful disease, develops. Much more dangerous is the tendency of the plaques to form blood clots inside the artery or break off themselves and block blood flow. If such an obstruction stops flow to the heart, it causes a heart attack. If it stops flow in an artery leading to the brain, it causes a stroke.

A controversy arising from statistics

That atherosclerosis is a disease of feast would seem to be apparent from extensive statistical studies, which show it to be unusually prevalent among well-fed people, and especially among those who eat certain foods. But despite such strong circumstantial evidence, the underlying cause of atherosclerosis has not yet been established beyond doubt. Exactly what causes the disease has, in fact, been the source of a great controversy among medical men for more than 50 years.

The incidence of atherosclerosis in the United States began to climb sharply during the 20th Century, accompanied by a parallel increase in the consumption of fats. At the start of the century, the average American diet included only about 30 per cent fat. Since then improvements in economic conditions have brought a sharp change in American eating habits, and a great increase in the consumption of beef and dairy products high in fat content.

Today, fats account for 40 to 45 per cent of the American diet, and with this increase of fat consumption atherosclerosis has become the No. 1 killer of American men. (Women, for reasons unknown, are much less susceptible.) In less prosperous countries, where the proportion of animal fats in the diet runs to less than 20 or 25 per cent of total calories, the incidence of the disease is substantially lower.

This relationship between fatty foods and disease turns up even in comparisons of disease statistics for people from the same nation who have different eating patterns. A recent study in South Africa contrasted diet and the incidence of coronary atherosclerosis—the most widespread form of the ailment—among three groups in that country. The Bantu, whose scanty diet contains very little fat, rarely suffer from coronary atherosclerosis. Among the "Cape colored," mulattoes who enjoy a some-

ANCIENT CANDYMAKERS, catering to the age-old craving for fattening sweets, are shown in a painting from an Egyptian tomb of about 3500 B.C. Early Egyptians had no sugar, but made their candy by mixing dough *(top)*, and then sweetening it with honey and dates *(center)*. Finally they cut the mixture into triangles *(bottom)*, which were probably as full of calories as today's fudge or caramels.

what better diet and eat more fats, the disease occurs more frequently. White South Africans, who have a rich diet and consume the highest proportion of fats, have the highest rate of coronary affliction.

The villain in the case of atherosclerosis appears to be cholesterol—a white waxy substance that exists in every animal cell, but not in plants. Analysis of the fatty arterial deposits found in atherosclerosis victims always reveals cholesterol content. However, while its presence in the arteries may be harmful, cholesterol is always found in the normal human body, particularly in nerve tissues, blood and bile (it takes its name from the Greek *chole*—bile, and *stereos*—solid). In fact, the body itself manufactures cholesterol to help in many of the reactions in the human chemical factory: cholesterol is one of the raw materials from which bile is made and it plays a part in the absorption of fats. Synthesized mainly in the liver, it may be released directly into the blood; it is also carried in the bile to the intestinal tract, from which it is absorbed into the bloodstream, where its presence can be measured.

The degree to which a high level of cholesterol in the blood influences atherosclerosis has long been a subject of dispute, fanned anew from time to time as scientists learned more about the disease and more about cholesterol itself. Until 1913 arterial ailments were generally considered to be an inevitable result of advancing age. But in that year a Russian medical scientist, Nikolai Anitschow, opened a new line of thought by feeding rabbits a diet high in cholesterol. The rabbits developed a circulatory disease.

When Anitschow examined the arteries of his experimental animals, he discovered the clue that continues to puzzle medical science. The arteries were lined with the now familiar fatty plaques with their heavy concentrations of cholesterol. Anitschow's findings led a number of physicians to conclude that a diet rich in cholesterol-containing foods produced atherosclerosis. The process, they reasoned, went like this: as the ingested cholesterol was added to the cholesterol that the body manufactured, a traffic jam was created in the arteries; some of the excess cholesterol clung to the arterial walls and started plaque formations. A high-cholesterol diet, they argued, equaled a high-cholesterol level in the blood and consequently a high incidence of atherosclerosis.

A false clue from rabbits

Despite its neat logic, the theory turned out to be a vast oversimplification. Taking a closer look at rabbit plaques, pathologists found that the injuries to the arteries were different from those formed in human arteries, and that atherosclerosis in rabbits was a different disease from atherosclerosis in man. A number of experiments with other types of animal—chickens, dogs, monkeys and rats—suggested that the rabbit was an exception, for it was very difficult to induce atherosclerosis in the other animals merely by feeding them high-cholesterol diets.

These animal experiments cast doubt on any connection between human diet and the concentration of cholesterol in human blood (and perhaps between human diet and atherosclerosis). But in the early 1950s the controversy flared again when new research began to show that cholesterol in the body was influenced not by eating cholesterol itself but by other eating habits. An unusually extensive series of studies, conducted by physiologist Ancel Keys of the University of Minnesota, amassed data on diets and cholesterol levels in several countries and revealed that the intake of food fats was definitely linked to the level of cholesterol in the blood. Later investigations—principally by L. W. Kinsell of Highland-Alameda County Hospital in Oakland, California, and by E. H. Ahrens Jr. of the Rockefeller Institute in New York City— narrowed the search for the cause of high blood-cholesterol levels first to animal fats and then to particular animal fats, the "saturated" fats.

In food chemistry, "saturation" refers to the molecular composition of a fat. All simple fat molecules are straight chains of carbon atoms, each accompanied by a number of hydrogen atoms. Whenever a carbon atom is surrounded or boxed in by hydrogen atoms, the fat is said to be saturated: that is, the carbon atoms are saturated by hydrogen. If, however, two adjacent carbon atoms each lack one hydrogen atom, the fat is a monounsaturate. And if still more hydrogen atoms are missing, the fat is polyunsaturated. These slight differences in chemical structure apparently influence the fats' ability to introduce cholesterol into the bloodstream. Saturates tend to raise the blood-cholesterol level, monounsaturates to be neutral, and polyunsaturates to lower it.

Why Danish arteries clog

Once these facts about fats and cholesterol became clear, several pieces of the atherosclerosis puzzle seemed to fall into place. Now there was a reason why atherosclerosis has always been rarer among Italians than Danes: the Italians eat less fat, and what they eat comes mainly from olive oil, which is largely polyunsaturated; the Danes eat much butter and hard cheese, which are rich in saturated fats. A similar explanation can account for the increase in atherosclerosis in 20th Century America; blame falls on the increased consumption of animal products, particularly of butter and beef fat and most particularly of "prime" beef. In the past, Americans ate comparatively little beef, and most of that came from range-fed cattle, whose flesh is tough and stringy, with only a little soft fat of low saturation. Today Americans are hearty beef-eaters, and they prefer prime beef from corn-fed steers; this meat is tender and tasty because it is "marbled" with hard, saturated fats.

Such deductions seem justified, but they hardly constitute proof that saturated fats and cholesterol are the only cause of heart disease. The search for unchallengeable evidence—for or against the supposed culprits—is now being pressed by a number of extensive research programs. In 1949, the U.S. Public Health Service enlisted 5,000 men and women in Framingham, Massachusetts, to take part in a study of arterial diseases. The volunteers were given a thorough examination when they joined the program and were asked to report every two years for a check-

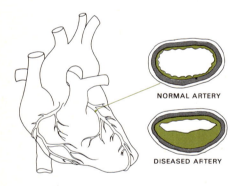

THE CORONARY ARTERIES, which supply the heart *(left)* with blood, are often seriously damaged by atherosclerosis, a disease that has been linked to the eating of certain fatty foods. The normal artery, seen in cross section *(upper right)*, has a wide opening and a relatively smooth inner lining *(green)*. In a diseased artery *(lower right)*, the lining is caked with deposits that narrow the opening. Frequently bits of the deposit break off or cause blood to clot, closing the artery. The result is the heart seizure called coronary occlusion, which may be fatal.

up. They were asked not to undertake any special dietary measures, but to go on living as they chose. Whenever heart disease struck a member of the group, the research team looked for its causes in the carefully compiled records of his life pattern.

The statistics collected at Framingham make cholesterol more highly suspect than ever. For instance, one set of figures compares the expected incidence of coronary heart disease among all men in the group with the actual incidence, classified according to each man's blood-cholesterol level. Men whose levels of blood cholesterol are low have few heart attacks—54 per cent less than the average incidence of coronary heart disease. But a group of men whose blood-cholesterol level was 50 per cent above the recommended value suffered nearly double the normal amount of heart disease.

The Anti-Coronary Club

A number of other investigations have borne out the Framingham study's results. New York City's 900-man Anti-Coronary Club, whose members volunteered to hold steadfastly to a diet low in saturated fats, suffered only one third as much heart disease as did a control group composed of men of similar ages and general patterns of life. The Anti-Coronary Club's members did not eliminate hard fat from their diets, but simply cut down on it: they were permitted beef four times a week, and eggs up to four times. But butter, ice cream and hard cheese were out, replaced by polyunsaturated-fat food such as "soft" margarine, sherbet and cottage cheese.

Over the years, research has built a strong case against cholesterol, but not strong enough to obtain a conviction. No one denies that it is an element in atherosclerosis, but debate still rages as to its relative importance. The Framingham study supports the belief that cholesterol in the blood is not the only villain. The same kind of statistical evidence implicates blood pressure and cigarettes as well. Both high blood pressure and high cholesterol levels have strikingly similar effects on heart disease: men whose blood pressure is about 50 per cent above normal suffer heart attacks more than twice as frequently as men with normal blood pressure. Those who smoke cigarettes experience a rate of heart disease 66 per cent above the nonsmokers' rate. And smokers who suffer from both high blood pressure and high cholesterol are the poorest risks of all. As the Framingham report points out: the significance of rising cholesterol level becomes more ominous when associated with other factors of risk. A combination of any two more than doubles the average risk, and all three together produce a risk more than five and a half times above the expected rate.

One thing seems certain: even if cholesterol is not the primary cause of atherosclerosis, it is a contributing factor. And that means that food influences heart disease, as it obviously does obesity. Too much food may not be as bad as too little, but that is scant comfort for those who become the victims of their own appetites.

SATURATED FAT

MONOUNSATURATED FAT

POLYUNSATURATED FAT

THREE FAT MOLECULES differ in the number of hydrogen atoms they contain. This variation is linked to their effects on the blood's content of cholesterol, often blamed for arterial disease *(opposite page)*. In a saturated-fat molecule *(top)*, each carbon atom grips two hydrogen atoms. Such a fat, found in animal products, tends to increase cholesterol. In a monounsaturated fat *(middle)*, contained in poultry and nuts, two of the carbon atoms each lack one hydrogen atom. These fats do not affect cholesterol. But in a polyunsaturated fat *(bottom)*, common in fish and vegetable oils, still more hydrogen atoms are lacking, and this lowers the cholesterol level of the blood.

Too Many Calories: A Gargantuan Problem

Throughout the ages, literature and art have pictured the fat man—from legend's Santa Claus to Shakespeare's hulking Falstaff—as a jolly soul, proud of his girth. But this fond picture is unlikely to be accepted by many of the millions of overweight Americans who have tried to lose the fat that impairs their appearance and health. Too often they have failed in their efforts to reduce because they could attack only the overt causes of excess weight—too much food and too little exercise—without affecting the elusive underlying forces that make people fat.

Today, research of many kinds in hospitals, schools and laboratories is beginning to disclose why people become overweight, that is, why they consume more calories in their food than they use up in daily activities. Studies of social customs and psychological needs, which strongly influence eating and exercise habits, are being pursued in programs for overweight schoolchildren. Hospitals are investigating the body's fat-storage mechanisms. Laboratory experiments with rats and other animals are revealing how the brain controls appetite —and this fundamental research may someday yield techniques to treat even the deepest-rooted causes of overweight.

PROFILE OF A PREDICAMENT
More than half of all American adults share the problem of girth with the man at the right. Each year waistlines stretch even further, as the increasing use of laborsaving machinery cuts down on exercise. Noting this trend, the National Academy of Sciences in 1964 reduced the recommended allowance of calories for men from 3,200 to 2,900 per day.

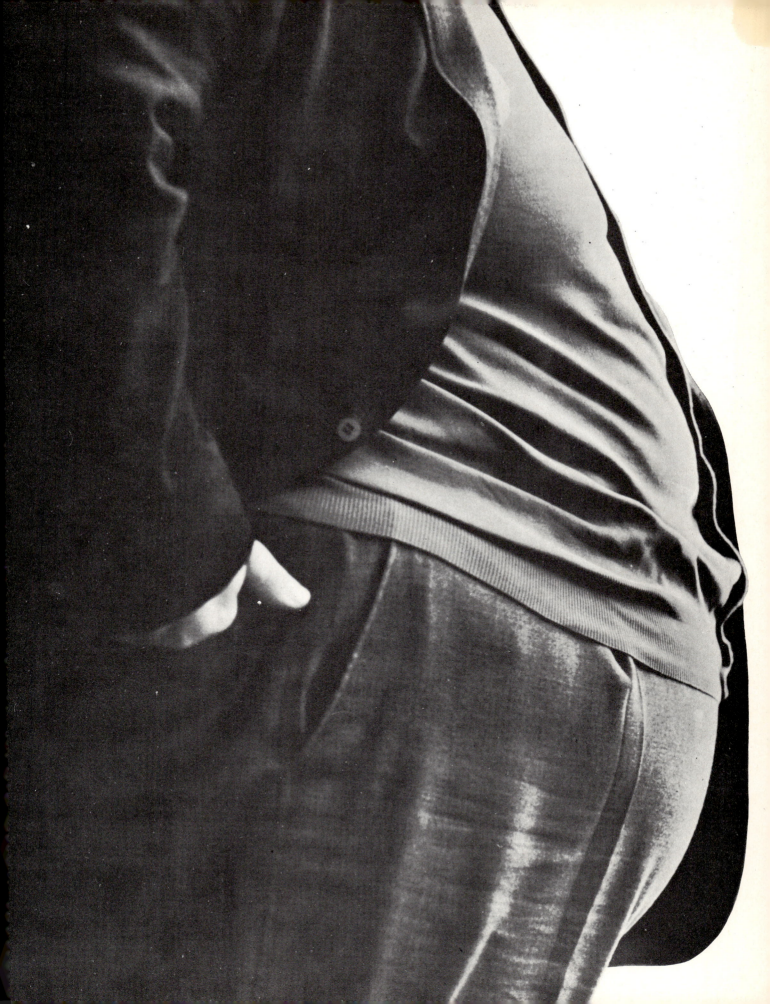

The Misguided Self-punishers

There is one guaranteed way to lose weight: eat less and exercise more. As simple as this prescription seems, many people find it impossible to follow, for it requires the willpower to sustain a permanent alteration in habits. Most overweight Americans seek quick cures, which do little or no good in the long run, and may put an unhealthy strain on their bodies.

The man above, strenuously exercising with a hoop, is burning calories and losing weight. But unless he exercises regularly, his weight problem will persist. If he simply walked 20 minutes more every day, he could lose a pound a month, and the pound would be more likely to stay lost.

Diet binges are usually as fruitless as these intermittent bursts of energy. Hoping for quick results, dieters swear off favorite foods and subsist on monotonous, unsatisfying meals —for a time. Soon they sneak pieces of cake or candy, and balloon back up to their former weight. If they continued to eat foods they like but reduced their intake by about 500 calories a day, they would lose a pound a week—and avoid the unhealthy cycle of glut and starvation.

But doctors know from experience that most people cannot stick to a prescription of fewer calories and more exercise. Thus new approaches to the weight problem are needed.

AN EXERCISE IN FUTILITY
The beauty salon's vibration machine *(above)* is pummeling a woman's hips in vain, for the reducing effects claimed for such machines are nonexistent. According to the federal Food and Drug Administration, "There is *no* device which will be effective for 'spot reducing,' for 'melting away fat,' or for 'breaking up fatty deposits.'"

THE UNHAPPY DIETER
Displeasure is evident on the face of a woman at a beauty resort who has just drunk her daily ration of food—a glass of Deer Milk, made with water, powdered skim milk, corn oil and honey. The near-starvation diet has shaved off pounds, but if the woman is typical she will soon return to her old eating habits and regain lost weight.

139

Shedding Pounds in Rock 'n' Roll Time

Obesity is a serious problem not only for adults but for an estimated three million American teenagers. A study of this age group has turned up one of the most useful clues to better reducing programs. This research, conducted by Jean Mayer of Harvard, has shown that youngsters gain weight not because they eat more than their thinner schoolmates (in fact, they eat an average of 350 few-er calories a day) but because they exercise so little. The obese children in the Mayer study were inactive 90 per cent of the time—three times as inactive as normal teenagers.

These findings have already been put to use at a junior high school near Boston where overweight girls are taught the importance of exercise. Many of the girls were afraid of activity because their awkwardness

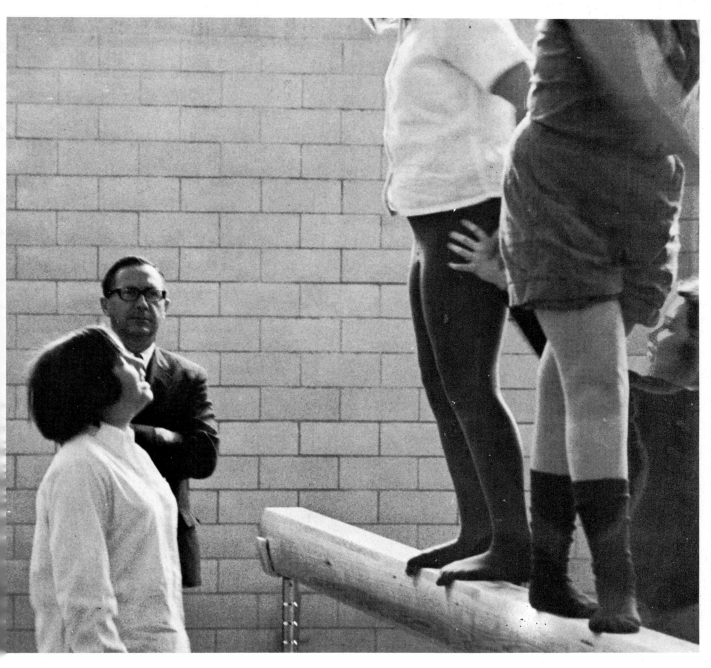

GYM CLASS FOR REDUCING
Overweight girls teeter on a wooden bar in a special gym class at Meadow Brook Junior High School in Newton, Massachusetts, as Harvard nutritionist Jean Mayer *(above, left)* observes. In his program, girls not only lose excess weight but learn grace performing such exercises as the balancing act shown above and the stretching calisthenics pictured opposite.

made them *feel* fat. To encourage them to move, Mayer accompanied the exercises with the commanding rhythms of rock 'n' roll. The girls gained a new sense of their own grace and steadily lost weight. The programs included lectures on nutrition and the caloric values of foods, thus giving the girls the knowledge they needed to fight off fat before it became a permanent part of their lives.

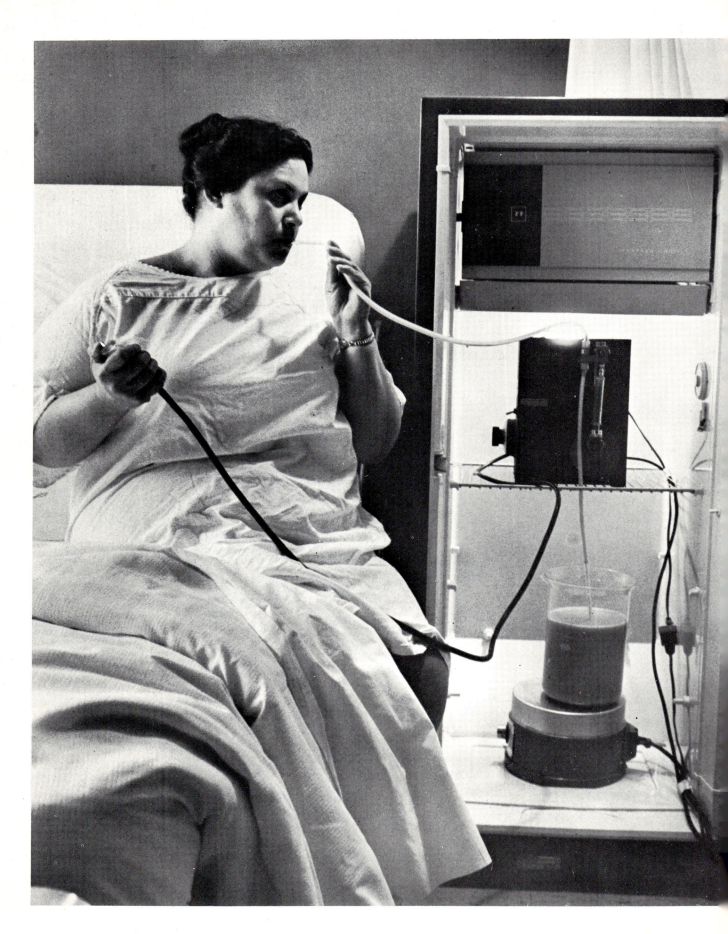

Isolating the Urge to Overeat

If people get fat because they eat too much, they eat too much mainly because of the complex of psychological attitudes and social customs involved with every aspect of food. The enormous effect of these purely mental forces on appetites of overweight people is only now becoming apparent. Ingenious experiments are slowly untangling the various influences affecting eating so that each can be gauged separately.

In one study at St. Luke's Hospital in Manhattan, a special apparatus (opposite) feeds obese patients in a rigidly mechanical fashion in order to avoid the psychological and social connotations of eating. Although the patients can eat whenever they want to, and as much as they want, the concentration of nutrients in their liquid diet is varied every day. This variation makes it impossible for the obese patients to tell from the appearance or quantity of the food how much nourishment they are getting. As a result, actual bodily hunger—not any mental desire for food—becomes the only guide for appetite. The body, unhampered by mental interference, responds in a dramatic fashion: patients who use this food machine tend to eat only what they really need and lose weight steadily.

A FOOD MACHINE
A feeding device at St. Luke's Hospital (opposite) operates at the push of a button, pumping liquid food from a jar in a bedside refrigerator. The patient's intake—consumed under conditions unaffected by social pressures—is monitored by an instrument in a separate room.

A WALKING MACHINE
The patients at St. Luke's Hospital have their daily exercise monitored as precisely as their diets. They exercise by taking walks on this conveyor-belt treadmill; since it can operate as fast as 18 miles per hour and be tilted up to 40°, differing amounts of effort can be demanded.

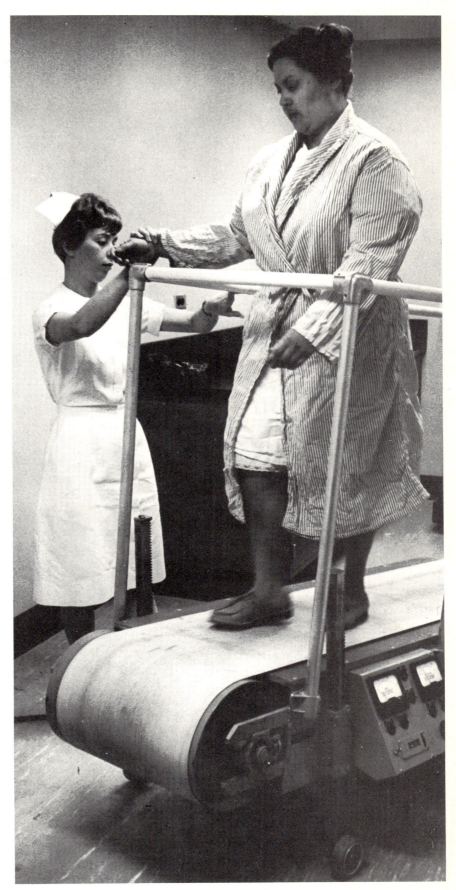

Peering into the Dieter's Body

The pajama-clad man shown on these pages weighed more than 300 pounds when he entered the hospital to begin reducing on a diet of nothing but water and vitamins. Besides melting him down toward a more healthful weight, this austere regimen yields important data on how fat cells inside his body are eliminated.

To control the loss of unwanted cells, researchers scan the natural radioactivity of the body, which is emitted almost entirely by nonfat tissue. As long as the man continues to sustain life by consuming only his own fat, the level of radioactivity remains constant. Any falling off in the level means that muscle is being used up by the body's energy-generating processes. By keeping track in this way, researchers can judge the merits of various diet and exercise programs.

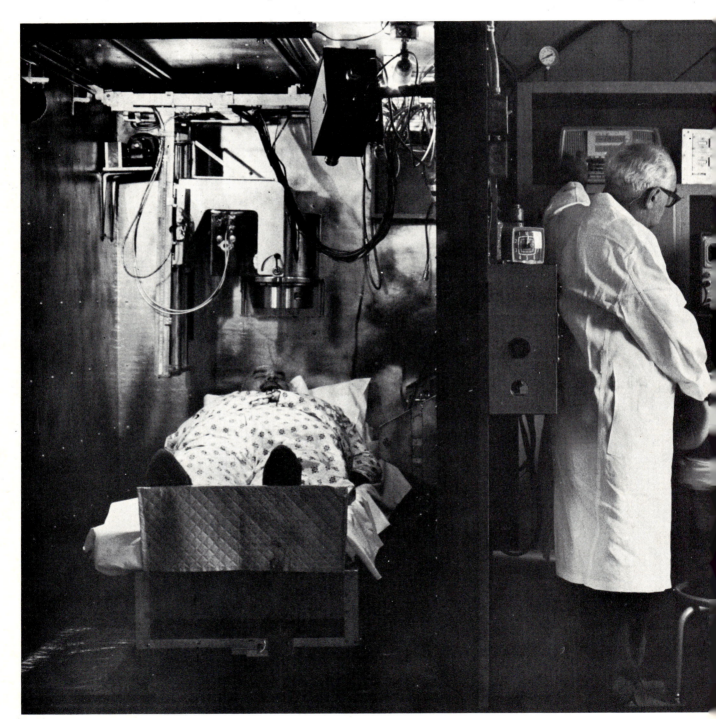

GAUGING FAT BY RADIOACTIVITY

Five tons of sophisticated equipment operated by two technicians compares fat and lean in a patient at Wadsworth Veterans Hospital in Los Angeles. The equipment measures the radioactivity level in the lean parts of the body, where potassium atoms emit rays that are then detected in a shielded chamber *(below, extreme left)*. Since fat gives off no radiation, any lessening of the rays picked up by the round detector *(right)* means that the body is burning up muscle.

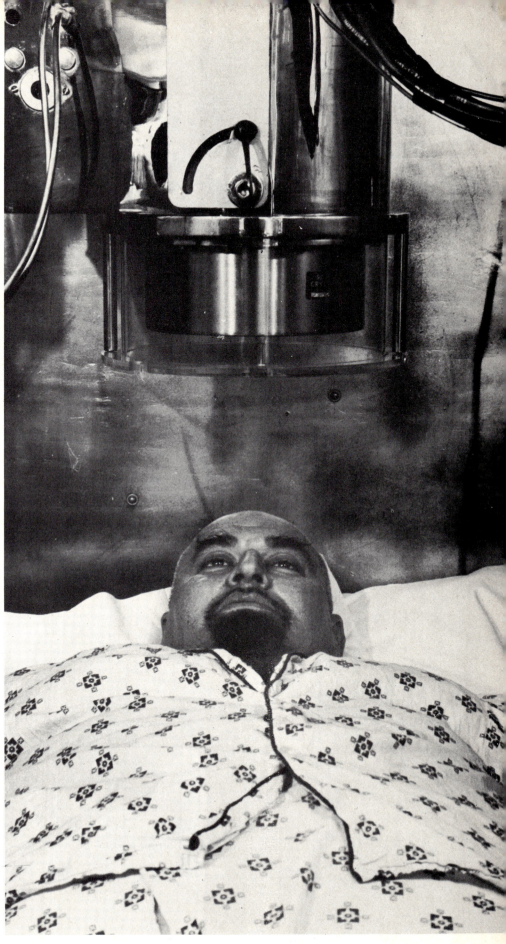

Hunting for the Basic Mechanism

Along with the mounting medical assault on obesity through studies of diet, exercise and psychology, scientists are exploring the brain to find an even more fundamental source of weight problems. For it is this complex organ that ultimately governs the intake and use of food.

The dominant role of the brain has been demonstrated by many experiments on animals. Damage to one part of the brain makes mice grossly obese (right). Furthermore, interference with an animal's normal eating habits, which are regulated by the brain, can radically alter the way its body uses food. Rats instinctively nibble, eating 20 or 30 snacks a day. But if the commands of their brains are overridden by force feeding, so that they get their food in a few large meals, their bodily use of the food changes. They do not gain weight, but the percentage of fat in their bodies increases relative to the content of protein and water.

These results have led some scientists to speculate that man, like the rat, is an instinctive nibbler—and to blame the distressing human tendency to get fat on the civilized habit of eating meals instead of obeying the brain's command to eat small amounts of food fairly frequently.

AN APPETITE THAT RAN AMOK
Dr. Jean Mayer of Harvard holds up two mice to illustrate the direct effect of the brain on eating. In the mouse on the left, the brain's appetite center—located in the hypothalamus —was destroyed by a fine surgical wire. The mouse began to eat without any relation to body need, and it now weighs more than twice as much as the normal mouse on the right.

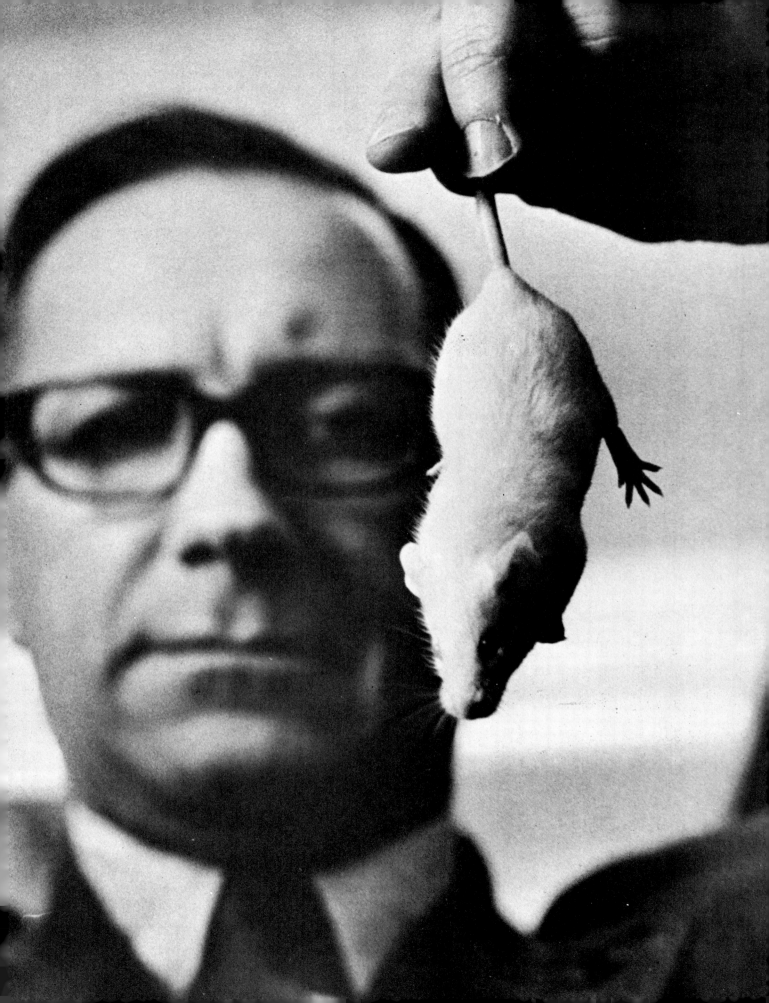

7

Food Fads and Frauds

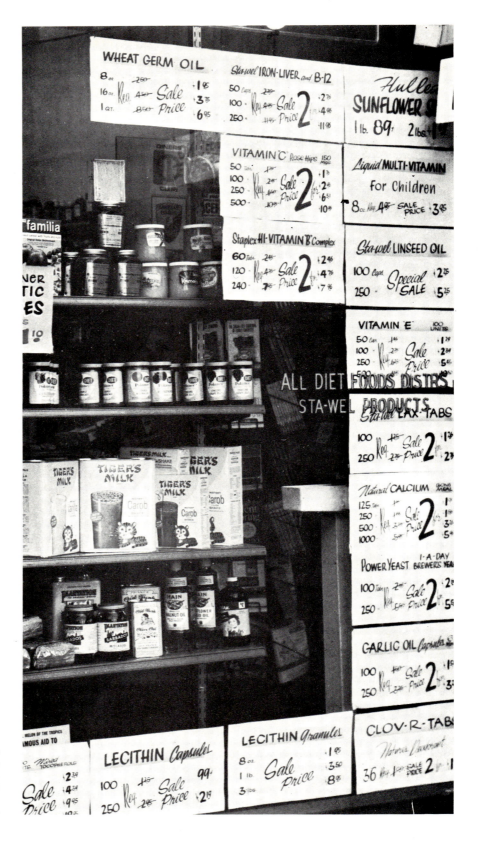

A health-food store in New York displays exotic foods favored by faddists. The prices on the window advertisement— $6.95 for a quart of wheat-germ oil and 89 cents for a pound of sunflower seeds— reflect the high cost of health-food diets.

EVER SINCE EVE bamboozled Adam into believing that a bite of the apple would bring him the knowledge of good and evil, people have attributed special powers to their foods. Egyptians of the Third Millennium B.C. fed garlic to the workmen who labored on the Great Pyramids because they thought it was a great body strengthener. The Greek physician Dioscorides of the First Century A.D. was convinced that a potion made of grasshoppers relieved bladder disorders, and that the liver of an ass was a cure for epilepsy. In Rome, Cato the Elder stuffed himself with cabbage, which he thought possessed special healing powers. And the eminent Roman scholar Pliny believed that the foot and snout of the hippopotamus would increase sexual potency—a prescription that was limited in its application by, among other things, a scarcity of hippos.

Just as some foods have been credited with health-giving benefits, others have been blamed for illness with scarcely more cause. At one time or another, oysters, cucumbers, carrots, pumpkins, apples, peaches, oranges and lemons have all been proscribed as dangerous. But few foods have suffered such capricious evaluation as the tomato. First cultivated by the Indians of South and Central America, it was taken to Europe—along with other loot—by the Spaniards who conquered Mexico in the 16th Century. When the tomato reached France, people there welcomed it with Gallic affection. They thought it was an aphrodisiac and called it the *pomme d'amour,* or "apple of love." Germans and Englishmen also valued it, but as a curiosity. They thought the tomato was poisonous because it belongs to the same family of plants as the deadly nightshade.

Not until 1820 did the tomato come into its own in the United States. In that year a fearless tomato lover named Robert Gibbon Johnson stood on the steps of the Salem County Courthouse in New Jersey and ate a whole tomato, while spectators gasped in awe. To the onlookers' surprise, Johnson survived this daredevil feat, and the tomato soon gained an honored place in the American diet.

Parallels to the ups and downs of the tomato can be found throughout history as people of one time or one place have found reasons for favoring or condemning particular kinds of food. Some of these fashions in eating have—or once had—a logical basis in nutritional fact or ethical belief. But most have been the work of misguided zealots who convinced themselves and their followers that they had discovered either hidden dangers or formulas for vigor and vitality. And a few are outright frauds, cynically promoted to line the pockets of unscrupulous quacks. The only attack effective against these nostrums is wide exposure of their falsity.

This leaves the food fads whose backers honestly believe that they aid health. Upon analysis these diets rarely prove to have a clear-cut advantage over an ordinary balanced diet, and in some instances they are harmful. They usually place too much reliance on certain foods at the expense of others that are equally or more valuable. Such restrictions on the variety of foods eaten may leave out of the diet nutrients that are essential to health, causing deficiency diseases—and even, in extreme cases, death. More often the danger is indirect, as it is in the reducing plans that promise easy ways to take off weight; the fact is that they do not work, and, by misleading people into relying on them, they prevent the use of effective treatments. However, the hazards of fad diets are not always serious. It makes little difference, nutritionally, if a man is convinced that he should not eat tomatoes; many other foods can supply the vitamins and minerals tomatoes offer. Nor will it matter if a person subscribes to the ancient Egyptian belief in the powers of the redolent garlic; any risk he runs is more likely to be social than physical. For most healthy people, the choice of foods to be eaten or avoided is a personal matter, heavily influenced by the social climate in which they live, and if their choices seem quaint to us it is usually because they differ so markedly from our own.

The genius who ate no meat

One of the oldest and most widespread fashions in eating is the vegetarian diet, which excludes meat and, in some cases, all animal products including milk, butter, cheese and eggs. Long established in India as a part of Hindu belief, vegetarianism has won many adherents elsewhere, including such illustrious enthusiasts as the British dramatist George Bernard Shaw. He gave up eating meat when he was 25 and never resumed for the rest of his 94 years. An egocentric and opinionated man, Shaw explained his objections to meat eating. First, he was extraordinarily fond of animals. Second, as he put it, "a man of my spiritual intensity does not eat corpses." Shaw also deplored the social connotations of a carnivorous diet: "It involves a prodigious slavery of men to animals . . . graziers, shepherds, slaughtermen, butchers, milkmaids and so forth, absorb a mass of human labor that should be devoted to the breeding and care of human beings." Finally, he was a firm believer in the alleged health-enhancing properties of the meatless diet, avowing that he was "seldom less than ten times as well as an ordinary carcass eater."

Vegetarians often point to Shaw's long life as evidence that their custom is conducive to good health, strength and longevity. Nutritionists know of no basis for these claims, although the practice need not be harmful. By forgoing meat, the vegetarian deprives himself of the primary source of high-quality protein. He makes it harder to obtain his nutrition. But theoretically he can get all the essential nutrients from a meatless diet—even if he abstains from eggs and milk as well. To do so he must select his vegetable foods carefully and know his nutritional requirements. The most elusive nutrient for the strict vegetarian is vitamin B_{12}. It can be synthesized by chemical fermentation processes, but otherwise comes almost entirely from animal sources. Lack of vitamin B_{12} recently caused serious health problems among a British vegetarian sect known as "vegans." Physicians who examined the group reported that a deficiency of this vitamin had stunted the growth of the children, while adults suffered sore tongues, stiff backs and nervous disorders.

While the vegetable diet may be questionable nutritionally, its ethical basis helps to explain its widespread acceptance. Far more difficult to understand is the popularity of other eating fashions that may not be particularly harmful but are often rather foolish.

One that swept the United States soon after the turn of the century seems plainly humbug now, but was taken very seriously at the time. The creation of a remarkable man named Horace Fletcher, the fad emphasized the way food was eaten rather than the foods themselves. As a youth, Fletcher ran away to sea. He later studied art in Paris and was art correspondent for the Paris edition of the *New York Herald,* managed an opera company in New Orleans, manufactured printers' ink, and imported Oriental silks and curios. In all, he made six trips around the world, 16 Pacific crossings and more transatlantic voyages than anyone can remember.

By the time he was 40, the strenuous life had taken its toll. Although he was only five feet six inches tall, Fletcher weighed 217 pounds; the slightest exertion caused his heart to pound like a hammer and made his breath come short. So he retired and took up the study of nutrition.

In the course of his studies he learned that British Prime Minister William Gladstone had once concluded that there was a logical reason for the fact that man was equipped with 32 teeth. It meant, said Gladstone, that every mouthful of food should be chewed 32 times.

The news hit Fletcher like a thunderclap. He decided that the trouble with the world was that it had been biting off more than it could properly chew. "Nature will castigate those who don't masticate," he said. Chewing is indeed healthful—it stimulates the digestive juices—but Fletcher was carried away by his discovery; he chewed so hard (and ate so little) that he lost 65 pounds.

When life was a steady grind

Before he knew it, Horace Fletcher had ground his way to national fame. "Fletcherism" and "Fletcherize" became national bywords as everyone took up the beat of Horace's jaws. West Point cadets chewed; John D. Rockefeller Sr. chewed; Thomas A. Edison chewed. Scientists at Cambridge University, the Sorbonne, Harvard, Yale and Johns Hopkins endorsed Fletcher's ruminations. By the time he died in 1919, the fad was almost an obsession in many countries. In the years that followed, however, Fletcherism slowly died away as its enthusiasts came to their senses.

It would be comforting to think that such excesses are a thing of the past, but such is not the case. When it comes to nutritional nonsense our own enlightened age is second to none. Today, people subscribe to an almost limitless variety of unfounded notions about food. Some of these misconceptions are old, some new. Many people believe that milk and fish, or pickles and milk should never be mixed. Others insist that citrus fruits make the blood acid, that white eggs are more nutritious than brown ones (or, in Boston, vice versa); that milk is devitalized by

"I THINK HE'S HAD ENOUGH."

Drawing by Geo. Price;
Copr. © 1953 The New Yorker Magazine, Inc.

THE VIRTUES OF SPECIAL FOODS, satirized in this cartoon, have long been endorsed by health faddists. They restrict themselves to raw vegetables, nuts, berries, yogurt, spinach and protein concentrates in their belief that these foods are endowed with unusual body-building powers. Their faith is misplaced, for while each of these foods is wholesome, the ordinary ingredients of a balanced diet will serve as well, supplying the body with all the nutrition it can use—and usually at less expense.

being pasteurized. Still others are convinced that beets make the blood richer, fish and celery make people brainier, and vegetable juices make the body stronger.

Even old Horace Fletcher has recently been resurrected. One health cult advocates chewing every mouthful of food at least 50 times and recommends as many as 100 or 150 chews. One of the cult's disciples, a Japanese girl, reportedly chewed an onion 1,300 times, a feat that may have strengthened her jaws but did nothing for her health.

Ideas of this kind, usually harmless but scientifically unsound, have led to the growth of what is probably the most popular food fad in America today. This is the vogue for the so-called "health foods," which are nutritious and useful but not unusually so. Its followers, like the vegetarians, believe strongly in the value of fruits, nuts and salads, but they also rebel against modern methods of growing and processing foods. They consider synthetic fertilizers harmful to crops; many health-food faddists will eat only vegetables grown "organically," that is, fertilized in the old-fashioned way by manure or garbage. They are enthusiastically in favor of certain simple foods, which they consider to be untainted by "over-refining."

Two of the most esteemed items in the list of health foods are yogurt, a custardy substance made by culturing milk with bacteria, and blackstrap molasses, the syrup left behind when sugar is extracted from sugarcane. Yogurt is supposed to be blessed with life-prolonging powers, mainly because it is a staple in rural Bulgaria, where, according to one report, many peasants have lived to be more than 100 years old. Blackstrap molasses is honored because it contains a substantial amount of iron, which is an essential mineral (also provided by foods like lean meats, somewhat more commonly encountered in American diets).

Catering to these beliefs has become big business, and most large cities have stores and restaurants that specialize in health foods. In New York City alone there are more than 80, and a description of one of them affords a view of a kind of eating that few people ever see.

Soybeans and grass for lunch

A visitor entering the health-food restaurant, which also sells packaged foods, walks past shelves of sunflower seeds, avocado honey, pumpkin seeds, rice polish, wheat germ, protein supplements and soy oil. At a table in the back of the restaurant, the menu offers him a selection utterly foreign to gourmet cuisine. For an appetizer, he might order a "mixed green" vegetable cocktail, a blend of parsley, celery and watercress juices. This concoction tastes like new-mown grass, and when the glass is set on the table, a sediment that does indeed look like chopped grass slowly settles to the bottom of the glass. From among the main courses he can choose a salad made of soybeans, which proves to be very tasty. And to wash it down, a favorite health-food drink is Tiger's Milk, a mixture of whole milk, skimmed milk, brewers' yeast and fruit juices; it smells like floor wax but tastes like soap. The visitor might then polish off his meal with the faddists' most popular dessert, yogurt seasoned with wheat germ and honey, a dish that is creamy in texture and piquantly sour in flavor.

The newcomer to health foods is likely to get up from such a luncheon and march off to the nearest hamburger counter for something more substantial. But the meal described above is an adequate one and nutritious.

The high cost of health foods

The health foods themselves are not harmful. They are expensive. A pound of "organically grown" peas costs almost twice as much as its equivalent in a supermarket. Honey is 75 cents a jar in a health-food store, 45 cents elsewhere. Many exotic commodities, possessing no unusual nutritional values, bring steep prices: pumpkin seeds $1.50 a tin, soy oil 83 cents a pint, rice polish 69 cents a pound. Others, equally costly, seem to be entirely useless. One popular item is "iodine ration," a dollar bottle of tablets made from kelp and "excipients," which are simply inert chemical binders that hold the kelp powder in tablet form. The tablets are intended to supply the element iodine, which is indeed essential to human nutrition. But most people acquire all the iodine they need from the iodized salt they ordinarily use to season their food —at a cost of less than two cents a month.

If the health-food fad and Fletcher's chewing craze are innocuous, the same cannot be said of many other special eating habits. At the least, they can interfere with the attainment of well-being; at worst, they may bring on illness. The possibility of harm usually arises when a so-called surefire diet is used to alleviate a physical ailment; since one of the most common afflictions in the United States is obesity, trick reducing schemes are among the frequent offenders against good health.

Fads win favor with the overweight simply because reducing is so difficult. The only way a fat man can get slim and stay slim is by decreasing his intake of calories and increasing his exercise—not temporarily, but permanently. This takes more willpower and tenacity than many fat persons can muster. They snatch at any promise of assistance, whether it comes from pills, unusual diets or special eating schedules.

These reducing aids can often help take off weight—if they are not complete frauds, as a few are—but they rarely provide a lasting solution to obesity. The popular liquid-meal-in-a-can, for example, provides a nutritious diet that is very low in calories but so monotonous that it usually defeats its purpose; the would-be reducer becomes so hungry for solid food that he may use up a week's allotment of calories in a one-hour eating orgy. A similar fate awaits those who try to lose weight by skipping meals; they often eat so much at their other meals that they gain instead of lose.

Some people believe that toasting bread lowers its calorie content. It does not; the application of heat causes a chemical alteration of the starch but does not make it any less fattening. Washing rice is another

A FAKE CURE FOR FATNESS, Allan's Anti-Fat was advertised in 1878 as a "concentrated fluid extract of sea lichens" that prevented the body from converting food into fat. While this preposterous claim would fool few people today, modern Americans spend $100 million each year on "medicated" caramels, chewing gum, cigarettes, fad diets, tonics and "reducing aids" that are no more effective than Anti-Fat.

trick that is supposed to help dieters; it simply washes out the water-soluble vitamins, not the calories. The reducing value of a between-meals snack of grapefruit is also a myth—except to the extent that the grapefruit, which is relatively low in caloric content, depresses the appetite so that less is eaten at the next meal. Grapefruit has no chemical component that will influence the fattening proclivities of other foods.

Nor do reducing pills have much more lasting effect. The "filler" (a chemically inactive substance like methyl cellulose, which is not absorbed by the body) gives a sensation of fullness and temporarily lessens hunger pangs. However, its efficacy lasts only so long as the dieter manages to exercise restraint at his next meal. A purpose somewhat similar to that of the filler is served by a quite different drug, the "depressant," usually an active chemical like amphetamine, which interferes with the appetite-controlling center of the brain to reduce the dieter's desire to eat.

One drug that does melt fat is the "stimulator," most often a thyroid extract, which acts as a sort of chemical exerciser, speeding up the body's reactions so that calories are consumed faster than usual. Another type of pill reduces weight without really affecting obesity. This is the "diuretic," a dehydrating material that stimulates the kidneys to drain water from body tissues. The loss is not in fat at all, only in water —the pill-taker may fool the bathroom scales, but not his tailor.

The drawbacks of reducing drugs

One or another of these drugs is sometimes prescribed by a physician as a morale booster; they help induce a weight loss that encourages the struggling reducer to stick to his slimming program a little longer. But many of them cause undesirable side effects such as nervousness and insomnia, and their value is in any case limited. To reduce, the patient must still restrict his intake of calories and increase his exercise; when he does so with the help of synthetic appetite-curbers or stimulants, he achieves nothing toward the development of sensible permanent eating and exercise habits. Almost invariably he will regain the lost weight— and frequently more—shortly after he stops taking the drugs.

Reducing schemes can be more than misleading. One that has enjoyed a vogue in recent years is potentially dangerous. This is the low-carbohydrate, "eat all you want" diet, sometimes known as the Mayo Clinic Diet or the Air Force Diet, although it has been disclaimed by both of these institutions.

The appeal of this diet is the claim that the reducer may eat all the fats and proteins he wants, so long as he limits his carbohydrate intake to 2.2 ounces a day, as opposed to the 11 ounces in the normal American diet. This seemingly painless way to lose weight rests on the notion that the body quickly uses up proteins and fats but does not readily dispose of carbohydrates, which tend to be stored as fatty tissue. The pseudoscientific explanation does not stand up to the facts: carbohydrates are *not* more readily stored by the body than other foods. Yet the diet may work, for a different reason: fats and proteins are more filling than carbohydrates, leading dieters to eat fewer calories.

This low-carbohydrate approach to reducing is risky, however, because the dieter may go overboard and cut his carbohydrate intake below the safety level. A certain amount of carbohydrate is essential to body chemistry in order to metabolize fat. If there is not enough carbohydrate to complete this metabolism, fat-derived compounds called ketone bodies build up in the bloodstream to induce ketosis, a dangerous condition evidenced by a general bodily discomfort. Moreover, a diet that is low in carbohydrate value probably lacks other essentials as well—including vitamin C, certain minerals and necessary roughage.

Quackery that can be fatal

Even more dangerous than the reducing fads are the quack diets that are frequently promoted as cures for serious illnesses. One young woman in New Jersey died some time ago, apparently because she fell prey to a widespread fad that limited her diet almost entirely to cereal grains. The unfortunate woman, who followed the faddist's instructions to the letter, tried to live on nothing but whole-grain cereal and tea. In the first month she lost 20 pounds but, convinced that the diet was ridding her body of poisons, she refused to give it up. Because the diet lacks vitamin C, she soon developed symptoms of scurvy; after nine months on the diet, she died.

According to pamphlets issued by the self-appointed expert behind this whole-grain cult, more than 80 ailments, from bedwetting, dandruff and toothache to leprosy, leukemia and cancer, could be cured within a few weeks without medicine or surgery, by faithful adherence to the cereal diet. The same diet with minor modifications—usually including a specialty sold at the group's headquarters—was said to correct apoplexy, appendicitis, arthritis, cataract, detached retina, diabetes, eczema, epilepsy, glaucoma, hemophilia, impotence, insomnia, meningitis, obesity, paranoia, schizophrenia and trachoma.

This is the worst form of nutritional quackery. The insistence that diet can cure such ailments encourages naïve or ignorant people to forgo necessary medical treatment that might alleviate grave illness.

The food charlatans who prey upon health fears bilk Americans of half a billion dollars every year. Cynical promoters of miracle foods, phony elixirs and misrepresented vitamin-mineral supplements use every technique of the hard- and soft-sell in advertisements, pamphlets,

ELOQUENT VEGETARIANS, the British poet Percy Bysshe Shelley *(far left)*, British dramatist George Bernard Shaw *(center)* and Russian novelist Leo Tolstoy all ardently opposed the eating of meat. In 1813 Shelley published a treatise declaring that man's digestive system was suited only to eating plant foods. Half a century later Shaw, influenced by Shelley's writings, also turned to vegetarianism. In 1876 Tolstoy proclaimed a new religion in which he rejected war, violence, drinking, smoking and the eating of animal flesh.

155

books and lectures. They tout their products by propounding four often-repeated myths of nutrition: that almost all disease is caused by faulty diet; that ordinary foods are nutritionally inferior because repeated planting has impoverished farm soils; that processed foods are "devitalized"; and that almost everyone is suffering from borderline nutritional deficiency.

The war against food frauds

A number of public and private organizations wage a continuing war on these frauds. The American Medical Association, for example, attempts to fight the false claims with facts, supplying community groups with information designed to combat food faddism and false nutritional claims. The American Dietetic Association sponsors a "Dial-a-Dietician" program; in major cities the Association publicizes telephone numbers that anyone may call to learn the truth about a food fad or a questionable product. The National Better Business Bureau and its local chapters keep a careful watch for deceptive practices. The U.S. Federal Trade Commission and the Post Office Department monitor food advertising for misrepresentations. But the primary job of removing fake cure-alls from the market and prosecuting their purveyors falls to the federal government's Food and Drug Administration.

This agency is charged with the enforcement of the Federal Food, Drug and Cosmetic Act, which requires that special dietary foods and vitamin or mineral preparations be truthfully and adequately labeled. The Food and Drug Administration (FDA) checks on new products and brings legal action to end the sale of "misbranded" products—those whose labeling is "false or misleading in any particular."

One of the most blatant cases in recent years involved a wonder capsule recommended in sales literature as a cure for a long list of ailments that included alcoholism, arthritis, anemia, frigidity, heart trouble, infections, nervousness, ulcers and even juvenile delinquency. For customers not afflicted with any of these, it also promised good health, beauty, athletic prowess, protracted youth and vitality. The sale of these capsules—containing a mixture of compounds, mostly unneeded by the body—was big business; the home office directed the operations of thousands of dealers all over the country.

The company's door-to-door salesmen, recruited from among customers, were organized in military fashion. For $10,000 a salesman could become a "general." The general was required to buy sales kits and a supply of the product. He recruited lieutenants, who lined up sergeants; the sergeants, in turn, formed their own platoons. Each level in the hierarchy took a large commission in sales. Eventually the army numbered more than 75,000 salesmen, selling the food supplement at $24 for a six-month supply.

When the FDA's inspectors compared the product's contents with its all-embracing claims, the FDA quickly took legal action against the company in Atlanta, Washington and a number of other American cities. Stocks of the product were condemned and the empire collapsed.

In many cases, nutritional quackery is not so easy to stop. By using ingeniously indirect sales approaches, the modern snake-oil purveyors can sometimes evade the charge of misleading labels. One best-selling book prescribed unpasteurized honey and apple-cider vinegar as a preventive or remedy for more than 60 ailments. Although the FDA termed the prescription "medical nonsense," it was powerless to act against the book. Only when a mixture of unpasteurized honey and apple-cider vinegar appeared on store counters alongside the book could the FDA move. The courts upheld its allegation that the implied connection between book and panacea constituted "misleading labeling."

The wiliest of the peddlers are careful to sidestep the law by avoiding a direct connection between exaggerated claims and their products. Not long ago, a "health" magazine carried an article extolling pumpkin seeds as a cure for disorders of the prostate gland. In the same issue of the magazine, but removed a few pages from the article, a pumpkin-seed packager advertised his product without any reference to its powers as a "cure." Prosecuting such a misrepresentation is difficult since a direct connection between an article and advertising can rarely be proved.

Catching the nutritional con men

The door-to-door pitchman is a persistent thorn in the side of the antiquackery forces. With fewer than 5,000 employees, the FDA does not have the manpower to check on the activities of the many thousands of "doorstep doctors." In some cases, however, the FDA has succeeded in obtaining tape recordings of incriminating sales spiels. One went like this: "Nutrition is the source of all difficulties. Hippocrates said, 'Let your food be your medicine, your medicine be your food,' and that the dietary deficiencies of youth are collected with compound interest 20 years later. Well, at 25 nobody could tell me nothin'. I had ulcerated stomach, arthritis, neuritis, pyorrhea, I wore glasses. I had a 44-inch waistline, high blood pressure. Well, I was finished. When everything else failed—doctors and all sorts of medication, chiropractors . . . everything failed—I got hold of this product through divine revelation." After that pitch the FDA "got hold" of both product and peddler.

That nostrum salesman will hardly be missed, however, for his place was quickly filled from the army of hucksters who prey on human gullibility. Nutritional quackery, food cults and phony diet fads flourish in the United States today as never before. In some ways they are encouraged rather than discouraged by the discoveries of modern food science. The demonstration by legitimate nutritionists that there is a vital need for a properly balanced diet has often helped to make more credible the claims of promoters and zealots, for these supersalesmen frequently use imaginative distortions of sober fact to convince prospective purchasers. There are, in truth, people who would benefit from special foods or diet supplements, but they need the help of a competent physician or nutritionist, not of a self-appointed food expert.

Nutrition Fit
for a King

"The discovery of a new dish," wrote the French gourmet Brillat-Savarin, "does more for the happiness of humanity than the discovery of a new star." More than happiness is at stake: an enjoyable dish also makes an essential contribution to nutrition, for even a well-balanced menu cannot fulfill its role in sustaining human well-being unless it tempts the palate. In the art of making food a pleasure, the French chef has few peers. In the Western world, he has made his haute cuisine—intricately prepared foodstuffs of the highest quality, embellished with delicate sauces, beautifully decorated and served with solemn grace—the standard against which fine food is gauged.

One of the most noted artists in food is 35-year-old Roger Fessaguet, who is head chef at New York's La Caravelle Restaurant. Fessaguet aims for perfection and works hard to achieve it. He spends 14 hours a day overseeing the preparation of an average of 300 meals a day. He rarely leaves his kitchen to witness the proof of his skill upstairs in the dining room. To him it is enough to know that few dishes return uneaten —sure evidence that he has demonstrated to his guests that food can be not only nutritious but one of life's chief delights.

GENERALSHIP IN THE KITCHEN
Proudly wearing his distinctive white cap—the *toque blanche* insigne of his eminent professional status—Roger Fessaguet issues instructions to the assistants who will fill the orders spread out on the counter. Before a meal is served, Fessaguet will sample the sauces, add a touch of decoration to a platter and help prepare the most difficult dishes.

For the Best Food, the Best Makings

The peak in flavor, like the utmost in nutrition, demands fresh food of excellent quality. Crates of fruit, vegetables and dairy products, mountains of meat and fish—ordered by telephone the night before—arrive at La Caravelle at 9 a.m. to be examined by Fessaguet's experienced eye. He checks beef to see that its meat is bright red and its marbled fat the color of fresh butter; he explores the lower layers of fruit crates to make sure that all oranges and lemons are of the specified size.

A formidable range of foods enters the kitchen of La Caravelle. In a two-week period, the restaurant offers more than 60 different main courses, which change with the seasons. Fessaguet creates this ambitious repertory with 40 varieties of vegetable, 20 kinds of fruit, 30 seafoods and 40 different kinds of meat. Many of the foodstuffs are expensive delicacies

with exotic origins: Beluga caviar from Caspian Sea sturgeon—a treat for which gourmets gladly pay nine dollars a serving; Brittany oysters, at $3.50 a portion, which Fessaguet prefers for their lack of any fatty flavor; *langouste,* or sea crayfish, from cold Atlantic waters, flown over from Paris weekly, which brings their cost up to nine dollars; venison from New York hunting clubs, listed on the menu at up to $12.50 for a single serving.

THE WARY BUYER

Sampling fruit from California, Roger Fessaguet studies the color and firmness of lemons and oranges that will supply sauce for roast duck, flavoring in pastries, garnishes for fish or a twist of peel in a cocktail. Each day he uses about $150 worth of fruit and vegetables.

Stern Devotion to a Great Tradition

To cook La Caravelle's noted dishes, a staff of six chefs—each a specialist in his department—works under Fessaguet's direction. The kitchen is organized around a division of duties traditional in haute cuisine. One chef creates the sauces, another prepares roasts in a minor inferno of heat that averages 130° F. near the front of the stoves; others concentrate on making fish, vegetable or pastry dishes.

Each of these men achieves high standards of taste by an instinct developed through long years of experience; many of them have worked at their particular branch of cooking for decades, and all had to pass examinations given by a board of chefs in France before emerging from their apprenticeships to become practicing chefs.

"We are in France here," Fessaguet says. The spoken language of La Caravelle's kitchen is French, most of the recipes are classic French creations, and the standards of culinary perfection are uniquely French. Fessaguet even sends his white chef's hat back to a Paris laundry to be washed, because "they are the only ones who know how to do it right."

THE CONSTANT SUPERVISION
Fessaguet confers with his *garde-manger* Max Avenet, who makes cold buffet dishes and supervises all meat cutting. Avenet will transform the striped bass *(foreground)* into a delectable dish for the buffet table. Both men, born in France, began their apprenticeships at 14. Fessaguet became a head chef at 29—an eminence usually not reached before the age of 45.

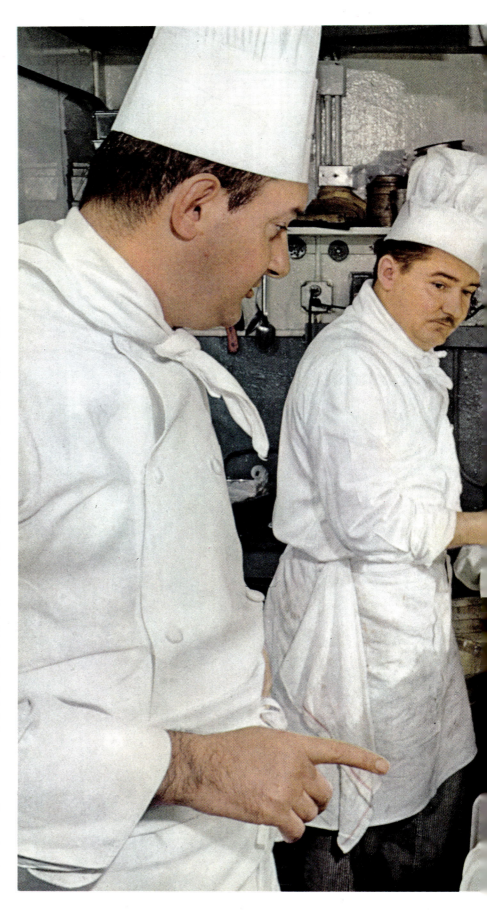

THE LONG LEARNING PROCESS
Fruit compote is prepared by a beginner in La Caravelle's kitchen, Angelo Saltares, who is also responsible for salads and coffee. After he learns enough to become an official apprentice, he will work under each department chef for several months before he is assigned a specialty.

THE MASTER PASTRYMAKER
Georges Keller, considered by Fessaguet to be one of the finest pastry chefs in the world, puts a frill of whipped cream on a many-layered pastry named *mille-feuille*, meaning "a thousand leaves." Keller, the senior among La Caravelle's six chefs, has made pastry since 1918.

A great dish begins as a pan is buttered.   Arranged in the butter is a decorative layer of carrots, turnips, and pork and garlic sausages.

After an hour in the oven has brought about a blend of the many flavors of the ingredients, the elegant dish is carefully flipped upside down.

Feasts for
Eye and Palate

Cooked cabbage and pheasant are added.

Appearance no less than flavor contributes to making good food into a great dish. And skill in decoration has long been the hallmark of the most famous French chefs. A century ago, they cared more about the look of food than its taste. They labored over sculptured pastries, huge architectural cakes, and dozens of extravagant variations on cold buffets of beef or fish.

Such baroque splendors have now given way to a simplicity that restores the preeminence of flavor. Today, chefs focus most of their energy on composing menus that will provide an interplay of tastes, or on devising an appropriate match between a dish and its sauce. But the decorative urge lives on. Roger Fessaguet makes certain that the colors of a dish—red of tomatoes, white of potatoes, green of string beans, for instance—are pleasingly arranged. With beef gelatin, hand-shaped truffles, cooked yolks of eggs, red pimentos, curving lines of leek leaves, he creates patterns of color tantalizing to the appetite.

For special occasions Fessaguet gives his fancy full rein—as in the dish shown here, a gaudy creation made with pheasants grouped on a bed of cabbage. This opulent dish takes him and his staff five hours to prepare, but the awed response of the diners makes it worthwhile.

Finally the awe-inspiring—and delicious—*Chartreuse de Faisans* is ready to be carried to the guests who are waiting expectantly upstairs.

The Rewards of Gourmet Dining

Dinner at a first-class French restaurant is a great occasion—esthetically and nutritionally. To a nutritionist, gourmet cooking is outstanding because its wide variety of foodstuffs offers a superior balance of ingredients, its attractive preparation guarantees that the balanced meal will be eaten, its flavors and aromas aid digestion. But such coldly scientific analysis of haute cuisine is rare, even among nutritionists. For them, as for La Caravelle's customers, its main reason for existence is pure pleasure.

Fessaguet believes that every aspect of the restaurant should serve to heighten enjoyment: the taste and appearance of the food, the décor of the dining room, the service, even the attitude of the guests (who, he insists, should eat unhurriedly and not smoke until after coffee). At La

ORDERING FOR TOMORROW

ORDERING FOR TOMORROW

At 10 p.m., as La Caravelle's late diners finish dinner upstairs, Fessaguet uses the kitchen telephone to dictate a cablegram to Paris, ordering *langouste* and oysters for the following week. At 10 a.m., he will be on the job again.

Caravelle the kitchen door opens quietly as the waiter sweeps in with the first course—perhaps caviar, or pastry filled with seafood; the meat course follows, then a light dessert —probably mousse or pastry.

Making each meal a leisurely pleasure occupies Fessaguet's long days, and late in the evening, while his guests are finishing up their dinners, he is planning for the days ahead.

8

Feeding the Family of Man

Riding a vertical conveyor inside a plastic-walled tower, potted plants receive full-time illumination and periodic doses of water and insecticide. This system, devised by Othmar Ruthner of Vienna, could grow rich crops in the harshest climates.

IN A LABORATORY in Newark, Delaware, biologist Morris H. Ross points to a cage of rats: fed a special diet, they have lived far beyond their usual span; men who accomplished a comparable feat would be 160 years old. Could men, by following similar diet principles, live to such an age?

In another laboratory, in Lavera, France, chemist Alfred Champagnat samples a nourishing sauce, rich in proteins, that he made from ingredients having a petroleum base. Could oil provide a new and plentiful source for the extra food the world so desperately needs?

Questions like these, intimately and immediately affecting human survival, challenge today's nutritional scientists. People still go hungry in many countries, and in some places they starve. Feeding the famished requires not only the imaginative application of modern farm technology but the development of new kinds of food that will put to use nutritional resources now largely ignored. Even where food is plentiful, gaps in our understanding of the mechanics of nutrition may shorten lives and aggravate illness.

Answers to the unsolved problems of food and nutrition are already being supplied by the laboratories of government agencies, food companies and universities the world over. Some solutions are tentative, their true value not likely to be established for years to come. Others, however, have had quick, beneficial effects on human well-being.

In a number of instances, these advances have been unexpected dividends of basic research. For example, when T. B. Van Itallie and Sami Hashim of Columbia University and St. Luke's Hospital in New York began their experiments, they were seeking fundamental knowledge of the way food fats are used in the body. The fat they were testing was an unusual one known as medium-chain triglyceride, or MCT. A synthetic derived from coconut oil, MCT has the molecular structure characteristic of all fats: carbon atoms accompanied by hydrogen atoms. But its three chains of carbon are shorter than usual; instead of 16, 18 or more carbon atoms, MCT has only 8 or 10 in each fatty-acid chain. This difference in structure was the reason Hashim and Van Itallie were investigating MCT, for they knew MCT would be absorbed differently from ordinary fats. While fats generally enter the bloodstream indirectly by way of a network of ducts containing lymph fluid, MCT moves directly into the bloodstream. The two researchers were astonished at the speed with which the medium-chain fats were absorbed by this direct route.

This discovery soon helped to save a life. A patient at St. Luke's Hospital, where the MCT studies were going on, had suffered from an infection caused by a tropical parasite that left him with an abnormal network of lymph ducts. When he ate fat it was digested normally, but instead of going into his bloodstream a large fraction of the vitally needed fat escaped through the diseased lymph passages, starving him of needed nutrients and causing painful symptoms. The physicians tried him on MCT—and the fat entered the bloodstream directly and bypassed the abnormal channels, so that the malnutrition was corrected. Since inability to absorb fats normally can also arise from other causes, such as pancreas malfunction and bile-duct obstruction, knowledge of MCT's action gives doctors a new tool to combat nutritional disease.

While research projects like the MCT study have developed new ways to save lives, even more significant, in the long run, are broad-gauge investigations of diets that suggest how foods can extend the active lives of healthy people. Research of this kind has already indicated that the human life-span may be doubled or even tripled by proper diet.

This extraordinary possibility has been raised by long-term experiments on animals, such as the series of tests on rats begun in 1948 by Dr. Ross of the Institute for Cancer Research in Newark, Delaware. Ross, seeking to learn how nutrition affects the onset of old age, has reared groups of rats on different kinds of diet in environments so carefully controlled that the only factors affecting the rats' health and life-spans are the amounts and types of food eaten. Some of the rats are allowed to eat as much or as little as they like; others are restricted to short rations. Each of these diets also varies in its proportions: one group of rats may be given food with 51 per cent protein, another group 22 per cent protein, a third only 8 per cent protein, and so on.

Eating less for longer life

From his long series of experiments, Ross has found that both the amount of food and its composition influence the rats' well-being, the kinds of disease they contract, the severity of their ailments and, especially, their longevity. The longest-lived animals are those that eat less than average, existing on a diet low in calories but not particularly low in protein. Among the worst diets is the one that would ordinarily be thought the best: the diet designed for maximum rate of growth. The largest animals, particularly those that grew the most when young, are more prone to diseases associated with old age than their litter mates.

After nearly 20 years of tests Ross had not been able to set an absolute limit to the rats' longevity. Many of his rats, 80 years old or more in human terms, still appear youthful, vigorous and healthy. When they die, it is most often not from disease or senile deterioration, but from blockage of their digestive systems caused by the hair they swallow as they groom their coats with their tongues. If this difficulty can be avoided, their life-spans may be extended far beyond anything yet achieved, probably to the equivalent of 200 years of human life.

How directly these results may apply to human beings is still unknown, although the rat has proved a reliable stand-in for man in many other nutritional experiments. And some support for the value of sparse diet for humans is given by life-insurance statistics: they show that slimmer people, who are presumably light eaters, are healthier and live longer than heavier people.

Proof of the benefits of skimpy meals would surely seem the ultimate irony to many of the world's people. Their lives are shortened and their energy is sapped, not by too many calories and proteins but by too few. Today at least half the population of the earth suffers in one way or another from lack of food, mainly because food production has not kept pace with mushrooming populations. The situation will almost certainly worsen before it improves. World population continues to expand at a rate that is hard to believe. It took all the years of history up to 1840 before the number of humans reached one billion; in the following 90 years the figure doubled; 30 years later, in 1960, it reached three billion. Now, demographers estimate that the planet will have four billion inhabitants by 1975 and five billion only a decade later.

In the highly developed areas of the world, food production is still on the rise, but not on a scale sufficient to meet the nutritional needs of the earth's people in the years ahead. The surpluses of the "have" nations, which annually give or sell millions of tons of food to the "have nots," are being depleted or eliminated; in any event handouts are not the long-term answer. Adoption of modern farming techniques can substantially increase the productivity of land. More acreage might also be put to work. The land that is tillable today represents only about 30 per cent of the earth's dry surface, and investigation now underway might turn large areas, at present considered wasteland, into useful farms. With the development of an economical method of removing plant-killing salt from seawater, irrigation of millions of acres of fertile desert soil would become feasible. Jungle land could be cleared and farmed if scientists can find some way to make the soil fertile and keep the soil's nutrients from being leached away by heavy rainfall.

The desperate need for protein

Such advances, if and as they come to pass, can multiply the world's agricultural output. But that output is mainly in grains—carbohydrate foods whose calories are not enough by themselves to satisfy the world's nutritional needs. There must also be an adequate supply of protein-containing calories, for it is possible for a human to get enough calories to satisfy his body's energy requirement, and still die from lack of protein. The shortage of protein in the underdeveloped countries is tragic because this lack kills so many children. According to one estimate, almost half of all deaths between the time of weaning and five years of age can be blamed on protein and calorie deficiency.

The best sources of protein are animal products—meat, fish, milk and eggs. But only wealthy nations can afford enough of these foods. Producing one pound of beef may require that a steer be fed as much as 15 pounds of plants. This extravagant consumption of vegetable food is

WORLD CROPLANDS, the principal source of human food, are located primarily in the temperate zones and comprise only about 10 per cent of the globe's land area. An additional 15 or 20 per cent of the earth's nonoceanic surface is devoted to pastures and meadows supporting animals that provide meat and dairy products. The rest of the world's land is either too forested, too rocky, too dry or too wet, too hot or too cold to be suitable for agricultural development.

intolerable where food and money are scarce; in such lands, people, not steers, must eat the plants.

Vegetables contain some proteins, but unlike meat they cannot normally satisfy the human need for protein, for no single plant contains the necessary combination of protein components—amino acids—that the human body requires. For example, wheat flour alone cannot sustain life for it lacks the two essential amino acids, lysine and threonine. But if wheat is bolstered by the addition of synthetic lysine and threonine it becomes just about as good a protein source as milk. Lysine alone provides a considerable increase in protein quality; it can be made synthetically in large amounts at low cost. Threonine has also been synthesized, but not on a commercial scale.

A mixture for balanced nutrition

A usually simpler way to increase the protein value of plant foods is to combine several different kinds of vegetable into a nutritious mixture. Their amino-acid components can then be balanced to achieve the proportions needed by the human body. Such protein mixtures are readily compounded from plant products—cottonseed, soybeans and peanuts with other ingredients such as beans, peas and cereal grains—that are cultivated abundantly in many parts of the world, and they are cheap: while a pound of beef protein cost $4.44 in 1966, its protein equivalent in cottonseed cost 17 cents and in soy flour only 11 cents.

However, no matter how nutritious these mixtures may be, they are useless if people are repelled by the strange taste, and often the flavor of these compounds is so unfamiliar that malnourished people will refuse to touch the stuff. The problem is compounded by the fact that people suffering from protein deficiency may not even experience the hunger pains that would usually drive them to eat.

Through intensive experimentation, research teams in several parts of the world have begun to produce nutritious protein mixtures that are not only inexpensive and easily manufactured from locally available resources but are also flavorsome. In the Middle East, a research team at Beirut, Lebanon, has developed a nutritious combination of parboiled wheat, chick-peas and skimmed-milk powder *(pages 116-125)*. Different mixtures are being tried in Africa, Asia and South America. The most successful of these vegetable-protein products is called Incaparina, named for the organization that developed it, the Institute of Nutrition of Central America and Panama (INCAP). A mixture compounded mainly of cornmeal, yeast and cottonseed or soy flour, Incaparina is now a commercial success in Latin America. In 1964, 1.7 million pounds were sold, providing 30 million servings—each containing the protein equivalent of a glass of milk—at one half cent per serving.

Nevertheless, the introduction of new foodstuffs still presents so many frustrating problems that scientists are trying a different tack. Instead of struggling to overcome the human prejudice against novel foods, they are searching for familiar vegetables with naturally occurring high-quality protein. One plant of this kind has already been found: a high-quality protein corn that could prove invaluable in Latin America, where corn is the basic foodstuff. The value of the new corn was discovered by E. T. Mertz and his associates at Purdue University when they decided to analyze a type of corn that has opaque rather than the normally translucent kernels. Mertz found that the opaque kernels were unusually rich in lysine, a nutrient usually in short supply in vegetable diets. Preliminary tests indicate that this Opaque Number Two corn may provide a source of protein almost as good as milk. Similar research is now being conducted to determine whether other grains such as rice and millet may not also have especially nutritious strains.

Another approach to the problem of feeding the world can be found in imaginative studies of potential food resources—animal, vegetable and even mineral—that are now largely untapped. The sea could be harvested much more intensively and efficiently than it has been in the past. Fish farming—that is, the raising of fish in enclosures—is impractical in the open sea; there is no economical way to pen the fish and no way to stimulate the growth of their food with fertilizer, which sinks uselessly beneath the fish-inhabited levels. But food fish are already raised on a small scale in farm ponds and rice paddies. And on the northwestern coast of Spain, mussels are being "sown" and grown in the calm waters of Vigo Bay. The "seeds"—immature mussels—are attached to ropes that are suspended from large anchored rafts; when the mussels mature they are harvested by raising the ropes.

Raising whales on a ranch

One of the most unusual ideas for getting additional food from the sea was suggested recently by Gifford B. Pinchot of Johns Hopkins University in Baltimore. He proposed the domestication of whales, which, like their distant relatives, cattle, are rich sources of tasty protein. To assemble a herd, Pinchot would attach radio transmitters to whales in the Antarctic and follow them on their annual migration north until they approached a coral atoll. The whales would then be shepherded into an atoll's central lagoon—a natural ocean "pasture"—and fenced in by stretching nets across the channels that pierce the surrounding reefs. Inside the lagoon, the whales would feed on the tiny sea creatures called plankton, which could be grown in quantity by fertilizing the lagoon's shallow waters. Pinchot estimates that at the outset meat from penned-up whales would cost about the same as beef, but that it might someday be produced for much less.

Whales are already used for food, and Pinchot's scheme would merely domesticate animals now hunted. But many scientists are looking for future food supplies far beyond currently accepted sources of nutrition. The green leaves of ordinary trees, for example, contain about 3 per cent protein, which can be concentrated by a process developed by N. W. Pirie of the Rothamsted Experimental Station in England, England's oldest agricultural-research establishment. Pirie started his search for a leaf food during World War II, when the British feared that the German U-boat blockade might starve them into submission. He ultimately devised a mass-production method of crushing leaves, extracting their juices and coagulating the protein into a dark green block having the texture of cheese and a flavor reminiscent of tea. "For many years," he reports, "we have been eating five-to-ten-gram quantities of leaf protein and giving it to visitors . . . in ravioli, rissoles and similar dishes."

Food from oil wells

The least likely source of edible protein is petroleum. But if some fertilizers are added to it and air is bubbled through, it will grow yeast, which is about 50 per cent edible protein. This is what has been done by Alfred Champagnat of the Société Française des Pétroles BP in France and other oil companies elsewhere. The process is efficient: one pound of oil yields about a half pound of protein and produces it several thousand times faster than farm animals can synthesize protein from fodder. The product, a tasteless and odorless powder, has already been made into meatlike concentrates and aromatic fish sauces. Its potential as a source of protein is enormous. Champagnat estimates that only about 3 per cent of the annual world output of petroleum would be needed to produce 20 million tons of pure protein—more than triple the protein now supplied by the world's catch of fish.

New food-making processes like Champagnat's are among the outstanding achievements of modern science. But how quickly they can be put into practical use is questionable. It is one thing to develop a method of increasing food production but quite another to persuade impoverished, uneducated people to adopt it. Acceptance of new ideas is slow because of the combined influence of local custom, ignorance and illiteracy, poverty, superstitions, taboos and religious restrictions. The best aid that can be given to millions of malnourished people is to offer them incentives to overcome their food shortage through their own efforts.

The success that can be achieved by such a bootstrap operation has been demonstrated by a Haitian physician, Dr. William Fougere, and a U.S. professor of biochemistry, Dr. Kendall King of Virginia Polytechnic Institute. Their project was started in 1964 in a remote and backward village in southeastern Haiti called Fond-Parisien, a town that could hardly be less Parisian in situation or spirit. The 3,500 natives lived in dilapidated thatched huts; water for drinking had to be carried from a spring more than a mile away. There was abject poverty, minimal food production and malnutrition in a variety of forms.

Fougere and King focused their attention on children six and under, the age range when children are growing most rapidly and hence are most subject to the ravages of malnutrition. The two doctors rented a hut in which they set up a combined classroom and cafeteria, and began feeding a test diet to the 30 most undernourished children in the village, always using foods locally available. A Haitian girl with some education was taught the rudiments of nutrition and cooking; she in turn served as instructress to the mothers of the children, who were required to attend "eating school" and to take turns preparing food.

The feeding program, specifically designed to treat protein-calorie malnutrition, quickly proved its worth. In three to four months, children who had had no better than a 50-50 chance of surviving were completely cured of basic nutritional illnesses and were growing healthier every day, scampering about the village in active testimony to the efficacy of proper diet. The mothers, encouraged by the seemingly miraculous cures, began to practice the basic principles of nutrition they had learned, and vastly improved the family diets. Without increasing their food budgets they were able to feed their children 100 per cent more protein and 50 per cent more vitamins than had previously been provided.

As one group of children completed its schedule of supervised meals, the experimenters started anew with another 30 subjects, with the same happy outcome. The astonishing improvement in health impressed the leaders of the community so deeply that they were very receptive when Fougere approached them with the second phase of the plan: to insure continued good health, the villagers would have to increase food production, to provide not only more food but the right kinds of food. Obviously, the primary need was a supply of water, and there was available a deep well that had fallen into disuse for want of a pump. The project's backers, an American foundation, offered to advance money for the pump—as a loan, not a donation. A small livestock breeding operation was also begun; the villagers raised rabbits, which eat things of little human nutritional value and do not compete for food with their breeders.

Small successes, great hopes

Fond-Parisien did not move overnight into the ranks of food-abundant societies, but it climbed a couple of rungs on the ladder. Building on the initial success, the experimental methods were applied in six more villages with the same gratifying results; as soon as the word spread, most of the people of the adjacent areas asked to participate. The cost to the supporting foundation, the Williams-Waterman Fund, has been low—about $25 for each child restored to health.

Further imaginative efforts, like the one that has transformed Fond-Parisien, are desperately needed. The nutritional outlook for the years ahead is bleak. Technology cannot work its wonders overnight, especially when it must combat age-old customs, nor can research be translated rapidly into food on the table. Shipments of surplus foods will provide emergency relief for the predictable local famines, but these represent only temporary assistance and contribute little toward solution of the basic problem. Barring some massive check on population growth, such as wide adoption of birth control, deaths from malnutrition will increase rather than decline. And yet, beyond the crisis of the next few decades, there is hope that the world can be decently fed. The earth has by no means exhausted its food resources; given time, modern food science can support a level of civilization now only dreamed of.

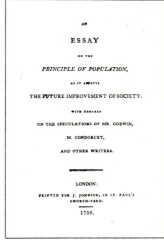

A PROPHET OF DOOM, the English cleric Thomas Malthus influenced public thought on population and food in 1798 with the essay whose title page is reproduced above. Malthus predicted that people would always multiply faster than their food supply and that populations would be "kept equal to the means of subsistence by misery and vice." In modern terms, the restrictive factors at work are —primarily—the starvation and pestilence that threaten underdeveloped nations. But advanced nations, benefiting from developments Malthus did not appreciate, such as birth control and farm technology, produce more food than they can use.

The Race
to Beat Famine

Ominous statistics tell the story: between 1964 and 1966 total world production of food remained fairly constant, but population increased by some 70 million people. The mouths to be fed are multiplying too rapidly for food output to keep up; as the gap between supplies and needs grows larger, the ancient specter of famine once again haunts the world.

Already half the world's population suffers from hunger or malnutrition. In the underdeveloped nations of Africa, Asia and Latin America, population is soaring so rapidly that by the year 2000 these countries must produce at least twice as much food as they do today simply to hold their present dietary levels, poor as those are. This is an overwhelming task: ignorance, outmoded agricultural practices and lack of the capital to support modern technology stand in the way of its accomplishment.

For the moment, famine is being averted by massive transfusions of food from the granaries of the richer nations. But this can only be a stopgap. In the long run, the hungry nations must learn to feed themselves—not only by improving their agriculture but also by limiting population growth and thus achieving a vital balance between people and food.

LOW YIELD FROM PARCHED LAND
Behind a pair of scrawny oxen and an outmoded plow, an Indian peasant tills his employer's dusty fields in the drought-stricken state of Uttar Pradesh *(right)*. Even when monsoon rains are normal, Uttar Pradesh does not produce enough grain to feed its people. When drought cut the rainfall 70 per cent in 1966, thousands found themselves near starvation.

Obstacles to Ending Starvation

The age-old terror of starvation, painfully familiar to mankind, contorts the faces of Congolese men struggling for food *(below)* and haunts the despairing eyes of an old Indian peasant *(below, right)*. From the time, hundreds of thousands of years ago, when man began his relentless expansion over the face of the earth, his rapidly growing numbers have stretched his food resources to the limit. Any sudden reduction in sup-plies—whether the result of warfare, insect plagues, flood or drought—has brought disaster. In Ireland between 1846 and 1849, the dreadful potato blight caused the death of more than a million people; in India a series of famines in the last half of the 19th Century killed 15 million people; in the Soviet Union three million people starved to death during the famine from 1932 to 1933.

The 20th Century's great achieve-

ments in agricultural technology have now ended such horrors in the advanced nations. But in other countries, where modern practices are not the rule, the threat of mass starvation looms larger than ever. The population explosion, poverty, ignorance and tradition block needed reforms. In India 30 per cent of all grain is eaten by rats and insects that might be eliminated if money could be spared for pesticides. In some areas people starve rather than violate custom by eating plentiful fish.

Until such obstacles are overcome, the benefits of new food-production methods cannot be applied where they are needed most. Modern technology—fertilizers, pesticides, high-yield plants, controlled irrigation, land management, mechanized farming—must be brought to bear if the underdeveloped nations are to raise enough food to feed their populations.

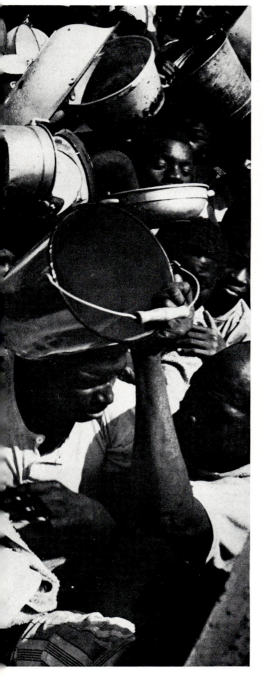

THE ANGUISH OF THE RAVENOUS
Baluba tribesmen *(left)*, uprooted in 1961 by the civil war in the Congo, fight for scant rations of cornmeal and flour issued at a refugee camp in Katanga. Normally peaceful, Balubas were reportedly driven to cannibalism by hunger.

THE HOPELESSNESS OF HUNGER
A despairing Indian peasant, his face a study of anguish, is one of thousands of people subsisting mainly on a dole of four ounces of grain daily, after a bitter drought in 1966 ruined three fourths of the harvest in the state of Bihar.

Famine's Roots in Backward Farming

Nutritionally speaking, the gulf between have and have-not peoples reflects their relative effectiveness as farmers. The charts on these pages, which compare agricultural efficiency in 20 countries, show the extent to which each of these lands is able to fill the food needs of its population.

In both the amount of food consumed by each person, and the production of food per farm worker, the United States ranks the highest. It has taken advantage of its natural fertility, advanced technology and a highly organized farm system (*pages 42-55*) to make available an

abundant diet—3,150 calories per person per day—through the labor of only 8 per cent of its workers and the use of only 20 per cent of its land. But smaller and less affluent nations have also achieved comparable abundance and efficiency. Israel, for example, feeds its 2.56 million people

CALORIES PER PERSON PER DAY

OUNCES OF ANIMAL PROTEIN PER PERSON PER DAY

TOTAL POPULATION

U.S.A.
FRANCE
U.S.S.R.
YUGOSLAVIA
SPAIN
MEXICO
BRAZIL
CHILE
COLOMBIA
NIGERIA
TANZANIA
UNITED ARAB REPUBLIC
ISRAEL
JORDAN
TURKEY
JAPAN
PAKISTAN
THAILAND
INDIA
PHILIPPINES

4,000   2,500   1,000   3   1.5   0   0   250,000,000   500,000,000

POPULATION FIGURES, 1965. ALL OTHER FIGURES, 1959-1961 AVERAGES.
STATISTICS FROM U.S. DEPT. OF AGRICULTURE AND UNITED NATIONS

adequately—2,840 calories each per day, and 1.2 ounces of animal protein —using only 20 per cent of its land.

A sharp contrast is found in India. About 70 per cent of its working population is engaged in agriculture. Yet for all this massive application of labor, the average diet comes to only 2,060 calories a day (780 fewer than in Israel), which contain only one fifth of an ounce of protein (one ounce less than in Israel).

Agricultural advances in India and many other countries are retarded by tradition and poverty—and are periodically halted entirely by such disasters as a locust attack *(background photograph)*. Yet many nations have overcome similar obstacles to provide enough food for their citizens. Among the most efficient food producers are Japan and Israel, which not only feed more people now than a decade ago but feed them better.

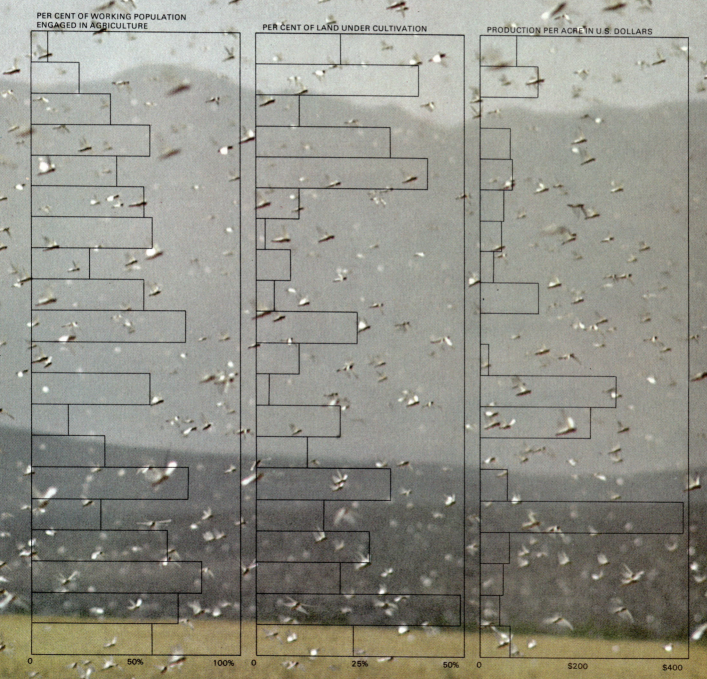

PER CENT OF WORKING POPULATION
ENGAGED IN AGRICULTURE

0   50%   100%

PER CENT OF LAND UNDER CULTIVATION

0   25%   50%

PRODUCTION PER ACRE IN U.S. DOLLARS

0          $200 $400

Food from Abroad to Stall a Crisis

To counter the immediate threats of mass hunger, countries blessed with agricultural surpluses have been shipping large quantities of food to stricken nations, sometimes donated, sometimes sold for the national currency to finance local construction projects. Often the aid comes from international agencies—such as the United Nations' UNICEF, which distributes food in 120 countries.

The largest of the food-shipment efforts has been America's Food for Peace program, which has sent surplus produce to every corner of the globe. In the 13 years following its inception in 1954, Food for Peace dispatched more than $16 billion worth of food to needy nations; shipments in 1965 alone were worth $1.4 billion.

The principal beneficiary of this Food for Peace program has been India, to which a "bridge of ships" has brought U.S. grain in an uninterrupted stream. In 1966 some 600 ships were engaged in this traffic, carrying 750,000 tons of wheat and other cereals over 8,000 miles of ocean monthly.

The years of grain shipments to India and other countries cut so deeply into U.S. surpluses that in 1966 President Johnson ordered some 30 million acres of fallow land, ordinarily held in reserve, returned to active cultivation. And Secretary of State Dean Rusk warned that a major crisis was bound to occur unless underdeveloped nations made a greater effort to increase their own food production.

A CARGO OF VITAL WHEAT
Wheat, part of the nine million tons sent to India in 1966 under the U.S. Food for Peace program, is bagged by local workers in a dockside warehouse *(left)* in Bombay Harbor. The grain will be shipped by truck, train or bullock cart to villages where it will be ground into flour.

A PAYMENT IN GRAIN
Wheat shipped from the United States is distributed *(right)* at a village in the state of Rajasthan in northwest India. This food is not given free to the villagers; it is payment for their labor on public-works projects such as roads, irrigation canals and community wells.

From a New Dam, More Cropland

If starvation is to be avoided in many parts of the world, vast areas of land still untilled must be brought under the plow. Much fertile land that is now useless only because it is too dry could be made productive by large-scale irrigation projects like the High Dam near Aswan, Egypt. This dam, by directing waters of the Nile River into complex systems of irrigation canals, is reclaiming about 1.3 million acres of tillable soil from the surrounding deserts—increasing Egypt's farmland by one third.

For ages the Nile has been a mixed blessing for Egyptians. Its annual flooding has brought tons of rich silt to farmlands, but it has also brought frequent destruction. Now the 360-foot-high dam, more than a decade in the building, realizes a dream of Egyptians since the Pharaohs: the taming of the Nile. Floods will be blocked and irrigation controlled to permit the growing of three crops per year on some land.

As beneficial and majestic as the huge Aswan Dam is, its effect on the nation's food problem will not be as great as originally anticipated. By the time the dam is fully in use, Egypt's population will have increased by 25 per cent or more—and the nation will still be unable to feed all its people properly. If the population continues to increase at its present rate, Egypt will be able to grow the food it needs only by adopting greatly intensified scientific farming methods.

A TASK WORTHY OF A PHARAOH
Man-made spits of land jut into the Nile River near Aswan, Egypt, early in the High Dam's construction. When these spits were joined, they blocked the river, diverting it beyond the cliffs in the background. Then construction of the rock-fill dam began. A 360-foot pile of stones 1,000 yards thick at the base makes up the bulk of the dam, while a core of cement and clay prevents seepage. The dam was designed to create a storage lake 300 miles in length.

DOUBLING HARVESTS QUICKLY

A farmer in the Philippines, under the guidance of a chemical company's agronomist, uses an over-the-shoulder applicator to spread fertilizer on his muddy rice paddy. Rice is the most important crop of the Philippines, but not enough can be raised there to feed the islands' population. Programs designed to increase production are heavily dependent on chemical fertilizers, pesticides and weed-control sprays. Recent experiments on Philippine farms have shown that, with proper fertilizer treatment, crop yields can be increased by as much as 100 per cent.

Chemicals to Raise Yields

The fastest way to expand the world's food supply is by treating land and crops with chemicals. Fertilizers enrich spent soil to such an extent that it produces more than it did before the first crop was sown in it. Pest-killing dusts and sprays attack the insects and diseases that harm growing plants, while poisons control vermin that ruin stored grain.

Plant diseases and voracious insects take a tremendous toll everywhere. Even in the United States, where chemical sprays are in common use, pests and diseases claim more than 20 per cent of the annual grain crop. In countries where sprays are not widely used, the losses are often as high as one third of the entire crop. It is estimated that proper chemical treatment could give the entire world an extra 200 million tons of grain a year without adding a single cultivated acre.

When pest control is combined with correct use of fertilizers the results can be dramatic. One example of the miracles worked by fertilizers and mechanized-farming methods is furnished by Japan. Unable to feed her people after World War II, Japan completely modernized her agriculture. Equipment especially adapted to small fields was introduced, and the application of fertilizer was increased in a single decade from an average of 145 pounds per acre of arable land to 270 pounds—a rate that is exceeded only in such intensively farmed lands as the Netherlands and Italy. Today Japan is the most efficient producer of rice in all Asia, harvesting 4,500 pounds an acre, two and a half times the world average.

CHORES BY FLYING HORSES

A helicopter, flying low in the misty rain, sprays a Japanese rice paddy with insecticide. Spraying is important in Japanese farming; during the growing season herbicides fight weeds and fungicides prevent the blight called rice blast. Before harvest, another spray helps dry the paddy's mud so that the ground will be firm enough to support the heavy reaping machines.

187

Two workers at the International Rice Research Institute walk between fields of the old-style rice plants *(left, above)* and the new shorter,

More Food from Better Plants

A bright hope for increases in basic food supplies is now offered by the improvement of existing crops: the development of plant varieties that resist diseases, mature faster and produce larger yields. Rice, for example, is the staple food of most of the nations of Asia, but it is difficult to grow. It takes many man-hours of care; it is susceptible to diseases, and sometimes its harvested grains lack needed nutritional substances.

One attempt to develop stronger, more nutritious strains of rice is now underway in the Philippines in the experimental fields of the International Rice Research Institute. The Institute's goal is to produce short,

stiff plants that will not be beaten down by wind, will be easy to harvest, will be resistant to the attacks of pests and disease, and will contain essential nutrients. Development of a superstrain of rice entails thousands of plant crossbreedings.

While these experiments are going on, field testing proceeds with chemical fertilizers and pesticides, and workers in special kitchens cook the different strains of rice to compare their flavors and textures. Although this work began only in 1962, it has led to new plants that, when grown in irrigated soil laced with fertilizers, yield at least four times more rice per acre than was previously possible.

sturdier rice *(right)*. The old-style rice plants droop, causing many kernels to fall to the ground.

CREATING PLANTS TO ORDER
To create a new type of plant, intricate cross-pollination of two varieties is necessary. The pollen-bearing stamen of one variety is cut off *(top)*. Then the stamen from a different variety is placed on the clipped plant *(middle)* where it can fertilize the seeds contained in the ovary. This cross-mating produces a hybrid *(bottom)* that displays the strengths of both varieties.

The Vital Balance
of Food and People

Improvements in agriculture alone cannot guarantee a food supply large enough to keep up with the world's exploding population. Throughout the world more than two babies are born every second—190,000 more mouths to feed every day. At this rate, the world population, which was 3.3 billion in 1966, will swell to more than seven billion by the year 2000. Ironically, most of this increase is likely to occur in Asia, Latin America and Africa, where food production is already dangerously low.

Many experts believe that the only way to achieve a proper balance between population increases and food production is through family planning. Oral contraceptives and mechanical devices *(right)* now make birth control dependable, cheap and simple enough for widespread use. In Taiwan and Japan—countries with high postwar birthrates—nationwide programs have proved remarkably effective. But in many nations religious and moral objections bar the way to population planning; in those parts of the world the specters of overpopulation, mass starvation and political chaos become more frightening daily.

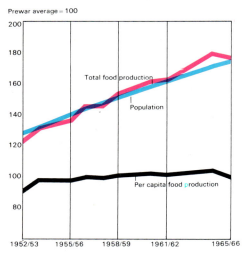

Prewar average = 100

A WORSENING SHORTAGE

Food production kept pace with population in underdeveloped countries *(top lines above)* until 1965, when food output dropped, reducing the food available per person *(bottom line)*.

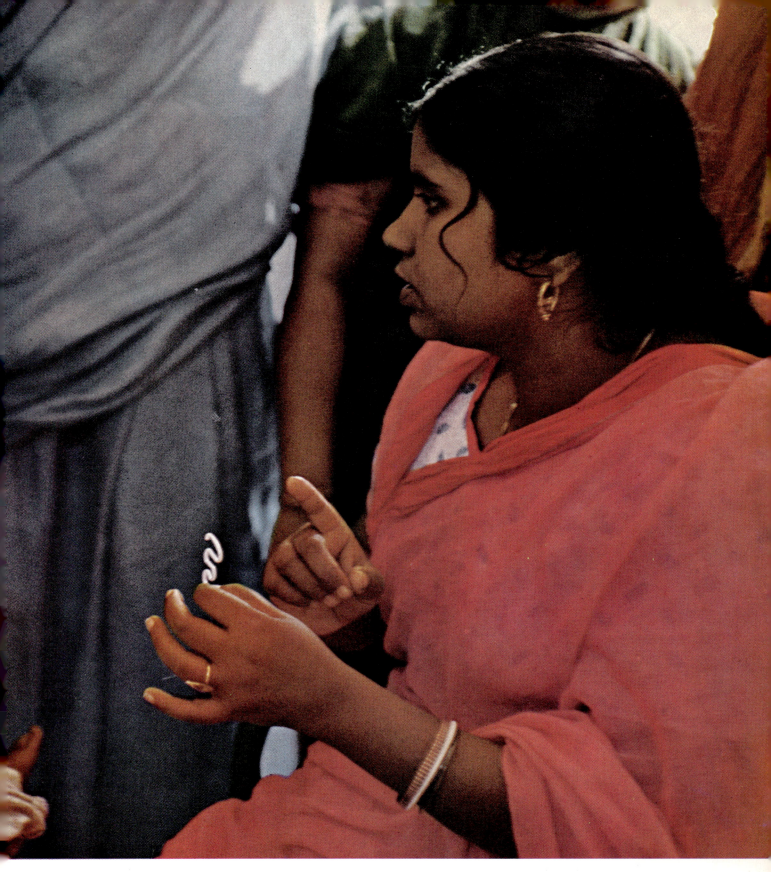

THE PROMISE OF A PLASTIC LOOP

The wife of an Indian farmer receives instructions from a nurse prior to being fitted with a plastic intrauterine device, or loop, in a village in West Bengal. More than one million Indian women use such devices, which prevent conception effectively although their principle is not yet fully understood; in addition two million men have chosen to undergo sterilization, for which they receive a small government payment. But this is small progress toward population control in a land that has about 500 million people, including 90 million women of childbearing age.

The Origins of Foodstuffs

Mankind, with a two-million-year history of gathering and hunting wild foods, made the critical turn toward civilization when food crops were first cultivated around 7000 B.C. One of the first plants to be brought under cultivation was wheat, domesticated in the Middle East. Almost simultaneously, farming was invented in Central America with the domestication of vegetables like squash, and later farming arose independently in China. The secret swiftly spread to nearly every temperate, fertile part of the Old and New Worlds, and crops were swiftly diversified as men took the basic idea of cultivating plants and tried it out on the varieties that were native to each new area. By 1500 B.C. all the major food plants known today were being grown.

With the aid of a technique called carbon dating, which measures the age of ancient seeds and tools found in archeological excavations, scientists can draw up a timetable and map (below) that show where foods were first raised. Today, many nations subsist on crops that originated in distant lands—and the secret of farming has been learned by every group of people on earth except the most primitive tribes, such as Australia's Warramunga aborigines.

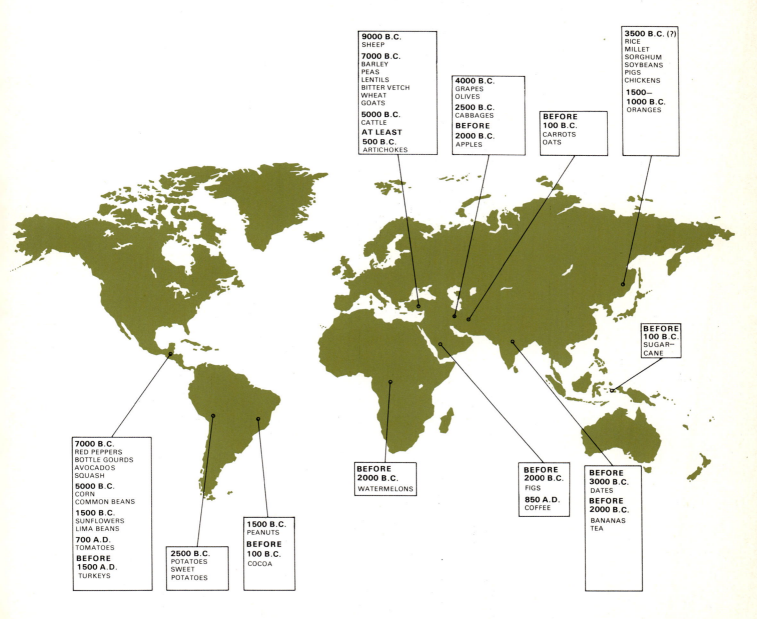

9000 B.C.
SHEEP

7000 B.C.
BARLEY
PEAS
LENTILS
BITTER VETCH
WHEAT
GOATS

5000 B.C.
CATTLE

AT LEAST
500 B.C.
ARTICHOKES

4000 B.C.
GRAPES
OLIVES

2500 B.C.
CABBAGES

BEFORE
2000 B.C.
APPLES

BEFORE
100 B.C.
CARROTS
OATS

3500 B.C. (?)
RICE
MILLET
SORGHUM
SOYBEANS
PIGS
CHICKENS

1500—
1000 B.C.
ORANGES

BEFORE
100 B.C.
SUGAR—
CANE

7000 B.C.
RED PEPPERS
BOTTLE GOURDS
AVOCADOS
SQUASH

5000 B.C.
CORN
COMMON BEANS

1500 B.C.
SUNFLOWERS
LIMA BEANS

700 A.D.
TOMATOES

BEFORE
1500 A.D.
TURKEYS

2500 B.C.
POTATOES
SWEET
POTATOES

1500 B.C.
PEANUTS

BEFORE
100 B.C.
COCOA

BEFORE
2000 B.C.
WATERMELONS

BEFORE
2000 B.C.
FIGS

850 A.D.
COFFEE

BEFORE
3000 B.C.
DATES

BEFORE
2000 B.C.
BANANAS
TEA

The Composition of Familiar Foods

Four principal ingredients—fat, protein, carbohydrate and water—make up the bulk of all foods, as indicated in the table below. The table gives the calorie value of many common foods, together with the weights of their most important nutrients. The

NAME	MAJOR NUTRIENTS					MINERALS					VITAMINS					AVERAGE PORTION		
	CALO-RIES	WATER GM.	PRO-TEIN GM.	FAT GM.	TOTAL CARBO-HY-DRATES GM.	CAL-CIUM MG.	PHOS-PHO-RUS MG.	IRON MG.	SO-DIUM MG.	PO-TAS-SIUM MG.	A (RETI-NOL) I.U.	B1 (THIA-MINE) MG.	B2 (RIBO-FLAVIN) MG.	NIA-CIN MG.	C (ASCOR-BIC ACID) MG.	TOTAL CALO-RIES	MEASURE	WEIGHT IN GRAMS
DAIRY PRODUCTS																		
BUTTER	716	15.5	.6	81	.4	20	16	0	980	23	3300	trace	.01	.1	0	100	1 TBSP.	14
CHEDDAR CHEESE	398	37	25	32.2	2.1	725	495	1	700	92	1400	.02	.42	trace	0	113	1 OZ. (1" CUBE)	28
COTTAGE CHEESE	95	76.5	19.5	.5	2	96	189	.3	290	72	20	.02	.31	.1	0	27	1 OZ.	28
CREAM CHEESE	371	51	9	37	2	68	97	.2	250	74	1450	.01	.22	.1	0	106	1 OZ.	28
CREAM, WHIPPING	330	59	2.3	35	3.2	78	61	0	40	56	1440	.02	.11	.1	1	50	1 TBSP.	15
ICE CREAM, PLAIN	207	62.1	4	12.5	20.6	123	99	.1	100	90	520	.04	.19	.1	1	167	1 SLICE	81
MILK, WHOLE	68	87	3.5	3.9	4.9	118	93	.1	50	140	160	.04	.17	.1	1	166	1 CUP	244
SHERBET	123	68.1	1.5	0	30	50	40	0	174	218	0	.02	.08	trace	0	118	½ CUP	96
FATS, OILS AND SHORTENINGS																		
MARGARINE	720	15.5	.6	81	.4	20	16	0	1100	58	3300	0	0	0	0	100	1 TBSP.	14
MAYONNAISE	708	16	1.5	78	3	19	60	1	590	25	210	.04	.04	0	0	92	1 TBSP.	13
OILS, SALAD OR COOKING	884	0	0	100	0	0	0	0	.2	.1	0	0	0	0	0	124	1 TBSP.	14
SALAD DRESSING, FRENCH	394	39.6	.6	35.5	20.3	0	0	0	*	*	0	0	0	0	0	60	1 TBSP.	15
FRUITS																		
APPLES	58	84.1	.3	.4	14.9	6	10	.3	.2	74	90	.04	.03	.2	5	87	1 MEDIUM	150
AVOCADOS	245	65.4	1.7	26.4	5.1	10	38	.6	3	340	290	.06	.13	1.1	16	280	½, 3½" X 3¼"	114
BANANAS	88	74.8	1.2	.2	23	8	28	.6	.5	420	430	.04	.05	.7	10	132	1 MEDIUM	150
CANTALOUPES	20	94	.6	.2	4.6	17	16	.4	12	230	3420	.05	.04	.5	33	37	½ MELON	385
CHERRIES, RAW	61	83	1.1	.5	14.8	18	20	.4	1	260	620	.05	.06	.4	8	94	1 CUP, PITTED	154
DATES, DRIED	284	20	2.2	.6	75.4	72	60	2.1	1	790	60	.09	.10	2.2	0	505	1 CUP, PITTED	177
GRAPEFRUIT	40	88.8	.5	.2	10.1	22	18	.2	.5	200	trace	.04	.02	.2	40	77	1 CUP, SECTIONS	194
HONEYDEW MELON	32	90.5	.5	0	8.5	17	16	.4	*	*	40	.05	.03	.2	23	49	1, 2" X 7" WEDGE	150
LEMONS	32	89.3	.9	.6	8.7	40	22	.6	.7	130	0	.04	trace	.1	50	20	1, 2" DIAMETER	100
ORANGES	45	87.2	.9	.2	11.2	33	23	.4	.3	170	190	.08	.03	.2	49	70	1 MEDIUM	215
PEACHES	46	86.9	.5	.1	12	8	22	.6	.5	160	880	.02	.05	.9	8	45	1 MEDIUM	114
PEARS	63	82.7	.7	.4	15.8	13	16	.3	2	100	20	.02	.04	.1	4	95	1, 3" X 2½" DIAMETER	182
RAISINS	268	24	2.3	.5	71.2	78	129	3.3	21	720	50	.15	.08	.5	trace	430	1 CUP	160
STRAWBERRIES	37	89.9	.8	.5	8.3	28	27	.8	.8	180	60	.03	.07	.3	60	54	1 CUP	149
WATERMELON	28	92.1	.5	.2	6.9	7	12	.2	.3	110	590	.05	.05	.2	6	97	½ SLICE	345
FRUIT COCKTAIL, CANNED, SWEET	70	80.6	.4	.2	18.6	9	12	.4	9	160	160	.01	.01	.4	2	180	1 CUP	257
FRUIT PRODUCTS																		
APPLE JUICE, FROZEN OR CANNED	50	85.9	.1	0	13.8	6	10	.5	4	100	40	.02	.03	trace	1	124	1 CUP	249
APPLESAUCE, FROZEN OR CANNED	72	79.8	.2	.1	19.7	4	8	.4	.3	55	30	.02	.01	trace	1	185	1 CUP	254
OLIVES, GREEN	132	75.2	1.5	13.5	4	87	17	1.6	2400	55	300	trace	*	*	*	72	10 "MAMMOTH"	65
OLIVES, RIPE, MISSION	191	71.8	1.8	21	2.6	87	17	1.6	980	23	60	trace	trace	*	*	106	10 "MAMMOTH"	65
ORANGE JUICE, FRESH	44	87.5	.8	.2	11	19	16	.2	3.6	182	190	.08	.03	.2	49	108	1 CUP	246
TOMATO JUICE, CANNED	21	93.5	1	.2	4.3	7	15	.4	230	230	1050	.05	.03	.8	16	50	1 CUP	242
GRAIN PRODUCTS																		
CORN FLAKES	385	3.6	8.1	.4	85	11	58	2.2	660	160	0	.41	.10	2.2	0	96	1 CUP	25
FLOUR, WHEAT	364	12	10.5	1	76.1	16	87	2.9	1	86	0	.44	.26	3.5	0	400	1 CUP, STIRRED	110
OATMEAL, COOKED	63	84.8	2.3	1.2	11	9	67	.7	.3	55	0	.10	.02	.2	0	150	1 CUP	238
PUFFED WHEAT	355	3.8	10.8	1.6	80.2	46	329	4.2	4	340	0	.56	.18	6.4	0	43	1 CUP	12
RICE, WHITE	362	12.3	7.6	.3	79.4	24	136	.8	2	130	0	.07	.03	1.6	0	692	1 CUP	191
WILD RICE	364	8.5	14.1	.7	75.3	19	339	*	7	220	0	.45	.63	6.2	0	593	1 CUP	163
WHEAT GERM	361	11	25.2	10	49.5	84	1096	8.1	2	780	0	2.05	.80	4.6	0	246	1 CUP	68
BAKED AND COOKED PRODUCTS																		
RAISIN BREAD	284	30.2	7.1	3.1	57.8	80	104	1.8	*	*	10	.24	.15	2.2	0	65	1 SLICE	23
RYE BREAD	244	35.3	9.1	1.2	52.4	72	147	1.6	590	160	0	.18	.08	1.5	0	57	1 SLICE	23
WHITE BREAD	275	34.7	8.5	3.2	51.8	79	92	1.8	640	180	0	.24	.15	2.2	0	63	1 SLICE	23
WHOLE WHEAT BREAD	240	36.6	9.3	2.6	49	96	263	2.2	930	230	0	.30	.13	3	0	55	1 SLICE	23
ANGEL FOOD CAKE	270	31.6	8.4	.3	58.7	6	24	.3	*	*	0	.01	.14	.2	0	110	2" SECTION	41
SPONGE CAKE	291	31.8	7.9	5	54.4	28	110	1.4	*	*	520	.05	.15	.2	0	117	2" SECTION	40
GRAHAM CRACKERS	393	5.5	8	10	74.3	20	203	1.9	710	330	0	.30	.12	1.5	0	55	2 MEDIUM	14
SALTINE CRACKERS	431	4.6	9.2	11.8	71.1	19	92	1	1100	120	0	.06	.04	1	0	34	2, 2" SQUARE	8
DOUGHNUTS	425	18.7	6.6	21	52.7	73	286	.7	*	*	140	.16	.13	1.2	0	136	1 DOUGHNUT	32
GINGERBREAD	327	30.4	3.9	12	51.6	114	71	2.5	*	*	100	.04	.08	1	0	180	1, 2" CUBE	55
PANCAKES, WHEAT	218	55.4	6.8	9.2	26.6	158	154	1.3	*	*	200	.18	.21	1.3	trace	60	1, 4" DIAMETER	27
APPLE PIE	246	47.8	2.1	9.5	39.5	7	24	.4	*	*	160	.03	.02	.2	1	330	1 SLICE	220
MINCE PIE	252	43	2.5	6.9	45.6	16	40	2.2	*	*	10	.07	.04	.4	1	340	1 SLICE	135
PUMPKIN PIE	202	58.9	4.2	5.6	25.8	54	81	.8	*	*	1910	.03	.12	.3	0	265	1 SLICE	131
PRETZELS	369	4.6	9.2	3.2	74.5	12	71	.7	1700	130	0	.01	.04	.7	0	18	5 SMALL STICKS	5
SPAGHETTI, COOKED	149	60.6	5.1	5	30.2	9	65	1.1	*	*	0	.17	.10	1.4	0	220	1 CUP	148
WAFFLES	287	40	9.3	10.6	37.8	192	204	1.8	*	*	360	.18	.27	1.3	0	216	1, 4½" X 5⅝" X ½"	75

weights of major nutrients are specified in grams, weights of minerals and vitamins in milligrams. Vitamin A is an exception; it is listed in the nutritionist's International Units (I.U.), each unit equaling .0003 milligram of vitamin A from animal food or .0006 milligram of vitamin from vegetable food.

For purposes of comparison, the table lists the amounts in a serving of 100 grams (about three and one half ounces), except in the last three columns, which give figures for average-size portions of food.

NAME	MAJOR NUTRIENTS					MINERALS					VITAMINS					AVERAGE PORTION		
	CALORIES	WATER GM.	PROTEIN GM.	FAT GM.	TOTAL CARBOHYDRATES GM.	CALCIUM MG.	PHOSPHORUS MG.	IRON MG.	SODIUM MG.	POTASSIUM MG.	A (RETINOL) I.U.	B1 (THIAMINE) MG.	B2 (RIBOFLAVIN) MG.	NIACIN MG.	C (ASCORBIC ACID) MG.	TOTAL CALORIES	MEASURE	WEIGHT IN GRAMS
MEAT AND MEAT PRODUCTS																		
BACON, FRIED	607	13	25	55	1	25	255	3.3	2400	390	0	.48	.31	4.8	0	97	2 SLICES	16
BACON, CANADIAN, RAW	231	56	22.1	15	.3	13	210	3.3	*	*	0	.91	.25	5.2	0	262	4 OZ.	115
CHILI CON CARNE	200	66.9	10.3	14.8	5.8	38	152	1.4	*	*	150	.02	.12	2.2	*	170	⅓ CUP	85
CORN BEEF HASH, CANNED	141	70.4	13.7	6.1	7.2	26	146	1.3	540	200	trace	.03	.14	2.9	0	120	3 OZ.	86
DRIED OR CHIPPED BEEF	203	47.7	34.3	6.3	0	20	404	5.1	4300	200	0	.07	.32	3.8	0	115	2 OZ.	56
FRANKFURTER, COOKED	248	62	14	20	2	6	49	1.2	1100	220	0	.16	.18	2.5	0	124	1	51
HAM, CURED, COOKED	397	39	23	33	.4	10	166	2.9	1100	340	0	.54	.21	4.2	0	340	3 OZ.	86
HAMBURGER, COOKED	364	47	22	30	0	9	158	2.8	107	345	0	.08	.19	4.8	0	316	3 OZ.	86
LAMB, RIB CHOP, COOKED	418	40	24	35	0	11	200	3	*	*	0	.14	.26	5.6	0	480	4 OZ.	115
LAMB, LEG ROAST, COOKED	274	56	24	19	0	10	257	3.1	*	*	0	.14	.25	5.1	0	314	3 OZ.	86
LIVER, BEEF, FRIED	208	57.2	23.6	7.7	9.7	8	486	7.8	*	*	53500	.26	3.96	14.8	31	118	2 OZ.	57
PORTERHOUSE STEAK, COOKED	342	49	23	27	0	11	170	3	69	334	0	.06	.18	4.7	0	293	3 OZ.	86
RIB ROAST, BEEF, COOKED	319	51	24	24	0	10	185	3	107	345	0	.06	.18	4.3	0	266	3 OZ.	86
SAUSAGE, PORK, RAW	450	41.9	10.8	44.8	0	6	100	1.6	740	140	0	.43	.17	2.3	0	158	2, 3½" LONG	35
FISH AND SEA FOODS																		
BLUEFISH, BAKED	155	69.2	27.4	4.2	0	23	293	.7	*	*	*	.12	.11	2.2	*	178	4 OZ.	115
CAVIAR, STURGEON	243	57	26.9	15	*	30	300	1.4	*	*	*	*	*	*	*	208	3 OZ.	86
CLAMS, RAW	81	80.3	12.8	1.4	3.4	96	139	7	180	240	110	.10	.18	1.6	*	92	4 OZ.	115
FLOUNDER, RAW	68	82.7	14.9	.5	0	61	195	.8	*	*	*	.06	.05	1.7	*	78	4 OZ.	115
HADDOCK, COOKED	158	66.9	18.7	5.5	7	18	182	.6	*	*	*	.04	.09	2.6	*	158	1 FILLET, 4" X 3" X ½"	100
HALIBUT, COOKED	182	64.2	26.2	7.8	0	14	267	.8	*	*	*	.06	.07	10.5	*	230	1 FILLET, 4" X 3" X ½"	126
HERRING, KIPPERED	211	61	22.2	12.9	0	66	254	1.4	*	*	0	trace	.28	2.9	*	211	1 SMALL	100
LOBSTER, CANNED	92	77.2	18.4	1.3	.4	65	192	.8	*	*	*	.03	.07	2.2	*	78	3 OZ.	86
OYSTERS, RAW	84	80.5	9.8	2.1	5.6	94	143	5.6	73	110	320	.15	.20	1.2	*	200	13-19 MEDIUM	238
SALMON, CANNED	203	64.7	19.7	13.2	0	154	289	.9	540	300	230	.03	.14	7.3	0	120	3 OZ.	86
SARDINES, CANNED	214	57.4	25.7	11	1.2	386	586	2.7	510	560	220	.02	.17	4.8	0	182	3 OZ.	86
SHRIMP, CANNED	127	66.2	26.8	1.4	*	115	263	3.1	140	220	60	.01	.03	2.2	0	110	3 OZ.	86
TUNA, CANNED	198	60	29	8.2	0	8	351	1.4	800	240	80	.05	.12	12.8	0	170	3 OZ.	86
EGGS AND POULTRY																		
CHICKEN, ROASTERS, RAW	200	66	20.2	12.6	0	14	200	1.5	110	250	0	.08	.16	8	0	227	4 OZ.	115
EGGS, WHOLE, RAW	162	74	12.8	11.5	.7	54	210	2.7	81	100	1140	.10	.29	.1	0	77	1 MEDIUM	54
TURKEY	268	58.3	20.1	20.2	0	23	320	3.8	40-92	310-320	trace	.09	.14	8	0	304	4 OZ.	115
SUGARS AND SWEETS																		
BUTTERSCOTCH	410	5	0	8.9	85.6	20	7	1.8	*	*	0	0	trace	trace	0	20	¾" SQUARE X ⅜"	5
CARAMELS	415	7	2.9	11.6	77.5	126	90	2.3	*	*	170	.02	.14	.1	trace	42	⅞" SQUARE X ½"	10
CHOCOLATE, SWEETENED, MILK	503	1.1	6	33.5	55.7	216	283	4	86	420	150	.10	.38	.8	0	30	¾" X 1½" X ¼"	6
COCOA, BREAKFAST	293	3.9	8	23.8	48.9	125	712	11.6	57	1400	30	.12	.38	2.3	0	15	2 TSP.	5
FUDGE, PLAIN	411	5	1.7	11.3	81.3	48	67	.3	*	*	220	.01	.07	.1	trace	185	2" SQUARE X ⅝"	45
HONEY	294	20	.3	0	79.5	5	16	.9	7	10	0	trace	.04	.2	4	62	1 TBSP.	21
JAMS, MARMALADES, ETC.	278	28	.5	.3	70.8	12	12	.3	7-13	8-78	10	.02	.02	.2	6	55	1 TBSP.	20
JELLIES	252	34.5	.2	0	65	12	12	.3	*	*	10	.02	.02	.2	4	50	1 TBSP.	20
MARSHMALLOWS	325	15	3	0	81	0	0	0	41	6	0	0	0	0	0	98	5, 1¼" DIAMETER	30
PEANUT BRITTLE	441	2	8.3	15.5	72.8	38	124	2	*	*	30	.09	.05	4.9	0	66	1½" X 3"	15
SUGARS, CANE OR BEET	385	.5	0	0	99.5	*	*	*	.3	.5	*	*	*	*	0	48	1 TBSP.	12
SYRUP	286	25	0	0	74	46	16	4.1	68	4	0	0	.01	.1	0	57	1 TBSP.	20
VEGETABLES																		
ASPARAGUS, COOKED	20	92.5	2.4	.2	3.6	19	53	1	*	*	1040	.13	.17	1.2	23	36	1 CUP	175
BEANS, BAKED, PORK AND MOLASSES	125	70	5.8	3	19.2	56	113	2.1	480	210	30	.05	.04	.5	2	325	1 CUP	260
BEANS, LIMA, COOKED	95	74.9	5	.4	18.3	29	77	1.7	*	*	290	.14	.09	1.1	15	152	1 CUP	160
BROCCOLI, COOKED	29	89.9	3.3	.2	5.5	130	76	1.3	*	*	3400	.07	.15	.8	74	44	1 CUP	150
CARROTS, RAW	42	88.2	1.2	.3	9.3	39	37	.8	51	410	12000	.06	.06	.5	4	45	1 CUP, GRATED	110
CELERY, RAW	18	93.7	1.3	.2	3.7	50	40	.5	110	300	0	.05	.04	.4	7	18	1 CUP	100
CORN, SWEET, COOKED	85	75.5	2.7	.7	20.2	5	52	.6	*	*	390	.11	.10	1.4	8	85	1 EAR	140
LETTUCE, HEADED	15	94.8	1.2	.2	2.9	22	25	.5	12	140	540	.04	.08	.2	8	7	2 LG. OR 4 SM. LEAVES	50
MUSHROOMS, RAW	16	91.1	2.4	.3	4	9	115	1	5	520	0	.10	.44	4.9	5	8	½ CUP	50
ONIONS, MATURE, COOKED	38	89.5	1	.2	8.7	32	44	.5	*	*	50	.02	.03	.2	6	79	1 CUP	210
PEAS, GREEN, COOKED	70	81.7	4.9	.4	12.1	22	122	1.9	*	*	720	.25	.14	2.3	15	111	1 CUP	60
POTATOES, WHITE, BOILED	83	77.8	2	.1	19.1	11	56	.7	*	*	20	.10	.04	1.2	15	120	1 MEDIUM	142
POTATOES, SWEET, CANDIED	179	57.4	1.5	3.6	36.2	36	45	.9	*	*	6250	.04	.04	.5	9	270	1, 6" X 1¾"	150
SPINACH, COOKED	26	90.8	3.1	.6	3.6	124	33	2	*	*	11780	.08	.20	.6	30	46	1 CUP	80
TOMATOES, RAW	20	94.1	1	.3	4	11	27	.6	3	230	1100	.06	.04	.5	23	30	1 MEDIUM	150
MISCELLANEOUS																		
BEER (4% ALCOHOL)	20-48	90.2	.6	0	4.4	4	26	0	8	46	0	trace	.03	.2	0	72-173	12 OZ.	360
COFFEE, BLACK	4	99	.2	0	.7	4	4	.5	.03	16.2	*	*	*	*	0	9	1 CUP	230
COLA BEVERAGES	46	88	*	*	12	*	*	*	1	52	*	*	*	*	0	83	6 OZ.	180
POPCORN	386	4	12.7	5	76.7	11	281	2.7	2000	240	0	.39	.12	2.2	0	54	1 CUP, POPPED	14
POTATO CHIPS	544	3.1	6.7	37.1	49.1	30	152	1.9	340	880	50	.18	.11	3.2	11	108	10 MEDIUM	20

*NO RELIABLE DATA AVAILABLE.

FURTHER READING

Agriculture

Curwen, E. C., and G. Hatt, *Plough and Pasture*.† Collier Books, 1961.

Food and Agriculture Organization of the U.N., *The State of Food and Agriculture 1966*.† 1966.

Rasmussen, Wayne D., ed., *Readings in the History of American Agriculture*. University of Illinois Press, 1960.

Soth, Lauren, *An Embarrassment of Plenty, Agriculture in Affluent America*. Thomas Y. Crowell Co., 1965.

U.S. Dept. of Agriculture, *The Yearbook of Agriculture 1958, 1966*. Government Printing Office.

U.S. Economic Research Service —Dept. of Agriculture: *Century of Service; The First 100 Years of the U.S. Dept. of Agriculture*. 1963. *Changes in Agriculture in 26 Developing Nations 1948 to 1963*.† 1965.

Zeuner, F., *A History of Domesticated Animals*. Harper & Row, 1964.

The Attack on Hunger

Cépéde, M., and others, *Population and Food*. Sheed & Ward, 1964.

Food and Agriculture Organization of the U.N., *Freedom from Hunger Campaign Series*.†

U.S. Economic Research Service —Dept. of Agriculture: Brown, Lester R.: *Increasing World Food Output*.† 1965. *Man, Land & Food*.† 1963. *The World Food Budget 1970*.† 1964.

Man's Food and History

Drummond, J. C., and A. Wilbraham, *The Englishman's Food*. Jonathan Cape, 1958.

Graubard, Mark, *Man's Food*. Macmillan, 1943.

McCollum, E. V., *A History of Nutrition*. Houghton Mifflin, 1957.

Parry, John W., *The Story of Spices*. Chemical Publishing Co., 1953.

Pfeiffer, J., and C. Coon, *The Search for Early Man*. Horizon, 1963.

Miscellaneous

Blumenfeld, A., *Heart Attack: Are You a Candidate?* Hill & Wang, 1964.

Deutsch, Ronald D., *The Nuts Among the Berries*.† Ballantine Books, 1967.

Lehner, E. and J., *Folklore and Odysseys of Food and Medicinal Plants*. Tudor Publishing, 1962.

Wyden, P., *The Overweight Society*. Wm. Morrow and Co., 1965.

The Science of Food

Altshul, Aaron, *Proteins: Their Chemistry and Politics*. Basic Books, 1964.

Burton, B., ed., *Heinz Handbook of Nutrition*. McGraw-Hill, 1965.

Davidson, S., and R. Passmore, *Human Nutrition and Dietetics*. Williams & Wilkins, 1959.

Gerard, Ralph, ed., *Food for Life*.† University of Chicago Press, 1965.

Sherman, H. C., *Chemistry of Food and Nutrition*. Macmillan, 1962.

†Available only in paperback edition.

ACKNOWLEDGMENTS

The editors of this book are indebted to the following: Dr. Suad Azhari Abu-Khadra, Dr. J. Cowan, Mary Gheblikian, Dr. Donald S. McLaren, American University of Beirut, Lebanese Republic; Charles Y. Arnold, Prof. of Vegetable Crops and Horticulture, University of Illinois, Urbana; Moises Behar, Director, Instituto de Nutrición de Centro America y Panama, Guatemala, C.A.; Robert J. Braidwood, Prof. of Archeology, University of Chicago; Confrérie des Chevaliers du Tastevin, N.Y.C.; Staff of Crèche St. Vincent de Paul, Beirut, Lebanese Republic; Fred Decre, Robert Meyzen, Roger Fessaguet, La Caravelle Restaurant, N.Y.C.; J. S. Dixon, Hormone Research Laboratory, University of California Medical School, San Francisco; John Gulland, Fish Stock Evaluation Branch, Alain Vidal-Naquet, Food and Agriculture Organization of the United Nations, Rome; Martha Haymaker, Beverly Hills; Douglas Hewitt, Farm and Industrial Equipment Institute, Chicago; Ronald Hill, Sr. Engineer, Dr. Lester Tepley, UNICEF, United Nations, N.Y.C.; Dr. Sami Hashim, Dr. Peter Holt, Dr. Theodore Van Itallie, Director of Medicine, St. Luke's Hospital, N.Y.C.; Susanna Icasa, Columbia University Teachers College, N.Y.C.; Alan H. Jacobs, Prof. of Anthropology, Dr. Janice M. Smith, Chairman, Dept. of Home Economics, University of Illinois, Urbana; Wallace F. Janssen, Margaret Nicholson, Paul Scheutte, Food and Drug Administration, National Library of Medicine, Dept. of Health, Education, and Welfare, Washington, D.C.; Dr. Graham H. Jeffries, Dr. Walter Rubin, Cornell Medical College, N.Y.C.; Mary Kaylor, N.Y.C. Dept. of Health, Bureau of Laboratories, N.Y.C.; Barbara Lawrence, Prof. of Archeology, Museum of Comparative Zoology, Harvard, Cambridge; Dr. Guy Livingston, Dr. Jamila Rana, Dr. Barbara Underwood, Institute of Nutrition Sciences, Columbia University, N.Y.C.; Staff of Luzmila Hospital, Amman, Jordan; Dr. George Mann, Vanderbilt University, Nashville; Oscar Mastin, U.S. Patent Office, Washington, D.C.; Dr. Jean Meyer, Harvard Medical School, Boston; Bruce B. Miner, Conn. Agricultural Experimental Station, New Haven; N.Y. Academy of Medicine, N.Y.C.; Mary Nuñez, Marco Aurelio Rodriguez, Standard Oil of New Jersey, N.Y.C.; J. W. Overholt, D. Robinson, Campbell's Soup Co., Camden, N.J.; W. Overman, International Harvester Corp., Chicago; Col. Jim Reid, USAF, N.Y.C.; Staff of St. John Ophthalmic Hospital, Jerusalem, Jordan; Dr. J. T. Schlebecker, Curator of Agriculture, Smithsonian Institution, Washington, D.C.; Dr. John T. Sessions, Jr., University of North Carolina, School of Medicine, Chapel Hill; Dr. S. A. Shafiq, Institute for Muscle Disease, N.Y.C.; Ralph Solecki, Prof. of Archeology, Columbia University, N.Y.C.; Lil Stuckey, American Spice Trade Association, N.Y.C.; Dr. J.A.G. Rhodin, N.Y. School of Medicine, N.Y.C.; C. G. Thomas, Environmental Science Services Administration, U.S. Dept. of Commerce, Silver Spring, Md.; Olivia Trivelli, Downstate Medical Center, Brooklyn; Dr. Robert E. Wise, New England Baptist Hospital, Boston; the following people from the U.S. Dept. of Agriculture, Washington, D.C.: M. L. Upchurch, Administrator, Economic Research Service; Robert Albert, Consumer and Marketing Service; Glen T. Barton, Chief, Production Adjustment Branch, Economic Research Service; Emmet B. Collins, Chief, Division of Budgetary and Financial Reporting; Wayne V. Dexter, Director of Information, Office of Management Services; Jerald C. Fitzgerald, Consumer and Marketing Service; Hubert W. Kelley, Asst. Director of Information, Agriculture Research Service; M. L. Koehn, Secretary, Crop Reporting Board; Dr. James L. Matthews, Agricultural Economist, Economic Research Service; Earl Miller, Head, Statistical Services Section, Economic Research Service; Kyle C. Randall, Chief, Farm Income Branch, Economic Research Service; Dr. Wayne D. Rasmussen, Executive Secretary, Agricultural History Society; James E. Reynolds, Chief, Current Information Branch, Agricultural Research Service; W. H. Scofield, Group Leader, Production Resources Branch, Economic Research Service; Robert L. Tontz, Chief, Trade Statistics and Analysis Branch; Gordon Webb, Deputy Director, Division of Information.

INDEX

Numerals in italics indicate a photograph or painting of the subject mentioned.

PICTURE CREDITS

The sources for the illustrations which appear in this book are shown below. Credits for the pictures from left to right are separated by commas, from top to bottom by dashes.

Cover—Neal Slavin.

CHAPTER 1: 8—UNICEF photo by Marc and Evelyn Bernheim from Rapho Guillumette. 10—Drawing by John and Mary Condon. 12—Drawing by Leslie Martin. 13—Courtesy Comtesse de Chabrol, Paris. 15—Drawing by John and Mary Condon. 17 through 31—Paintings by Paul Davis.

CHAPTER 2: 32—Douglas E. Wilkinson. 34—Drawing by Gloria Cernosia. 37—Reproduced from Frederick E. Zeuner, *A History of Domesticated Animals*, Hutchinson Publishing Group Ltd. 38, 39—Drawings by Shelley Sachs. 40, 41—Drawings by Nicholas Fasciano. 43—Photo by Edward Clark and Edstan Studio; Graph by Otto van Eersel courtesy USDA, Washington, D.C. 44, 45—Photo by John Phillips and Edstan Studio; Graph by Otto van Eersel courtesy Mr. M. L. Koehn and Earl Wilson, USDA, Washington, D.C. 46, 47—Maps by Otto van Eersel. 48, 49—Graph by Otto van Eersel courtesy Earl Wilson, USDA, Washington, D.C.—Bill Lilley for the Walla Walla Union Bulletin and Edstan Studio. 50, 51—Chart by Otto van Eersel. 52—Edstan Studio—Frank Scherschel and Edstan Studio. 53—Table by Ray Ripper courtesy C. Kyle Randall and Wylie D. Goodsell, USDA, Washington, D.C. 54, 55—Drawings by Otto van Eersel.

CHAPTER 3: 56—Courtesy New York Public Library Rare Book Collection. 58—Map by John and Mary Condon. 62—The Bettmann Archive. 65—USDA, Washington, D.C. 66, 67—Arthur Rickerby. 68, 69—Arthur Rickerby except top left Jon Brenneis. 70, 71—USDA, Washington, D.C.—Arthur Rickerby. 72, 73—Arthur Rickerby. 74, 75—USDA, Washington, D.C., Arthur Rickerby. 76, 77—Arthur Rickerby except left Borden Company. 78, 79—Arthur Rickerby.

CHAPTER 4: 80—Courtesy Denver Art Museum. 82—Courtesy Novosti Press Agency. 84—Drawing by Ray Ripper. 86—Reproduced from Sanctorius, Sanctorius, *Medicina Statica*, courtesy The New York Academy of Medicine. 89—Visible Man courtesy of Renwal Products, Mineola, New York, photo by Arthur Sellers. 90, 91—Joseph D. McKenzie courtesy R. E. Wise, M.D., Chairman, Department of Diagnostic Radiology, Lahey Clinic Foundation and New England Baptist Hospital. 92, 93—Graham H. Jeffries, M.D., Cornell Medical College. 94, 95—Dr. Roman Vishniac, Walter Rubin, M.D., Cornell Medical College courtesy *Laboratory Investigation*. 96, 97—Johannes A. G. Rhodin, M.D. 98, 99—Photos by Johannes A. G. Rhodin, M.D.; right courtesy W. B. Saunders Company. 100—Dr. S. A. Shafiq courtesy Institute for Muscle Disease. 101—Dr. Roman Vishniac.

CHAPTER 5: 102—Courtesy Mrs. E. V. McCollum. 104—The Bettmann Archive. 105—Williams-Waterman Fund of Research Corporation. 107—By courtesy of the National Gallery, London. 111—Map by Gloria Cernosia. 117 through 125—Robert Mottar.

CHAPTER 6: 126—Hannes Betzler. 129—Chart by Gloria Cernosia. 130—Drawing by John and Mary Condon. 132—Adapted from Norman de Garis Davies, *The Tomb of Rekh-Mi-Re at Thebes*, New York, 1943. 134, 135—Drawings by John and Mary Condon. 137—Joe Baker for *Medical World News*. 138—Bill Bridges. 139—Frank Denman—Julian Wasser. 140, 141—Ted Polumbaum. 142, 143—Alfred Eisenstaedt. 144, 145—J. R. Eyerman. 146, 147—Ted Polumbaum.

CHAPTER 7: 148—Lee Boltin. 151—Drawing by George Price; Copr. © 1953 The New Yorker Magazine, Inc. 153—"100 Years of Harper's Bazaar" exhibition at The Hallmark Gallery. 155—Drawings by James Barkley. 159 through 167—Richard Meek.

CHAPTER 8: 168—Ormond Gigli for TIME. 171—Map by Donald and Ann Crews. 175—Radio Times Hulton Picture Library—Courtesy New York Public Library. 177—Raghubir Singh from Nancy Palmer Photo Agency. 178, 179—Terence Spencer, Raghubir Singh from Nancy Palmer Photo Agency. 180, 181—Photo by James Burke; Chart by Otto van Eersel. 182—David Channer from Nancy Palmer Photo Agency. 183—Raghubir Singh from Nancy Palmer Photo Agency. 184, 185—Ralph Crane. 186—Reproduced from *The Lamp*, Standard Oil of New Jersey. 187—Arthur Rickerby. 188, 189—Richard Swanson. 190, 191—Graph by Gloria Cernosia, Raghubir Singh from Nancy Palmer Photo Agency. 193—Map by Otto van Eersel. Back cover—Drawing by Donald and Ann Crews.

A
STONEHENGE
BOOK